MW00364907

Islam and the Last Day

Christian Perspectives on Islamic Eschatology

Edited by

Brent J Neely and Peter G Riddell

Occasional Papers in the Study of Islam
and Other Faiths No. 4 (2013-2014)

The Centre for the Study of Islam
and Other Faiths (CSIOF)
Melbourne School of Theology

Occasional Papers in the Study of Islam and Other Faiths

No 4. (2013-2014)

ISSN 1836-9782

ISBN 978-0-9924763-1-1

Editors
Brent Neely and Peter Riddell

Production and Cover Design
Ho-yuin Chan

Publishing Services
Published by Melbourne School of Theology Press.
Thank you to Richard Shumack for his publishing services.

Centre for the Study of Islam and Other Faiths
Melbourne School of Theology
5 Burwood Highway, Wantirna, Victoria 3152, Australia.
PO Box 6257, Vermont Sth, Victoria 3133, Australia
Ph: +61 3 9881 7800, Fax: +61 3 9800 0121
csiof@mst.edu.au, www.mst.edu.au

People involved in the Christian interface with other religions are welcome to submit related items to the Editor for consideration for publishing in the CSIOF Occasional Papers.

Introduction

On one level, it is patently obvious that eschatology is a crucial element of the religion of Islam. The Qur'an virtually thunders with warnings of impending cataclysm; it issues shrill warning of certain judgment; and it promises rewards as exhortation to the pious. 'The Hour' (of the resurrection to judgment) relentlessly impresses itself on the listener. The 'Fire' and 'Paradise' are famous motifs of the book (particularly the Meccan suras). On the other hand, some elements of Islamic teaching on the interim state of the individual between death and final judgment, or aspects of Islamic expectation about the earth's last days are much less well known.

When it comes to the events ushering in the Final Day, the unpredictable energy of Muslim apocalyptic may be compared to the preparation of traditional Arab coffee which is brought to a frothy boil and then allowed to settle back again prior to the next surge: that is, apocalyptic tumult periodically erupts onto the canvas of Muslim society and then recedes, but never disappears, ready to burst out once again at a later time. For some it will be a surprise to discover that a number of scholars attribute the incredible energy and success of the early Islamic conquests to apocalyptic fervour, that is, to the conviction that the end-of-the-world was imminent. A certain type of eschatological dynamic and disruptive energy has been unleashed by apocalyptic expectation throughout Islamic history (both Sunni and Shi'i), including considerable 'latter-days' agitation associated with the recent conflicts in both Iraq and Syria.

In its broadest sense, eschatology is a concern of most religious worldviews. That is, eschatology is related to 'last things' or, we might say, 'ends,' goals, or those things of utmost significance. For most religious systems there is a sense that ultimate meaning and purpose transcend our mere temporal physical existence. In the monotheistic religions in particular the importance of eschatology is very pronounced, sometimes with a rather 'sharp edge.' This is so because Judaism, Christianity, and Islam all hold to a more-or-less 'historical' or 'meta-narratival' construction of history and proclaim the one God as personal, as creator, and as judge: the human story is, at some level, under divine supervision and will one day be brought to conclusion, humanity held to account.

Eschatology is a notoriously slippery word, but generally the term is used (in monotheist settings) in reference to one of three major concerns:

a) what happens to an individual after death;

b) the events of a universal, final judgment before God (usually subsequent to 'resurrection');

c) the cataclysmic happenings and portents of the world's final history just prior to the events of item 'b'.

Muslim eschatology, from each of the three main arenas, must be examined with some sensitivity, for just as 'eschatology' is a slippery term, so too is 'Islam' itself. What for example is 'Islamic expectation' with respect to a latter-days Messiah for Twelver Shi'is? Or, what might a Muslim woman expect when she thinks of ultimate rewards and punishments? Where do specific Muslim 'sects' like the Ahmadiyya fit into this picture? What about non-Arab Muslim views of the End? What about those who used to be Muslims? The possible questions are endless.

Each of the three aspects of eschatology, and each of the many angles of approach, are important in our attempts to understand Islam better. Such understanding is critical for interpersonal and inter-communal relations in our (in)tensely inter-connected world. It is also of value for Christians who would represent themselves, and their Lord, to a Muslim neighbour with fairness, humility, and effect. In this volume we are happy to present a broad array of studies that touch on issues in Muslim eschatology. The authors bring creative and diverse perspectives to this engaging and complex field of study. All write as persons concerned to engage Islam with fairness and faithfulness, all from within the boundaries of Christian conviction and experience. The opinions expressed are those of the individual authors only, but we believe these essays taken together are an insightful and cohesive collection.

Amanda Parker devotes her paper to a consideration of the experience in the grave of the deceased, a period known in Islamic terminology as the *barzakh*. She draws on Islamic texts, including Qur'an and hadith,[i] commentary on the Quran, and modern

---

[i] Numbering systems for hadith collections are complex and varied. In this volume, consistency has been sought within individual papers, though different hadith referencing systems are used across the full set of papers. The reader should be able to identify the specific edition of hadith books used by each author in the endnotes.

scholarship, to paint a graphic portrait of Muslim understanding of the deceased's experiences. The picture for the unbeliever, or indeed the lax Muslim, is frightening in its detail; in contrast, the experience of the faithful believer is idyllic. Therein lies the dilemma for Muslims, as their fear of the terror presented of the torments of the grave is a key factor in encouraging them to follow the rules of the faith, as it were.

Parker concludes her paper with elements of a Christian response to the Islamic understanding of the experiences of the grave. While Islamic teaching on the intermediate stage between death and resurrection is a cause for trepidation among Muslims, biblical teaching offers believers direct entry to the divine presence upon death. Parker argues that the contrast could not be more stark.

Bernie Power presents a concentrated selection of traditions from the Sunni Muslim apocalypse. Sometimes the importance, prevalence, and vitality of apocalyptic (intense focus on the events ushering in 'the last day') in the Sunni world are under-appreciated. This, even though belief in 'the last day' is a fundamental doctrine in Islam (cf. Q 2.62). Of course, the vast majority of the apocalyptic content is derived not from the Qur'an but from the profuse, diverse, and bewildering books of prophetic traditions/Hadith. Power provides a sort of tour through the raw materials of Sunni Muslim apocalyptic, mediated *primarily* through the lens of the most prestigious collection of Hadith, that of al-Bukhari, particularly the section *Afflictions and the End of the World*.[i]

Power's arrangement of the material is a very handy précis of the basic components of classic Sunni apocalyptic eschatology. With a minimum of commentary, Power provides a collection of translated primary source material pertaining to penultimate happenings and to the End itself.[ii]

Power brings a variety of traditions, 'signs of the Hour,' which highlight the major and minor events that herald the coming of God's fearsome judgment. There are generalized trends, such as increasing corruption, irreligion, and immorality in society; there

---

[i] Arabic title: *Kitab Al-Fitan* (*fitan* = trials, afflictions).

[ii] Of course, the presentation is necessarily selective, based on a culling from the massive (and sometimes apparently contradictory) conglomerations of *hadith*, and this mainly from only one (Bukhari) of the six major tradition books.

are cataclysmic portents and changes in nature; there is the proliferation of warfare (with Jews, Christians, and others) and, most acutely, internal strife. There are also a host of key apocalyptic characters ranging from the Mahdi to Gog and Magog.

The panorama continues to unfold with the *hadiths* about the events of Judgment Day itself, for example, the horrific spectacle of humanity massed together, naked, interminably awaiting judgment. The terrifying accounting includes both exacting justice and also mysterious, if not arbitrary, fiat. Unusual components of this Day abound—angels, records of deeds, scales of judgment, a razor fine bridge over hell, and perhaps even a glimpse of 'God's shin.'

Power concludes with an examination of some of the acts of intercession which will extract many otherwise 'unworthy' Muslims from the fires of Hell.[i] In this way Hell becomes for many something of a gruesome purgatory. Power has invited the reader to a first-hand taste of the Muslim apocalypse, opening the door to further study.

Brent Neely sets out to examine a very specific element of Sunni Muslim apocalyptic, namely the Muslim Antichrist, the Dajjal, as he is described in the work of the fourteenth-century Syrian theologian, Ibn Kathir. Apocalyptic is often the domain of marginal or non-conformist societal groups, but also is part of the 'formal doctrines' of the faith, and the religious elites (e.g., Ibn Kathir) may also seek to bend the apocalypse towards more 'mainstream' ends.

Neely points out that apocalyptic theology is usually more than mere future-oriented speculation and fascination; it is very often a polemical theology (sometimes a 'protest theology') deployed amidst the ideological, ethnic, moral, social, political, or religious[ii] battles of the day. The 'history of the future' is often in reality a contest for the spiritual heart of the *umma* (the Muslim community) of 'today.' Thus, many of the apocalyptic *hadiths* Ibn Kathir brought seem calibrated to correct or attack an array of groups and influences perceived as a threat to a puritanical Sunni ethos (e.g., Shi'is, Christians, Jews, antinomian Sufis).

---

[i] The elaborate and graphic depictions of Hell and Paradise are an important part of the larger picture, but are not a major focus of Power's presentation.

[ii] Of course, in Islam in particular there are no hard-and-fast lines between these categories.

Neely's extended article is primarily about a portion of Ibn Kathir's eschatology, based largely on the established traditions from the famous Six Books of Sunni Hadith.[i] Thus, this study is about a facet of Medieval Islam, with only passing consideration of the modern scene.

And yet both the author, Ibn Kathir, and the subject matter, the Dajjal, are appropriate fare for those interested in contemporary Islamic eschatological thought. This is because Sunni Islam is very much oriented towards the example and authority of the pious forebears. *'The way forward is to look back.'* Ibn Kathir himself eventually became an authoritative contributor to this influential Sunni construct, being a particular favorite of the so-called *'salafis'* today.

As for the Dajjal figure, this character looms large (often described in massively deranged and caricatured terms) in the classical literature, and is arguably the most prominent figure in some of the wildest and politically bitter speculation in the Muslim world today. [For example, in ways *partially* analogous to the confessional contests of the fourteenth century, the Dajjal is often unleashed today as a negative symbol in anti-Jewish or anti-Zionist invective.] Ibn Kathir, the Muslim Antichrist, and the events of our own day continue to converge, though predicting where the torrent will flow is no straightforward matter.

Peter Riddell devotes his paper to a series of snapshots from the different stages of the eschatological continuum. Drawing on a range of textual materials, including sacred text, classical Arabic theological writings and, interestingly, writings by Muslim scholars from Southeast Asia, the paper first considers the actual experience of dying and the temptations presented to the Muslim believer as he/she passes away. Consideration is then given to a theme addressed earlier by Amanda Parker: the experience of the grave, and debates among scholars regarding the nature of that experience. The remainder of the paper is devoted to a consideration of resurrection, judgement, and the eternal punishments and rewards that follow.

Riddell's paper draws a link between the dire warnings articulated in ancient writings and the way that modern Islamist radicals play

---

[i] These apocalyptic traditions are deployed in both his Qur'an commentary and a book he devoted entirely to the events of the End.

on the resulting fears. A sincerely believing Muslim who takes a literalist approach to the various Islamic writings on eschatological themes is likely to have a highly exclusivist view of their faith. Such a Muslim is also likely to hold negative views of other faiths, because of negative portrayals of those faiths in the historical Islamic writings.

Anthony McRoy argues that contemporary political attitudes and actions among Shia communities are informed in significant ways by eschatological perspectives and beliefs. He traces the emergence of the figure of the Mahdi among the Shia, seen as the ultimate defender of the oppressed. This figure is the focus of a leadership line among Shia that stands in contrast with Sunni Caliphal leaders; indeed, Shia reject Sunni rulers as usurpers. McRoy points to the Shia hope that the Mahdi will end sinful governance in this world.

While awaiting the return of the Mahdi, contemporary Shia leadership among the majority Twelver community is entrusted to the institution of the *Vilayet-i Faqih*. This institution provided the vehicle for the Iranan revolution of 1979. McRoy also considers other Shia resistance movements driven by eschatological fervour, such as Hezbollah and its conflict with Israel in southern Lebanon and the Shia resistance to longterm Sunni dominance in Iraq. He also considers the ongoing issue of the Iranian nuclear program in the context of Shia eschatological perspectives and Western responses.

Steven Masood unpacks the relevant teachings of Mirza Ghulam Ahmad and of the late 19th-century reformist Muslim movement, the Ahmadiyya, that sprang up around him. As with so many aspects of Ahmadi thought, much of Ghulam Ahmad's eschatology deploys rather traditional terminology and concepts, but explicates them in a quite non-traditional fashion. Many verses from the Qur'an are taken to mean things previously unheard of in Muslim interpretation. For example, the Qur'an is held to point towards the advent of Ghulam Ahmad, the great restorer, himself.[i]

Masood provides a compelling exposition (based primarily on Ghulam Ahmad's own writings) of a sectarian, reformist Islam in which many qur'anic passages are taken as 'eschatological' but in a

---

[i] The *hadith* too come in for creative, esoteric reinterpretation, providing, for example, unprecedented understandings of the state between death and resurrection.

wholly non-conformist way.[i] The Ahmadis saw their age (late 19th C.) as the promised era, hailing their leader as Mahdi and Messiah; in many respects Ghulam Ahmad further demoted, not only the traditional Muslim Mahdi, but also the Muslim *and* Christian 'Jesus' in favor of himself.[ii] Throughout Masood's article we encounter an Ahmadi hermeneutic which frequently spiritualizes, generalizes, or moralizes scriptural passages which otherwise have been taken to be literal, apocalyptic, or highly specific.

In Ahmadi Islam, the period of nineteenth-century colonial hegemony in the non-European world is seen to be anticipated in the Qur'an as the day of the ultimate renewal in the person Ghulam Ahmad himself. The heavy impact of colonialism, industrialization, and modernity on Ahmad is quite evident in his exegesis of qur'anic eschatological passages. For example, the qur'anic reference to the 'abandoning of camels' because of Judgment Day is not taken to be indicative of the fearsomeness of the Day—such that even one's precious resources lose all meaning—but, rather, it is taken to point to the age of mechanization which displaces the use of beasts of burden.[iii] For the Ahmadi 'progress' is a vital motif, applicable even in heaven.

In a fascinating juxtaposition with NT eschatology and christology, Ahmad assertively places *himself* at the center of qur'anic expectation, at the turning of an age, with a decidedly anti-Christian slant. Masood introduces the reader to a fascinating and easily overlooked world of 'marginal Islam' and to an eschatological theology which underscores the wide, diverse, and multi-layered world of Islam, 'orthodox' or otherwise.

Moyra Dale's study of women in Islamic eschatology is a bracing investigation of the right topic for the right time: too little is known of the role, the place, and the expectations of/for women in Muslim theology generally, and women's voices have long been under-represented. Dale ably discusses issues with respect to Muslim women and 'the End,' and she does so not only by investigating sacred writings but also by bringing to bear research experience at

---

[i] Of course, Islam's various sects and movements have long battled over the right framework for interpreting the allusive and oblique text that is the Qur'an; the Ahmadiyya are not alone in 'heterodox' exegesis.

[ii] Recall the comments above and in Neely's article on the polemical edge of apocalyptic exegesis.

[iii] Or, Gog and Magog may be associated with England and Russia.

a women's program in a Middle Eastern mosque. The spectrum of Dale's sources ranges from theological texts to the teaching of a *shaykha* (female religious teacher) to the popular ideas of the 'common woman.'

While some qur'anic passages do proffer equal possibilities for requital and reward to men and women, Dale points out that many factors in Islamic life and faith radically differentiate on the basis of gender; matters of the end of life, death, and 'final things' are no exception. Dale explores Islamic teaching on the final fate of women and the factors that influence a woman's destiny. Such factors include martyrdom, the degree to which a woman pleased her husband, Qur'an memorization, Muhammad's intercession, and God's foreordination (*qadr*).

Drawing on her extensive research, Dale looks into women's place, experience, and limitations in funerary rites and into hopes *and fears* with respect to the 'time in the grave' and also with respect to Judgment Day itself. Of real interest is the issue of female thought (and thought about females) when it comes to Hell and Heaven.

Dale touches on highly relevant matters pertinent to women in the Islamic Paradise: What precisely are *their* rewards in the seemingly sensual and male-oriented heaven? How do Muslim women relate to the famous '*huris*' of Paradise? Dale also brings out the more spiritualizing and metaphorical strand in some interpretations of Paradise. Questions of motivation towards piety (e.g., pure devotion or fear) are also addressed. This is a nicely balanced study that brings the reader in touch with Muslim women and their theology of 'ultimate things.'

Alex Miller concludes the collection with an original and captivating look at eschatological thought among people who were formerly Muslims, that is, Ex-Muslim Christians (or CMBs[i]). The study of CMB theology is an important, pioneering (and potentially controversial) endeavor; this discipline is emerging in tandem with the historically recent trend of Muslims migrating to the Christian faith (in places such as Indonesia, Iran, and North Africa).

There is no universal 'core' theology to which CMBs adhere; the CMB theology which Miller investigates is, in fact, not a systematic

---

[i] Christians from a Muslim Background. Miller deals only with Muslim-background people who are self-professed converts to Christianity, leaving aside the issue of 'insider believers.'

theology, but an 'informal theology' extracted from interviews, poetry, autobiographical writings, and so on. It is, for all that, theology in its own right. CMB theology is presented as both 'wisdom theology' (a 'situational' or 'lived' theology) and 'liberation theology' (that is a theology whose end is the freedom of CMBs to, some day, express and practice their faith in their home contexts). Miller surveys the terrain of CMB theologies to highlight the eschatological instincts of these (often) suffering Christians.

Interestingly, for some CMBs, the remarkable influx of Muslims into the Church is itself a 'sign of the times.' A fascinating component of Miller's article is the glance at CMB hermeneutics—the choice of which biblical texts are taken as relevant to 'the End' and *how they interpret these passages.* In many cases an American Dispensational heritage may be discerned in the thought of these new adherents of the Church. According to Miller, when it comes to *eschatology* in particular (as opposed to other areas of theology), CMBs tend to radically differentiate their new theological convictions from their former Islamic tenets. Miller's essay presents material that is fresh and of natural interest for anyone concerned with mission or Global Christianity.

Brent Neely
Peter Riddell
September 2014

Part One:

The Texts and Eschatology

Torment in the Grave and a Christian Response

Amanda Parker[i]

The concept of what happens to a person after their death while in the grave is a fairly developed theme within Islam. This is evidenced by references to it in both the Qur'an and in the hadith literature. Many authors, both Islamic and not, have picked up on this theme and established it further in commentaries and assorted writings. By using these materials, this paper will aim to explore the concept of the torment that occurs in the grave for the disbeliever and for the Muslims who do not live up to God's standards contrasted with the pleasantries that will be experienced by the true believer. In addition, a concluding section will develop a Christian response to this topic.

While both the Qur'an and the hadith will be the primary sources used to understand this concept, it is helpful to cite broad commentaries on the Islamic understanding of what happens in the grave. Hussam S. Timani writes, 'Although the Qur'an is so explicit about the particulars of Paradise and Hell, it is left to early Muslim commentators to describe in detail what actually happens in that life in the grave, the stage between death and resurrection, often referred to in the Qur'an as the *barzakh*.'[1] This in-between state of being is commonly linked to Surah 23:100 which says, '...This will not go beyond his words: a barrier stands behind such people until the very Day they are resurrected'.[2] This is affirmed by Ibn Abbas who is reported as commenting, '(and behind them) in front of them (is a barrier) the grave (until the day when they are raised) from the graves.'[3] As can be seen, the *barzakh* is a time that stands between death and the Day of Resurrection.

The *barzakh* is a concept that is rooted within the Qur'an and was mentioned by the Prophet Muhammad himself.[ii] During the *barzakh* 'the soul does not enter into heaven or hell, since those two abodes will not be populated until after the Day of

---

[i] Amanda Parker is an independent scholar who has completed a Master of Arts in Muslim Studies. Amanda's studies were concentrated on Muslim women living in the Levant. She currently lives and works in the USA.

[ii] Ed: For the purposes of this paper the *hadith* are taken at face value as reflecting the words or thought of Muhammad. Of course, the historical setting of the *hadith* is a contested matter in scholarship.

Resurrection. It receives, however, a foretaste of its ultimate and permanent state. As the Prophet said, death is the 'lesser resurrection' and the grave is 'either one of the pits of hell or one of the gardens of paradise.'[4] Since the soul does not find permanent residence in either heaven or hell until the Day of Resurrection, the concept of what happens to a person in the grave has obviously attracted considerable interest within the Islamic community over the centuries.

One of the most famous hadith that is often cited in relation to the torment that may be experienced in the grave is found in Sahih Bukhari:

> Narrated Ibn 'Abbas: 'Once the Prophet, while passing through one of the grave-yards of Medina or Mecca heard the voices of two persons who were being tortured in their graves. The Prophet said, 'These two persons are being tortured not for a major sin (to avoid).' The Prophet then added, 'Yes! (they are being tortured for a major sin). Indeed, one of them never saved himself from being soiled with his urine while the other used to go about with calumnies (to make enmity between friends).' The Prophet then asked for a green leaf of a date-palm tree, broke it into two pieces and put one on each grave. On being asked why he had done so, he replied, 'I hope that their torture might be lessened, till these get dried.'[5]

In this hadith, Muhammad recognizes that there are people being tormented in the graves because they sinned while they were still alive.[i]

As Jane Smith writes, '*barzakh* has been interpreted to mean, among other things, the physical barrier between the Garden and the Fire or between this world and the life beyond the grave, as well as the period of time separating individual death and final resurrection.'[6] The most common interpretation of this concept, however, is the time between death and resurrection. It would be worth looking deeper into what this time in the grave entails.

The experience in the grave differs greatly depending on whether or not the deceased person was a true believer and followed Islam. One modern author states, 'If the person were a believer, he would enjoy his life in the grave and is promised the utmost happiness and comfort in heaven. On the contrary, the unbelievers will start

---

[i] Ed: Notice even here the range of concern with respect to what constitutes sin: not only what some might immediately deem "ethical" concerns (calumny) but also ritual purity.

suffering in the grave and are promised further and more severe punishment in hell.'[7] It is important to note, however, that this time in hell is seen by some Muslims not as eternal punishment but rather the opportunity for sinners to 'pay back what they owe their Lord,'[8] that is, their sin. Nevertheless, this eventual escape from punishment in hell is only offered to Muslims, not disbelievers. This is pertinent to the discussion of the *barzakh* because the punishment of the grave 'may then be subtracted from the sentence to hell incurred before the throne of judgment on the day of resurrection.'[9][i]

One commentator who recognizes this theme of a tormented disbeliever frequently is Ibn Abbas.[ii] In his tafsir on Sura 2:159 he writes:

> (Those who hide the proofs) the commands, prohibitions and the signs mentioned in the Torah (and the guidance) i.e. the description given there of Muhammad (pbuh) and his feature (which We revealed) exposited, (after We had made it clear) to the Children of Israel (in the Scripture) in the Torah: (such are accursed of Allah) Allah will torment them in the grave (and are accursed of those who have the power to curse) all created beings, save human beings and jinn, will curse them upon hearing their screams from the grave.[10]

Ibn Abbas also affirms the belief that there are two distinct times that the disbeliever will be tormented. One of those will be for the duration of their time in the grave and then another for the eternity of hell. His commentary on Surah 20:124 endorses this concept, 'he will be exposed to a severe punishment in the grave; and it is also said: he will be exposed to a severe punishment in hell, (and I shall bring him blind to the assembly on the Day of Resurrection).'[11] In addition, he comments that the disbeliever's time in the grave will be no comparison to the time and torment of hell.[12]

In agreement with Ibn Abbas, the Jalalayn commentary[iii] also writes that the punishment of the grave, while still terrible, will not compare to the punishment in hell. On Surah 20:127 al-Jalalayn

---

[i] Ed: In other words, a sort of "purgatory." The concept of purgation appears also in the chapters on *hadith* and eschatology, the Ahmadiyya, and women and eschatology.

[ii] Ed: Ibn Abbas is traditionally the "father of Qur'an commentary." Modern scholars generally dispute the attribution of the *Tanwir al-Miqbas* to him. Its value as a major source in qur'anic studies is indisputable.

[iii] Ed: Classic and brief medieval commentary, still very popular. Dated to the late fifteenth/early sixteenth century.

states, 'And the chastisement of the Hereafter is more terrible, than the chastisement of the life of this world and the punishment of the grave, and more enduring, longer lasting.'[13] The Qur'an gives graphic descriptions of what hell is like. For example Surah 4:56 states, 'We shall send those who reject Our revelations to the Fire. When their skins have been burned away,We shall replace them with new ones so they may continue to feel pain: God is mighty and wise.'[14]

While the time in the grave will not be as severe and is not eternal like hell is, there is still a strong sense that this period will be dreadful for the disbeliever. For instance, one hadith in Sahih Bukhari states, 'Narrated Asma' bint Abi Bakr: Allah's Apostle once stood up delivering a sermon and mentioned the trial which people will face in the grave. When he mentioned that, the Muslims started shouting loudly.'[15] Another translation of this hadith says that the Muslims started 'crying loudly.'[16] Just the mention of the trials that would face the disbelievers was enough to bring Muslims to tears, so there is a clear picture that the anguish of the grave is something horrible and to be avoided. Ibn Abbas describes the 'compression of the grave'[17] as part of the torture to be faced. Other experiences will include the stings of scorpions, snake bites, laying on hissing coals, and being beaten with a rod.[18]

This concept of suffering can easily be contrasted with what awaits the believer. According to al-Ghazali, 'The believer in his grave is in a verdant garden. For his sake his tomb is widened by seventy cubits, and he shines with light until he becomes as the full moon.'[19] In addition, Surah 56:89 says, 'he will have rest, ease, and a Garden of Bliss.' Ibn Abbas comments on this same verse and says that this rest will also include a pleasant time in the grave, '(Then breath of life) then rest for them in the grave.'[20]

While the concept of the fate that awaits a person in the grave is established, there is still the question of how a person knows whether they will be tormented or whether they will find rest. In the Qur'an, there is no doubt that the theme of good deeds outweighing the bad is core. Surah 101:6-10 states, 'the one whose good deeds are heavy on the scales will have a pleasing life, but the one whose good deeds are light will have the Bottomless Pit for his home—what will explain to you what that is?—a blazing fire.'[21] If *barzakh* is the barrier that exists between heaven and hell, then this verse applies to the intermediate time in the grave as well. A person has great motivation to do the deeds that are correct, as mentioned in the Qur'an, in order to escape the torment. Some scholars believe that the soul's memory will 'continue until the day of resurrection to affect and to remind the living soul who is in *barzakh* of his or her good and evil past deeds.'[22] This is most pointedly summed up by Smith who writes, 'Thus the main concern of this *barzakh* life, as with life on earth, is with activity and human responsibility.'[23]

In addition to the works that will be weighed, there are hadith that specifically mention how a believer can be relieved of this terrible fate. Muhammad is quoted as saying:

> 'O Allah! I seek refuge with You from miserliness; and seek refuge with You from cowardice; and I seek refuge with You from being sent back to geriatric old age; and I seek refuge with You from the affliction of this world (i.e., the affliction of Ad-Dajjal etc.) and seek refuge with You from the punishment in the grave.'[24]

Muhammad is asking for refuge for a wide array of things that will cause suffering and at the end he lists punishment in the grave as something to be protected against. Clearly, this reiterates the Islamic belief in the *barzakh*. In addition, it shows that Muhammad wanted to protect others from suffering as is seen in another hadith narrated by Aisha, 'And then he [the Prophet] ordered the people to seek refuge with Allah from punishment of the grave.'[25]

While Muhammad recommends that the people do these things before the grave, there is one thing that will happen after a person has died that cannot be prepared for here on earth, besides being convinced of the truthfulness of Islam and the validity of the Prophet Muhammad. This is the belief that two angels will come to every deceased person and question them. These angels are named Munkar and Nakir. One modern author describes them as 'fearsome to behold, black in appearance with green eyes, with voices like thunder and eyes like lightening. Their long fangs rend the ground.'[26] Support in the Qur'an for these two angels is often cited from Surah 6:111 which says, 'Even if We sent the angels down to them, and the dead spoke to them, and We gathered all things right in front of them, they would still not believe, unless God so willed, but most of them are ignorant [of this].'[27] Ibn Abbas' explanation of this verse implies that the dead will speak to the two angels and will answer questions about Allah's oneness, Muhammad being the final prophet and the Qur'an being the revealed speech of Allah.[28]

More specifically, Munkar and Nakir will 'ask the deceased about his or her knowledge of God, the Prophet Muhammad, and Islam. One's ability to answer these questions, easy for the righteous and impossible for the faithless, determines the quality of one's stay in awaiting the Day of Judgment.'[29] Commentators such as Ibn Abbas[30] and al-Tustari[31] both confirm this questioning by Munkar and Nakir. Most importantly, Muhammad himself is quoted as saying these angels will be a reality for everyone who dies.[32]

Christian Reflections

It is important for a Christian to be aware of this dimension of Islamic eschatology. The Gospel has much to offer in regards to responding to the fear Muslims have of this torment in *barzakh*. The fear that seems embedded in both theology and experience for many Muslims is not just a thing of the past. In fact, a psychologist cited in a New York Times article 'has found that preoccupation with the torture of the grave remains acute. The Egyptians and Kuwaitis he polled worried about this torture more than they feared losing a dear relative or succumbing to a serious, fatal disease.'[33] In orthodox Christian teaching, a believer's death is not to be a time of fear and uncertainty, but of joy in getting to spend eternity with God. A great example from the New Testament is when Paul writes, 'Therefore we are always confident and know that as long as we are at home in the body we are away from the Lord. We live by faith not by sight. We are confident, I say, and would prefer to be away from the body and at home with the Lord.'[34] Paul is longing to be away from this life and into the immediate presence of the Lord.

In addition, Jesus gives a picture of what happens to a believer after death while he is still on the cross. Luke 23:43 states, 'Jesus answered him, 'I tell you the truth, today you will be with me in paradise.' The use of this verse is relevant to show the contrast between *barzakh* found in Islam with the immediacy of entering God's presence, for the believer, in Christianity. Commenting on this verse, Robert H. Smith writes, 'The criminal—and all penitents—are promised the company of the king in the king's own royal park without any intervening period of waiting, without any abandonment in Hades. There is no speculation on the interim state here...The word is promise and assurance.'[35] Through this promise of Christ from the cross, the Christian has full confidence that at death they will be ushered into the presence of God without fear of experiencing torment in the grave or suffering in an intermediate period.[i]

As has been seen, the time period between death and the Day of Resurrection is full of uncertainty and fear for a Muslim. Depending on how a person lived their life here on earth, it could be full of rest or a terribly painful experience that is just a glimpse of what hell will be like. The Qur'an, hadith and tafsir all support this theology and it has practical implications for a Muslim today. However, a Christian's assurance of immediately entering the presence of God could potentially have positive missiological implications. Theologian Wayne Grudem aptly describes a Christian's death this way, 'Once a believer has died, though his or her physical body remains on the earth and is buried, at the moment of death the soul (or spirit) of that believer goes immediately into the presence of God with rejoicing.'[36]

---

[i] Ed: This is not to deny that strands of Christian theology did in fact go on to develop a doctrine of purgatory.

The Sunni Hadith concerning the Last Day

Bernie Power[i]

The Hadith is a library of books detailing the sayings and actions of Muhammad and his early followers. The following account is a collation of the events preceding and taking place on the Last Day, according to the 'six books'[ii] of the Hadith collections generally accepted by most Sunni Muslims.[iii] The Hadith contain much detail[37] about the Day of Resurrection, or the Day of Judgement, and the events preceding and surrounding it.

Belief in the Last Day, or 'the Hour', is a requirement of faith for all Muslims.[38] The term 'believe/s in Allah and the Last Day' is a frequently occurring term throughout the Hadith, appearing nearly 40 times in the six collections.

This study will particularly draw on the collection of al-Bukhari, supplemented by input from the other five collections. There is a mass of eschatological traditions, not fully ordered or harmonized—even when only dealing with the six 'consensus' collections. The intention here is to present the Hadiths with a minimum of comment and explanation, thus introducing the reader to the undiluted experience of the Hadith.

This study will present the details of the Last Day in a schematic or tabular form, rather than a prose form. This sequential scheme is a rough tracking of what seems to have become the standard Muslim expectation. There is no absolute unanimity or authoritative single narrative on the Last Day for all Sunnis.

---

[i] Dr Bernie Power lectures at the Melbourne School of Theology in the CSIOF. Together with his family, Bernie lived and worked with Interserve in a range of Muslim countries in Asia and the Middle East for over 20 years. He holds degrees in science and theology and wrote his doctoral thesis on a comparative study of the Bible and al-Bukhari's Hadith collection. Bernie writes regularly for scholarly and popular journals, including *Quadrant* and *St Francis Journal*.

[ii] They are the collections of Al-Bukhari, Muslim, Abu Dawud, Tirmidhi, Al-Nasa'i and Ibn Majah. The numbering systems of each collection are problematic. We will use Mohsin Khan's method for Al-Bukhari (vol.X:account no Y) and Muhammad Fuad Abd al-Baqi's system for Muslim (nos 1 to 3033). The various websites (e.g. Searchtruth) and software programs (e.g. Alim and Islamic Scholar) all use different numbering systems. However it is easy to search for key words among the different collections.

[iii] The Shi'a collections differ from the Sunni Hadith and are much more extensive.

Events leading up to the Last Day

There is much detail in the Hadith about the events preceding the Last Hour. Sometimes this is presented as 'ten signs'[39]; however even a brief study uncovers many more. They are as follows:

1) Wars: Prior to the Last Day, there will be a series of military conflicts between various forces. Some of the antagonists are clearly identified but others are not.

(a) Amongst Muslims?

Muhammad said: 'The Hour will not be established till two big groups fight each other whereupon there will be a great number of casualties on both sides and they will be following one and the same religious doctrine.'[40] Muhammad had warned Muslims against fighting each other. 'When two Muslims fight (meet) each other with their swords, both the murderer as well as the murdered will go to the Hell-fire.'[41]

(b) Against Jews:

Muslims will fight against the Jews, and gain victory over them. If a Jew seeks shelter behind a rock, the rock will betray him, saying: 'There is a Jew hiding behind me: kill him.'[42]

(c) Against Christians:

Muhammad gave very specific details to one of his followers of a great battle between the Muslims and 'Rome'. By this he meant the Christian Byzantine Empire which included Syria. He said: 'The Last Hour will not come until the people divide inheritance and rejoice over booty. Then he said pointing towards Syria, with a gesture of his hand like this: 'The enemy will muster strength against the Muslims and the Muslims will muster strength against them (Syrians).' I said: 'You mean Rome?' He said: 'Yes, and there will be a terrible fight. The Muslims will prepare a detachment (for fighting unto death) which will not return unless victorious. They will fight until darkness intervenes. Both sides will return without being victorious and both will be wiped out. The Muslims will again prepare a detachment for fighting unto death so that they may not return unless victorious. When it is the fourth day, a new detachment from the remnant of the Muslims will be prepared and Allah will decree that the enemy will be routed. They would fight such a fight the like of which has not been seen, so fierce that even if a bird were to pass their flanks, it would fall down dead before reaching the other end. (There will be such a large scale massacre) that when counting will be done, (only) one out of a hundred men related to one another would be found alive.

So what can be the joy at the spoils of such war and what inheritance can be divided? They will be in this very state when they will hear of a calamity more horrible than this. A cry will reach them: The *Dajjal* has taken your place among your offspring. They will therefore throw away what is in their hands and go forward, sending ten horsemen as a scouting party.' Allah's Apostle (peace be upon him) said: 'I know their names, the names of their forefathers and the colour of their horses. They will be the best horsemen on the surface of the Earth on that day or among the best horsemen on the surface of the Earth on that day.'[43]

(d) Against non-Arabs:

Muhammad said: 'The Hour will not be established till you fight with the Khudh and the Kirman from among the non-Arabs, a nation wearing hairy shoes, and live in Al-Bariz, and till you fight the Turks, who will have small eyes, red faces and flat noses; and their faces will be like flat shields coated with leather.'[44]

(e) Against Gog and Magog:

The warlike peoples of Gog and Magog were imprisoned behind an iron wall built by Dhu al-Qurnain (thought by many Muslims to be Alexander the Great). They would not escape until the Last Day.[45] Then they would cause great devastation.[46] Muhammad fearfully described an opening in the wall of Gog and Magog, demonstrating it with his fingers.[47]

(f) Warfare to the end:

Muhammad expected and required that Muslims be involved in warfare until close to the end of history. He said: 'Jihad will be performed continuously since the day Allah sent me as a prophet until the day the last member of my community will fight with the Dajjal (Antichrist).'[48] There would be a short period of peace under Christ and the Mahdi before the End would come (see below).

2) **Political and social changes:** There will be a series of political and social events or trends which precede the Last Day.

---

[i] The *Dajjal* is the Antichrist who will appear on earth before the Last Day. For more on this, see the next chapter.

(a) The caliphate ruling in Jerusalem:

Muhammad placed his hand on the head of a man and said: 'When you see the caliphate has settled in the holy land, earthquakes, sorrows and serious matters will have drawn near and on that day the Last Hour will be nearer to mankind than this hand of mine is to your head.'[49]

(b) Moral decay:

There will be an increase in murders (*al-Harj*).[50] Honesty will be lost, and power or authority will be in the hands of unfit persons.[51] Honesty will gradually disappear.[52] Illegal sexual intercourse will be widespread, and the drinking of alcoholic drinks will prevail.[53]

(c) Demographic changes:

Muhammad claimed that '[m]en will decrease in number, and women will increase in number, so much so that fifty women will be looked after by one man.'[54]

(d) Growth of wealth:

Despite these changes, there will be unprecedented prosperity. Money will overflow[55] to such an extent that a wealthy person who wants to give *zakat* to the poor will find no-one who needs it. People will compete with each other in constructing high buildings.[56]

3) Unusual events:

(a) Physical changes in the earth: The military and social chaos of that time will be mirrored in the physical creation. The sun will be obscured and sky split asunder.[57] Frequent earthquakes will take place,[58] increasing in number.[59] There will be landslides in three places, one in the east, one in the west and one in Arabia at the end of which fire would burn forth from the Yemen, and would drive people to the place of their assembly.'[60] On the Last Day, the sun will rise from the West.[61]

(b) Strange communication: Muhammad said: 'The last hour will not come before wild beasts speak to men, the end of a man's whip and the thong of his sandal speak to him, and his thigh informs him what his family have done since he left them.'[62]

4) Challenges for Muslims:

Islam will face some great challenges.

(a) Internal division:

Muhammad stated that 'knowledge will be taken away'.[63] In its place, there will be false teachers. They will have shaved heads. 'Some foolish young people will use the best speech of all people, they will recite the Qur'an, and they will be so pious that you will consider your prayers inferior to their prayers, but their belief will not go beyond their throats, and they will abandon Islam. The last of them will accompany the Antichrist. So kill them, in order to get a great reward on the Day of Resurrection.'[64] About thirty liars (*dajjals*) will arise, and each will claim that he is Allah's apostle.[65]

(b) Idolatry returns:

Worship of idols will make a return. 'Allah's Apostle said, "The Hour will not be established till the buttocks of the women of the tribe of Daus move while going round Dhi-al-Khalasa." Dhi-al-Khalasa was the idol which the Daus tribe worshipped in the Pre-Islamic Period of ignorance.'[66]

(c) Ka'ba burnt and Hajj ended:

Symbols and rituals necessary for Islam will disappear. The *Ka'ba* will be burnt,[67] and *Hajj* to the *Ka'ba* will be abandoned.[68]

(d) Afflictions will appear:

These are unnamed, but they may be the combination of the events outlined above. They will be evident and widespread.[69] A believer is advised to seek refuge or shelter from these afflictions.[70] 'Some will take to the tops of mountains and to the places of rain-falls to run away with his religion in order to save it from afflictions.'[71] These difficulties[i] will be so severe that some will desire death. 'A man when passing by a grave of someone will say, "Would that I were in his place".'[72]

(e) Some Muslims will persevere:

Muhammad said, 'Some of my followers will remain victorious (and on the right path) till the Last Day comes.'[73] 'A group of people amongst my followers will remain obedient to Allah's orders and they will not be harmed by anyone who will not help them or who will oppose them, till Allah's Order (the Last Day) comes upon them.'[74]

---

[i] Ed: See comments on *fitna/fitan* in the next chapter.

(f) Too-late believers rejected:

On the day that the sun rises in the west, when it becomes obvious that all the prophecies are being fulfilled, people will want to believe and embrace Islam, but it will be too late. 'That will be the time when: (As Allah said,) "No good will it do to a soul to believe then, if it believed not before, nor earned good (by deeds of righteousness) through its Faith".' (Q 6.158).[75]

5. The Mahdi:[i] There is some information about the 'Mahdi' ('the guided one'). Muhammad is reported to have said: 'If only one day of this world remained. Allah would lengthen that day ... till He raised up in it a man who belongs to me or to my family whose father's name is the same as my father's, who will fill the earth with equity and justice as it has been filled with oppression and tyranny.' This hadith adds: 'the Arabs [will be] ruled by a man of my family whose name will be the same as mine.' [76] This man is described as 'of the descendants of Fatima.'[77] His physical description will be unlike Muhammad: he 'will have a broad forehead [and] a prominent nose.'[78] He will come from Medina. He will be unwillingly co-opted as leader, following the death of the Caliph. A military force from Syria sent to oppose him, will be swallowed up[ii] in the desert. Allegiance will be pledged to him from Iraq and Syria, but a man from the Quraysh 'whose maternal uncles belong to Kalb' will send a force against him and be defeated, and Kalb's booty will be distributed. Every person who requests will receive as much as he can carry.[79] This new leader 'will govern the people by the Sunnah of their Prophet ...and establish Islam on Earth.' [80] The He will reign for seven years,[81] after which he will die and the Muslims will pray over him.[82]

6. The coming of Al-Dajjal: Since the next chapter will give more detail about Al-Dajjal, the Antichrist, he is only briefly mentioned here for the sake of chronology. He will live on the earth for a period described as 'forty', although it is unclear if this is 40 days or weeks or years,[83] but another hadith has a more specific time frame. He will be on earth 'for forty days, one day like a year, one day like a month, one day like a week, and the rest of the days will

---

[i] The title 'Mahdi' does not appear in the two famous Sahih collections, though the term and/or descriptions of this figure do appear at least briefly in other collections such as Abu Dawud, Tirmidhi, and Ibn Majah. Ed: The Mahdi traditions are more developed theologically in the Shi'i material (see Anthony McRoy's chapter on Shi'i eschatology).

[ii] Ed: The 'swallowing' [*khasf*] is itself an Islamic apocalyptic trope.

be like your days.'[84] Alongside Al-Dajjal will be another being called 'the beast of the earth'.[85]

7. Jesus' reign: Jesus will return to earth and kill Al-Dajjal. 'He will fight the people for the cause of Islam. He will break the cross, kill swine, and abolish *jizyah*. Allah will perish all religions except Islam.' Jesus will establish a rule of justice and prosperity. He 'will descend as a just ruler and ... there will be abundance of money and nobody will accept charitable gifts.'[86] For a seven year period there will be no rancour between any two persons.[87] After 40 years on earth, Jesus will die and the Muslims will pray over him.[88]

8. The death of all believers:[i] A pleasant wind, a cold wind from the direction of Syria, will come, and Allah will take the life of every Muslim, everyone having a speck of good or faith in him.[89]

9. The period of the unbelievers: Some will be left behind. 'Only the wicked people will survive and they will be as careless as birds with the characteristics of beasts. They will commit adultery like asses. They will never appreciate good nor condemn evil. Then Satan will come to them, in human form, and would say: "Don't you respond?" They will say: "What do you order us to do?" He will command them to worship the idols but, in spite of this, they will have an abundance of sustenance[ii] and lead comfortable lives.'[90]

10. The blowing of the two trumpets: 'Then the trumpet will be blown and he who hears it will bend his neck to one side and raise it from the other side. The first one to hear that trumpet will be the person who is busy in setting right the cistern meant for supplying water to the camels. He will faint and the other people will also faint. Then Allah will send or He will cause to be sent rain which will be like dew and there will grow out of it the bodies of people. Then the second trumpet will be blown and they will stand up and begin to look (around).'[91]

11. The timing of the end:

(a) It will be unexpected and sudden:

---

[i] Ed: In a sort of inverse of some Christian millennial schemes, there is an almost 'Isaianic' interlude of peace and then a sort of rapture of the faithful.

[ii] Ed: This is one of many instances in which apocalyptic expectation is not merely future fantasy, but is concerned with theology, justice, and ethics today. Here in particular a theodicy issue is raised: Why do the wicked prosper?

People will not have time to respond. 'And the Hour will be established while two men spreading a garment in front of them but they will not be able to sell it, nor fold it up; and the Hour will be established when a man has milked his she-camel and has taken away the milk but he will not be able to drink it; and the Hour will be established before a man repairing a tank (for his livestock) is able to water (his animals) in it; and the Hour will be established when a person has raised a morsel (of food) to his mouth but will not be able to eat it.'[92]

(b) Time will be shrunk:

Muhammad said: 'The last hour will not come before time contracts, a year being like a month, a month like a week, a week like a day, a day like an hour, and an hour like the kindling of a fire.'[93] Time will pass quickly.[94]

(c) The Last Day will take place on a Friday:

On a Friday 'the Last Hour will come,'[95] and the last trumpet will be blown.[96] Every beast looks each Friday fearing that it is the Last Day.[97]

(d) Perhaps in or near Muhammad's time:

Sometimes Muhammad had the impression that the end was very near, possibly even in his lifetime. 'The Prophet got up from his sleep with a flushed red face and said, "None has the right to be worshipped but Allah. Woe to the Arabs, from the great evil that is nearly approaching them. Today a gap has been made in the wall of Gog and Magog like this." (Sufyan illustrated this by forming the number 90 or 100 with his fingers.) It was asked, 'Shall we be destroyed though there are righteous people among us?' The Prophet said, "Yes, if evil increased".'[98] Muhammad was described as being in 'a state of fear' when he related this.[99] He explained: 'How can I be at ease when the one who blows the trumpet has put it to his mouth, inclined his ear and bent his forehead, waiting to see when he will be ordered to blow it?'[100] He often prayed to Allah: 'I seek refuge with you from the afflictions of Masih al-Dajjal',[101] implying that he thought he might be alive when Al-Dajjal came. When an adult slave passed by, Muhammad said: 'If this (slave) should live long, he will not reach the geriatric old age, but the Hour will be established.'[102] He also said: 'I have been commissioned when the end of time is near and I have preceded it as this has preceded that," indicating his forefinger and his middle finger.'[103]

(e) After two centuries: Islam's prophet announced:[i] 'The signs will come after the end of the second century.'[104]

12. Punishment in the grave:[ii] Between their deaths and the day of Judgement, people will be treated differently from each other.

(a) Non-believers will be punished according to their sins:

In a dream, Muhammad was taken to Jerusalem where he saw people being punished in their graves. He was told by the two men that were accompanying him that each of the people he saw 'will be punished like that till the Day of Resurrection.' A liar had an iron hook pushed continuously through his cheeks and ripped out. His cheek was restored after each tearing, so that it could be torn again. A man who had knowledge of the Qur'an but did not recite it at night, because he was sleeping, and did not act on it had his head continuously crushed by a rock, but his head returned to normal after each crushing, in preparation for the next crushing. Men and women who committed adultery were being roasted, naked and together, in a fiery hole. Those who dealt in *riba* (usury) were swimming in a river of blood and a stone was cast into their mouths when they tried to escape.[105] Judgement will come according to the sins that a person committed. For a person who did not pay his zakat from gold or silver, these metals will be beaten into plates, heated in the fire of hell, and his forehead, sides and back will be cauterised with them for a day that lasts 50,000 years until judgement is passed on him and he is sent to Paradise or hell. A man who did not pay zakat for his camels will be trampled and bitten by them, and a man who did not pay zakat for his cows and sheep will be gored and trampled by them for the same period of time.[106] 'This punishment will go on till Allah has finished the judgments amongst the people.'[107]

(b) Faithful Muslims will not be punished in the grave:

A person 'who is on the frontier (in Allah's path), for his deeds will be made to go on increasing till the Day of Resurrection, and he will

---

[i] Ed: There are different ways Muslims have harmonized these prophecies with the fact that the End has not yet come. For example, some have looked for a series of signs stretching out into history so that certain climactic historical events around the Islamic year 200 are interpreted as part of the on-going list of signs.

[ii] Ed: See Amanda Parker's chapter on the 'torments of the grave.'

be safe from the trial in the grave.'[108] Every person will be questioned in the grave by the angels about what they believe about Islam's prophet. 'If the person testifies: "He is Muhammad, Allah's Apostle, and he came to us with self-evident truth and guidance. So we accepted his teaching, believed and followed him." Then the angels will say to him to sleep in peace as they have come to know that he was a believer.'[109]

(c) Yet Muhammad prayed to be saved from the punishment of the grave:

This prayer was often on his lips. He regularly entreated: 'O Allah! I seek refuge with You from the punishment of the Fire, the afflictions of the grave, (and) the punishment in the grave.'[110] Aisha reported him 'seeking refuge with Allah from the punishment in the grave in every prayer he prayed.'[111]

Events of the Day of Judgment

1. The assembling: The people will be told: 'Go to your Lord'.[112] Muhammad said: 'On the Day of Resurrection Allah will gather all the first and the last (people) in one plain, and the voice of the announcer will reach all of them, and one will be able to see them all, and the sun will come closer to them.'[113] The sun will be so close that they will suffer such distress and trouble that they will not be able to stand or bear it.[114] Muhammad said: 'Mankind will be assembled on the Day of Resurrection in three classes, one walking, one riding and one on their faces.' He was asked how people could walk on their faces and replied, 'He who caused them to walk on their feet has power to make them walk on their faces. They will guard themselves by their faces from every acclivity and from thorns.'[115] Another account has them being dragged on their faces by the angels. Those riding will have food and clothing, but animals for riding will be difficult to obtain.[116] All people will be barefooted, naked and uncircumcised.[117] It will be a time of severe agony. 'Every pregnant female shall drop her load (have a miscarriage) and a child will have grey hair. And you shall see mankind as in a drunken state, yet not drunk, but severe will be the torment of Allah.' (Q 22.2)[118]

2. The grand assize: 'On the Day of Resurrection mankind will be reviewed three times, the first two consisting of disputing and excuses, but at the third the records of men's deeds will go quickly into their hands, some receiving them in their right hands and some in their left.'[119]

The basis for judgement will be one's deeds. Good deeds or acts of mercy will receive credit, but evil deeds or acts of oppression will result in some of the perpetrator's credit being transferred to those who suffered. On hearing this, one man who had been beating his slaves immediately set them free.[120] Every action that a person has performed has been recorded by the angels.[121] Deeds will be weighed in the scales.[122]

But for those who have recited the *shahada*, this will outweigh all their sins. 'Allah's Messenger (peace be upon him) said that on the Day of Resurrection Allah will separate a man belonging to his people in presence of all creatures and spread ninety-nine scrolls over him, each scroll extending as far as the eye could see, then say, "Do you object to anything in this? Have my scribes who keep note wronged you?" He will reply, "No, my Lord." He will ask him if he has any excuse, and when he tells his Lord that he has none, He will say, "On the contrary you have with Us a good deed, and you will not be wronged today." A document will then be brought out containing, "I testify that there is no god but Allah, and that Muhammad is His servant and Messenger," and He will say, "Come to be weighed." He will ask his Lord, "What this document along with these scrolls is? And He will reply, "You will not be wronged." The scrolls will then be put in one side of the scale and the document in the other, and the scrolls will become light ßand the document heavy, for nothing could compare in weight with Allah's name.'[123]

2. Separation of and judgement of non-Muslim religions

Allah will order the people to follow what they used to worship. So some of them will follow the sun, some will follow the moon, and some will follow other deities.[124]

The Jews will be asked who they worshipped. 'They will reply: "We used to worship Ezra, the son of Allah." It will be said to them, "You are liars, for Allah has neither a wife nor a son. What do you want (now)?" They will reply, "We want You to provide us with water." Then it will be said to them: "Drink," and they will fall down in Hell (instead).

Then it will be said to the Christians, "What did you use to worship?" They will reply, "We used to worship Messiah, the son of

Allah." It will be said, "You are liars, for Allah has neither a wife nor a son. What do you want (now)?" They will say, "We want You to provide us with water." It will be said to them, "Drink," and they will fall down in Hell (instead).' [125]

3. Seeing Allah's shin:

Only the Muslims will be left with the hypocrites – those who claimed to be Muslims.[126] The Muslims are told that they will definitely see their Lord as clearly as they can see a full moon.[127] They will see Him with their own eyes,[128] and they will have no difficulty seeing him.[129] 'The people said, "O Allah's Apostle! Shall we see our Lord on the Day of Resurrection?" He replied, "Do you have any doubt in seeing the full moon on a clear (not cloudy) night?" They replied, "No, O Allah's Apostle!" He said, "Do you have any doubt in seeing the sun when there are no clouds?" They replied in the negative. He said, "You will see Allah (your Lord) in the same way".'[130]

Initially they will deny it is Him, but He will insist, and they will agree.[131] The part of Allah's body which Muslims recognise will be his "shin" *saq*, which he will uncover at their request.[132] On that day His "shank"[i] will be uncovered.[133]

4. The order of judgment:

Muslims will be judged first, then Christians and Jews.[134] Muslims will be the foremost on the day of resurrection,[ii] even though they were the last to come into the world.[135]

5. Crossing the Bridge:

Muhammad said: 'Allah will call them, and *As-Sirat* (a bridge) will be laid across Hell and I (Muhammad) shall be the first amongst the Apostles to cross it with my followers. Nobody except the Apostles will then be able to speak and they will be saying then, "O Allah! Save us. O Allah Save us".'[136]

'There will be hooks like the thorns of Sa'dan in Hell, but nobody except Allah knows their greatness in size and these will entangle the people according to their deeds; some of them will fall and stay

---

[i] Ed: Cf. Q 68.42 which seems to imply that the judged sinner is 'exposed' or 'laid bare' before God and/or that 'running in fear' the robes must be hiked up, exposing the shins.

[ii] Ed: Throughout the *hadith*, as in the Qur'an, Islam defines itself frequently in relationship to and (usually) in favourable contrast against Judaism and Christianity.

in Hell forever.'[137] These will include the hypocrites, whose lights will be extinguished.

But the believers will 'secure salvation ...The first group to achieve it would comprise seventy thousand men who would have the brightness of the full moon on their faces, and they would not be called to account.'[i] Then the faces of the people immediately following them will be like the brightest stars in Heaven.'[138] This seventy thousand will enter Paradise without reckoning or punishment, with 'each thousand accompanied by seventy thousand and three handfuls added by my Lord.'[139] In another hadith, Muhammad claims that Allah 'has promised me that four hundred thousand of my people will enter Paradise without being taken to account.' These will represent two of Allah's handfuls.[140] These could the one sect or party of the Muslim *umma* (Community or nation) which will not be in the Hell-fire, whereas the other seventy-two sects of Islam will be in the Hell-fire.[141]

6. Most people will enter hell:

The Prophet said, 'On the day of Resurrection Allah will say, "O Adam!" Adam will reply, "*Labbaik*,"[ii] our Lord", and "*Sa'daik*."[iii] Then there will be a loud call (saying), "Allah orders you to take from among your offspring a mission for the (Hell) Fire." Adam will say, "O Lord! Who are the mission for the (Hell) Fire?" Allah will say, "Out of each thousand, take out 999." ...(When the Prophet mentioned this), the people were so distressed (and afraid) that their faces got changed (in color) whereupon the Prophet said, "From Gog and Magog nine-hundred ninety-nine will be taken out and one from you".'[142] People will continue to be thrown into hell until Allah puts his foot on it.[143]

7. Muhammad would be the first into Paradise: He said: 'I shall be the first to rattle the knocker of Paradise, and Allah will open for me and bring me into it accompanied by the poor ones among the believers, and this is no boast. I shall be the most honourable in Allah's estimation among those of earliest and latest times, and this is no boast.'[144]

---

[i] Ed: In their variant fashions Islam and Christianity both incorporate the notion of 'grace.' In Christianity it is expressed in the self-giving of Christ; here it seems to be mainly a matter of the exercise of divine fiat to forgo accounting for some (similar examples below).

[ii] This means 'Here I am at your service.'

[iii] This means: 'I am obedient to you.'

8. Muslims may be a minority in Paradise:

'Allah's apostle said: "You Muslims (compared to the large number of other people) will be like a black hair on the side of a white ox, or a white hair on the side of a black ox, and I hope that you will be one-fourth of the people of Paradise." On that, we said, "Allahu-Akbar!" Then he said, "I hope that you will be one-third of the people of Paradise." We again said, "Allahu-Akbar!" Then he said, "(I hope that you will be) one-half of the people of Paradise." So we said, "Allahu Akbar".'[145]

9. Some will come out of hell:

'Others will receive punishment (torn into small pieces) and will get out of Hell, till when Allah intends mercy on whomever He likes amongst the people of Hell, He will order the angels to take out of Hell those who worshipped none but Him alone. The angels will take them out by recognizing them from the traces of prostrations, for Allah has forbidden the (Hell) fire to eat away those traces. So they will come out of the Fire, it will eat away from the whole of the human body except the marks of the prostrations. At that time they will come out of the Fire as mere skeletons. The Water of Life will be poured on them and as a result they will grow like the seeds growing on the bank of flowing water.'[146] Some will be a very short time in hell and go straight to Paradise, like a flash of lightning, but others will stay there for a time and come out like a person walking, with many speeds in between.[147]

10. There will be intercession:

Some people will say: 'Don't you see, in what condition you are and the state to which you have reached? Why don't you look for a person who can intercede for you with your Lord?[148]

(a) **Adam:** 'Some people will say: "Appeal to your father, Adam." They will go to him and say: "O Adam! You are the father of all mankind, and Allah created you with His Own Hands, and breathed into you of His Spirit (meaning the spirit which he created for you); and ordered the angels to prostrate for you, and made you live in Paradise. Will you not intercede for us with your Lord? Don't you see in what (miserable) state we are, and to what condition we have reached?" On that Adam will reply, "My Lord is so angry as He has never been before and will never be in the future; (besides), He forbade me (to eat from) the tree, but I disobeyed (Him), (I am worried about) myself! Myself! Go to somebody else; go to Noah".[149]

(b) Noah: 'They will go to Noah and say; "O Noah! You are the first amongst the messengers of Allah to the people of the earth, and Allah named you a thankful slave. Don't you see in what a (miserable) state we are and to what condition we have reached? Will you not intercede for us with your Lord?" Noah will reply: "Today my Lord has become so angry as he had never been before and will never be in the future. I had (in the world) the right to make one definitely accepted invocation, and I made it against my nation. Myself! Myself! Go to someone else; go to Abraham".[150]

(c) Abraham: 'They will go to Abraham and say, "O Abraham! You are Allah's Apostle and His Khalil from among the people of the earth; so please intercede for us with your Lord. Don't you see in what state we are?" He will say to them, "My Lord has today become angry as He has never become before, nor will ever become thereafter. I had told three lies ... Myself! Myself! Myself! Go to someone else; go to Moses".[151]

(d) Moses: 'The people will then go to Moses and say, "O Moses! You are Allah's Apostle and Allah gave you superiority above the others with this message and with His direct Talk to you; (please) intercede for us with your Lord! Don't you see in what state we are?" Moses will say, "My Lord has today become angry as He has never become before, nor will become thereafter, I killed a person whom I had not been ordered to kill. Myself! Myself! Myself! Go to someone else; go to Jesus".[152]

(e) Jesus: 'So they will go to Jesus and say, "O Jesus! You are Allah's Apostle and His Word which He sent to Mary, and a superior soul created by Him, and you talked to the people while still young in the cradle. Please intercede for us with your Lord. Don't you see in what state we are?" Jesus will say, "My Lord has today become angry as He has never become before nor will ever become thereafter". Jesus will not mention any sin,[i] but will say, "Myself! Myself! Myself! Go to someone else; go to Muhammad".[153]

(f) Muhammad: The Muslims will meet Muhammad at a pre-arranged location. He told them: 'Your promised place to meet me will be Al-Haud (i.e. the Tank) (on the Day of Resurrection).'[154]

---

[i] Ed: The sinlessness of Jesus stands out, even in the *hadith.*

Another time he said it could be at 'the path', 'the scale' or 'the reservoir'.[155]

'Muhammad said, "I will be the chief of all the people on the Day of Resurrection... So they will come to me and say, "O Muhammad! You are Allah's Apostle and the last of the prophets, and Allah forgave your early and late sins. (Please) intercede for us with your Lord. Don't you see in what state we are?' The Prophet added, "Then I will go beneath Allah's Throne and fall in prostration before my Lord. And then Allah will guide me to such praises and glorification to Him as He has never guided anybody else before me. Then it will be said, "O Muhammad! Raise your head. Ask, and it will be granted. Intercede! It (your intercession) will be accepted." So I will raise my head and say, "My followers, O my Lord! My followers, O my Lord". It will be said, "O Muhammad! Let those of your followers who have no accounts, enter through such a gate of the gates of Paradise as lies on the right; and they will share the other gates with the people".'[156] Muhammad claimed that he had been given the choice between half of his people entering Paradise, or intercession, and he chose intercession.[157]

(g) Fellow Muslims: 'The Prophet said, "You (Muslims) cannot be more pressing in claiming from me a right that has been clearly proved to be yours than the believers in interceding with Almighty for their (Muslim) brothers on that Day, when they see themselves safe. They will say, "O Allah! (Save) our brothers (for they) used to pray with us, fast with us and also do good deeds with us."' Allah will say, "Go and take out (of Hell) anyone in whose heart you find faith equal to the weight of one (gold) Dinar." Allah will forbid the Fire to burn the faces of those sinners. They will go to them and find some of them in Hell (Fire) up to their feet, and some up to the middle of their legs. So they will take out those whom they will recognize and then they will return, and Allah will say (to them), "Go and take out (of Hell) anyone in whose heart you find faith equal to the weight of one half Dinar."' They will take out whomever they will recognize and return, and then Allah will say, "Go and take out (of Hell) anyone in whose heart you find faith equal to the weight of an atom (or a smallest ant), and so they will take out all those whom they will recognize." Abu Sa'id said: "If you do not believe me then read the Holy Verse: "Surely! Allah wrongs not even of the weight of an atom (or a smallest ant) but if there is any good (done) He doubles it." (Q 4.40)[158] This personal intercession will be numerically effective. Muhammad stated that 'more than the number of the B. Tamim [a large Arab tribe] will enter Paradise through the intercession of a man of my people,'[159] although other individuals may successfully intercede for a group or only one person.[160] Having given one of the inhabitants of Paradise water for ablutions could be grounds for intercession and release from hell.[161]

(h) Martyrs: Muhammad said: 'The intercession of a martyr will be accepted for seventy members of his family.'[162]

(i) Allah's intercession:

'The Prophet added, "Then the prophets and Angels and the believers will intercede, and (last of all) the Almighty (Allah) will say, "Now remains My Intercession." He will then hold a handful of the Fire from which He will take out some people whose bodies have been burnt, and they will be thrown into a river at the entrance of Paradise, called the water of life.

They will grow on its banks, as a seed carried by the torrent grows. You have noticed how it grows beside a rock or beside a tree, and how the side facing the sun is usually green while the side facing the shade is white. Those people will come out (of the River of Life) like pearls, and they will have (golden) necklaces, and then they will enter Paradise whereupon the people of Paradise will say, "These are the people emancipated by the Beneficent. He has admitted them into Paradise without them having done any good deeds and without sending forth any good (for themselves)." Then it will be said to them, "For you is what you have seen and its equivalent as well".'[163]

Theoretically, at least, Allah could save all of humanity from hell. Abu Bakr asked: "What harm would it do you if Allah were to bring us all into Paradise?" Umar said, "If Allah Who is Great and Glorious, wishes to bring all His creatures into Paradise simultaneously He can do so," and the Prophet said, "Umar has spoken the truth".'[164]

(j) Self-intercession: Muhammad said: 'Two men of those who enter Hell will shout loudly, and the Lord Most High will say, "Bring them out." He will ask them why they shouted so loudly and they will reply, "We did that in order that Thou mightest have mercy on us." He will say, 'My mercy to you is that you should go and throw yourselves where you were in Hell." One of them will do so and Allah will make it coolness and peace for him, but the other will stand and not do so. The Lord Most High will ask him, "What has prevented you from throwing yourself in as your companion did?" and he will reply, "My Lord, I hope that Thou wilt not send me back into it after taking me out of it." The Lord most high will then say to him, "You will have your hope realised," and they will both be brought into Paradise by Allah's mercy.'[165]

11. Last man out of hell:

The last person to be taken out of hell and allowed to enter Paradise will be a man whose minor sins are revealed in detail but his major sins will be overlooked and replaced by good deeds.[166]

'Then when Allah had finished from the Judgments amongst his creations, one man will be left between Hell and Paradise and he will be the last man from the people of Hell to enter paradise. He will be facing Hell, and will say, "O Allah! Turn my face from the fire as its wind has dried me and its steam has burnt me." Allah will ask him, "Will you ask for anything more in case this favor is granted to you?" He will say, "No by Your (Honor) Power!' And he will give to his Lord (Allah) what he will of the pledges and the covenants. Allah will then turn his face from the Fire.

When he will face Paradise and will see its charm, he will remain quiet as long as Allah will. He then will say, "O my Lord! Let me go to the gate of Paradise." Allah will ask him, "Didn't you give pledges and make covenants (to the effect) that you would not ask for anything more than what you requested at first?" He will say, "O my Lord! Do not make me the most wretched, amongst Your creatures." Allah will say, "If this request is granted, will you then ask for anything else?" He will say, "No! By Your Power! I shall not ask for anything else." Then he will give to his Lord what He will of the pledges and the covenants. Allah will then let him go to the gate of Paradise.

On reaching then and seeing its life, charm, and pleasure, he will remain quiet as long as Allah wills and then will say, "O my Lord! Let me enter Paradise." Allah will say, "May Allah be merciful unto you, O son of Adam! How treacherous you are! Haven't you made covenants and given pledges that you will not ask for anything more that what you have been given?" He will say, "O my Lord! Do not make me the most wretched amongst Your creatures." So Allah will laugh and allow him to enter Paradise and will ask him to request as much as he likes. He will do so till all his desires have been fulfilled. Then Allah will say, "Request more of such and such things." Allah will remind him and when all his desires and wishes; have been fulfilled, Allah will say "All this is granted to you and a similar amount besides".' Abu Said Al-Khudri said to Abu Huraira, 'Allah's Apostle said, 'Allah said, "That is for you and ten times more like it".'[167]

12. Muslims taking revenge on each other before entering Paradise:

After being saved from the (Hell) Fire, and crossing safely over the bridge across hell, 'the believers will be stopped at a bridge between Paradise and Hell where they will 'retaliate upon each other' for the injustices done among them in the world and for the wrongs they have committed against one another. After they are cleansed and purified from their sins (through the retaliation), they will be admitted into Paradise; and everyone of them will recognise and know his dwelling in Paradise better than he knew his dwelling in this world.'[168]

Some parallels between the eschatological teaching of the Bible and Al-Bukhari's Hadith (B. = Al-Bukhari)

Wars	B.4:787,788,789,790; 9:237	Mt.24:6; Mk.13:7,8; Lk.21:10
Earthquakes	B.2:146; 9:137,237	Mt.24:7; Lk.21:11
Celestial signs	B.6:159, 160; 8:513; 9:237	Mt.24:29;Acts.2:20 Lk.21:11,25; Joel 2:31
False prophets and deceivers appear among believers	B.6:577; 9:64,65,66,237	Mt.24:11; 2.Pet.3:3,17; Mk.13:6,21,22
Idol worship will reappear	B.9:232	Rev.9:20
Affliction will result in apostasy	B.4:799	Mt.24:8-13
Declining moral standards	B.1:56; 4:808; 6:577; 7:158; 8:503,504; 9:64	Mt.24:12; 2.Thess.2:10
Believers will flee to the mountains and remote places to preserve their faith	B.4:798; 9:210	Mt.24:16-21; Mk.13:14-16; Lk.21:21
People will seek shelter among the rocks	B.4:176, 177, 791	Rev.6:15,16 c.f. Isa.2:10
Gog and Magog will arise	B.2:663; 4:565,566,797; 6:265; 7:215; 8:537; 9:181,249,250	Ezek.38,39; Rev.20:8
The end will come quickly and unexpectedly. People unable to complete normal household tasks	B.9:237; 8:513	Mt.24:40-44; 1.Thess.5:2; 2.Pet.3:10
The perseverance of righteous people could be in jeopardy	B.4:565,797; 9:181,249	Mt.24:22; Mk.13:20
People will desire death	B.9:231,237	Rev.9:6

The Antichrist in Classical Islam: The Muslim Apocalypse, Ibn Kathir, and the Dajjal

Brent Neely[i]

PART ONE

Introduction

The recent popularity of certain best-selling titles in Christian publishing seems to confirm a surge in apocalyptic interest and eschatological speculation in Western Christianity. As it turns out, apocalyptic writings, and even fevered speculation, also have a long pedigree in historic Muslim literature and are thriving in contemporary Muslim society. Articulating the apocalyptic theology or the eschatology of Islam is hardly a simple matter of outlining 'what the Qur'an says.' Rather, mainstream Islamic thought is generally expressed by a historical collectivity of informally authoritative scholars (*'ulama'*) expositing the Qur'an by means of *hadith*, all this culminating in a roughly coherent (Sunni) consensus.[ii]

In the following study we propose to examine one of the dominant characters of the Islamic end-of-days landscape, the Dajjal (the false Messiah), as he is mediated to us through the lens of the prominent medieval theologian, Ibn Kathir (d. 1373). We begin with a general examination of the sources and building blocks of the Muslim apocalypse. Next, we briefly highlight the historical and polemical relevance of apocalyptic literature. Then, we introduce Ibn Kathir and his works, including a glance at the theological, social, and hermeneutical agenda he pursued. Thus far, Part One of

---

[i] Brent Neely has served in the Middle East for over fifteen years and is a faculty member of the Nazareth Evangelical Theological Seminary. He lives with his family in Israel where he is active in ministry with the Arabic-speaking church, inter-denominational evangelical associations, theological education, and humanitarian projects. In terms of study, his areas of interest include New Testament, Intercultural, and Middle Eastern studies.

[ii] There are important distinctions between the eschatological outlook of Shi'i and Sunni Islam. In this study we largely confine ourselves to the Sunni material. See the article by Anthony McRoy for discussion related to Shi'i eschatology.

our essay. Finally, in Part Two, we devote our attention to presenting the profile of the Dajjal in Ibn Kathir's apocalyptic writings.

Sources of Apocalypse in Islam

Resurgent Islam; Shi'i-Sunni tensions; West-East friction; the Arab-Israeli conflict—all these have served to stoke eschatological ferment and speculation in the Muslim world. In the torrent of modern Muslim apocalyptic publishing,[169] the nominal foundation is the classical, 'authorized' traditions (*hadith*) on Islam's last days, source material supposedly extending back to the prophet Muhammad himself. In reality, however, the surprising dynamic core of much *current* eschatological ferment in Muslim writing is actually drawn from sources both diverse and highly suspect from a conventional Muslim perspective. Especially important among these sources are biblical materials (along with their popular Christian interpretations) and anti-Semitic conspiracy theories.[170] Ironically, perhaps, popular Christian eschatology in the West has actually helped feed the apocalyptic resurgence in Islamic publishing.[171] The ancient Muslim *hadiths* on the 'end of the world,' then, are sometimes diluted and even overwhelmed by the volume of imported material and free speculation by popular authors. Nonetheless, this classical source material is avowedly authoritative for the Muslim community and it is to this bedrock of Muslim apocalyptic that we turn our focus.

Of course, when speaking of the textual bases of any aspect of Islam, the Qur'an comes first as the authoritative, miraculous 'sign' (*aya*) *par excellence*. The Qur'an, *especially the so-called Meccan suras*, certainly breathes in an air of apocalyptic. The theme of the coming Hour of resurrection and judgment reverberates through the pages. The proclamation of approaching End, and the attendant delights for the righteous and torment for the infidel, are among the most famous sections of the book.[i] 'Signs' of looming cataclysm or certain resurrection to judgment abound; dreadful portents shake the heavens, possibly including the splitting of the moon (Q 54.1).

---

[i] See further Peter Riddell's article in this volume.

In Q 19.88-91, whether the criticism is of traditional Meccan paganism or even of monotheist trinitarianism, the scandalized rhetoric is laced with apocalyptic imagery:

> And they say, 'The All-merciful has taken unto Himself a son.' You have indeed advanced something hideous! The heavens are wellnigh rent of it and the earth split asunder, and the mountains wellnigh fall down crashing for that they have attributed to the All-Merciful a son (Arberry).

For all that, the Qur'an is not really an 'apocalypse' in the classic literary sense. It is not an extended narrative, a heavenly travelogue, a sustained vision with angelic interlocutor[i] explaining either the structure of the cosmos or the course of holy history. The conflict of the final days and the ultimate vindication of the righteous are not worked out in a detailed narrative borne along by graphic symbolism and caricatured personae. Gog and Magog put in only a cameo appearance in typically allusive style (Q 18.94-96; 21.96). Jesus' association with the End is barely elaborated in the text (cf. Q 4.159; 43.61). As for other quintessentially apocalyptic players, the Mahdi and the Dajjal leave not even a trace.[ii] David Cook has well described the Qur'an as 'an eschatological book,' but not an apocalypse.[172]

Though the Qur'an holds primacy of place as sacred writ, there *is* of course another effectively 'inspired' source for Muslim faith and life, the *hadith.* The authoritative Sunni collections of prophetic traditions were compiled mainly in the third Muslim century. These reports (*hadiths*) speak of the life, actions, sayings, or rulings of the prophet Muhammad. Allegedly deriving from the prophet (or sometimes his closest followers) they appear as textual units backed up by a (ideally flawless) chain of transmitters [*isnad*] from the prophet to the compiler.[iii] They were meticulously and copiously gathered as divinely-mandated guides to Muslim belief and practice following the mode of the prophet himself (*sunna*). For the Sunnis the paramount collections are found in six works, headlined by those of Bukhari (d. 870) and Muslim (d. 875).

---

[i] Despite the traditionally assumed references to Gabriel as the bearer of the revelation.

[ii] Though, of course, Shi'i hermeneutics are well capable of descrying copious if covert allusions to 'Ali and their Mahdi throughout the book.

[iii] Here we sidestep the contested issue of the historical authenticity of the prophetic hadiths, noting only that, truly stemming from Muhammad or not, the body of traditions certainly was put to dynamic use in the early centuries of Islam and, thus, do represent a window on to the concerns of that primal community.

Guidance may be found herein on everything from the lives of the prophets to prayer ritual to sexual behavior to inheritance law and so on; also included are traditions on the last days, judgment, and paradise and hell. Other collections of lasting prestige (such as Ibn Hanbal's[173] *Musnad*), and many less illustrious, were also circulated.

When it comes to the Muslim apocalyptic storyline, the *hadiths* step in to fill the 'narrative gap' in the Qur'an. In fact, the *hadith* provide the actual foundation for the Muslim Apocalypse (i.e., the story of the 'last days'), more so than does the Qur'an. Though, for the most part, these traditions are short reports, mini-narratives, they do at least contain the elements of a last-days theology and provide the key characters to set in the ominous panorama. A common stencil for these traditions is Muhammad predicting a list of *ashrat al-sa'a* (signs of the Hour),[i] typically in groups of six or ten. Muslim scholars have categorized evidences of the oncoming *eschaton* as either 'greater' or 'lesser' signs. The lesser signs may deal with events in nature (sky portents, famine) or especially with moral trends, things like the tendency towards *fitna,*[ii] schism, violence, spiritual decline, and so forth in the last days. Sexual libertinism, neglect of prayer and *hajj,* the leadership of women,[iii] are all 'lesser' signs of the coming End. Lists of 'greater signs' are also enumerated, though the many lists are not mutually consistent[174] (cf. Bukhari 9.88.237[175]). Greater signs may be the splitting of the moon, the conquest of Jerusalem, the sun rising in the west, the rise of the Mahdi, the Dajjal, the Beast (*Dabba*[176]), the return of Jesus, Gog and Magog, a discovery of wealth at the Euphrates, the fall of Constantinople, the burning of the Ka'ba, and others.[iv] Large numbers of apocalyptic *hadith,* whether 'signs' lists or other types, were compiled in books most often titled *fitan* and/or *malahim* (apocalyptic battles). Some of these books formed part of the 'consensus' *hadith* collections referred to above, but many other apocalyptic works were written.[177]

---

[i] That is, signs to appear preceding the Hour of resurrection to judgment.

[ii] pl.: *fitan.* This key term has a broad semantic range including usages with both apocalyptic and non-apocalyptic overtones. The sense may be trials, schisms, violence, temptations, or seductions (to heresy or otherwise).

[iii] See further Moyra Dale's chapter in this volume.

[iv] Notably, some of the signs occurred long ago; some are debated (the splitting of the moon); some may have to occur again or be reinterpreted (the fall of Constantinople, destruction of the Ka'ba).

The exegetical relationship between Qur'an and *hadith* is intriguing. The terse and allusive nature of the qur'anic text practically begs for an 'unpacking,' an explanatory background. In contemporary Western scholarship there is plenty of debate as to whether the posited historical contexts appearing in *hadiths* that 'explain' the qur'anic text[178] are historical reportage or exegetical invention. In any case, it is often the case that qur'anic passages are alleged to be illuminated by *hadiths* which, by historical-critical standards, would appear to be only tenuously connected to the text at best.[179] In the apocalyptic realm, for example, *hadiths* about the final great sign, *the day the sun rises in the west*, are said to relate to the day in which repentance is no longer received in Q 6.158:

> What, do they look for the angels to come to them, nothing less, or that thy Lord should come, or that one of thy Lord's signs should come? On the day that one of thy Lord's signs comes it shall not profit a soul to believe that never believed before, or earned some good in his belief. Say: 'Watch and wait; We too are waiting.' (Arberry)

Nothing internal to the text makes the connection obvious. As noted above, a comparable narrative expansion and exposition occurs in the linking of apocalyptic *hadith* on Jesus or Gog and Magog to terse or highly ambiguous allusions in the qur'anic text (e.g. Q 43.61; 18.94; 21.96).

The *fitan* traditions number in the thousands. Harmonizing, sequencing, and flattening the mass of material into a single coherent storyline would be a herculean, if not impossible, task. The traditions are by no means consistent with one another, and any overarching metanarrative hardly emerges via clear and obvious induction. If the *hadiths* may be seen to relate to one another as part of a larger story, that story must in some degree be imposed on them with selecting, excluding, explaining, and flattening to bring harmony to the picture. This challenge remains, if ameliorated, even if one chooses only to work with the so-called 'sound' tradition collections. For the 'official' Muslim apocalypse, the authorized source material is more-or-less established; its ordering and exposition, much less so.[i] Our guide, then, to the Muslim apocalypse, specifically to the story of the Antichrist, will be the *hadith*-based works of the late medieval scholar, Ibn Kathir.

---

[i] While much the same could be said of Christian eschatology, the diffuse and disparate nature of the Islamic source material makes the Muslim case even more acute.

First, though, a word on the historical and polemical setting of apocalyptic writing.

Historical Context of Apocalypse and Polemics

There is an impulse in apocalyptic to *unveil* (*apokalyptein* in Greek) the hidden mysteries of salvation-history and to make stark an often confusing, depressing, and temptation-ridden moral order: to separate and to vivify the distinction between the pure and the corrupt. In the face of powerful evil, spiritual darkness, or moral seduction, a counter-intuitive revelation seeks to reinterpret history, the cosmos, or *the present* so that the believer might live accordingly.[180] The apocalyptic perspective is rarely a mere curiosity-driven attempt to predict the distant future. Typically, the unveiling of the 'history of the future' is thoroughly embedded in the concerns of a given place and time and often emerges from a matrix of conflict, tension, or inter-religious polemics; thus, for example, the frequent focus of the apocalyptic author on questions of immorality and social decline. Think too of the setting of early Christian and Jewish apocalypses against the backdrop of threatening pagan Roman power, or of the eschatological tumult in Europe and the Near East accompanying the era of Mongol advance. Or, at the genesis of Islam, 'Ishmael at the gates of Constantinople,' was a major catalyst for what David Olster calls the golden age of Byzantine apocalyptic, headlined by the versions of the *Apocalypse of Pseudo-Methodius.*[181]

Sometimes the inter-religious critique entailed in apocalyptic exhibits a sort of mirror effect in which one community's 'beast' is a parody of the rival community's 'savior.' For example, in Sunni-Shi'ite diatribes it has been claimed by some Sunnis that the alleged Mahdi of the Shi'i is in reality the Dajjal himself.[182] The would-be hero of some Umayyad revolts, the Sufyani, becomes in later Muslim apocalyptic a latter-days butcher and villain. In the early Islamic period, texts have the monk Bahira affirming the 'final age,' that of Muhammad, either as pious confirmation of divine purpose (Muslim texts) or as fraudulent instigation of ultimate heresy (Christian texts). In Medieval Jewish tradition the Armilos Antimessiah figure seems have negative connections to Byzantine Christian characters and concepts.[183] Conversely, throughout many ancient Christian and Muslim texts it is evident that the Antichrist is Jewish, perhaps hailing from the tribe of Benjamin or Dan.[184] The notion of the 'Jewish Dajjal' is also prominent in the *hadiths*, as we shall see.

Apocalyptic can manifest a sharply polemical edge. David Cook comments perceptively on a series of events which culminated in an 'apocalyptic explosion' in the Ottoman world in the later 1600's:

> [T]he Jews found that during a period of heightened messianic expectations they could become the targets of pogroms. When the Jews expected their Messiah, in this case Shabbetai Zvi, the Muslims feared the appearance of the Dajjal. For this reason riots and mass slaughter of Jewish children in the Yemen occurred in the immediate wake of the Shabbetian messianic interlude.[185]

The function of the Muslim Jesus in some of the most famous *hadiths* is anything but subtle: upon his return he kills the Antichrist, many of whose henchmen are Jews; breaks crosses; kills pigs; and brings Jews and Christians into submission to Islam (or death).[186] The *dhimmi* communities are ultimately put in their place by being abolished. We have here a dramatic co-opting of the lead figure from one faith community's theology into an alternative, even hostile, storyline of another community.

If apologetics and disputations aim at a confessional victory over rivals in the contested present, then apocalyptic discourse is also frequently enlisted in aid of such a struggle, all the while tuned to the 'approaching hereafter.' Theodicy, struggle, and the ultimate vindication of true believers are the lifeblood of apocalyptic. In our study (below) we might not draw *clear and absolute* connections between each detail of Ibn Kathir's Antichrist figure and his own historical, social, and religious context.[187] Nonetheless, this Muslim scholar's profile of the coming Dajjal is uncannily relevant to the theological agendas and sectarian contests of his day.

Ibn Kathir: Works and Ideology

In the nature of the case, there is no universally-acknowledged teaching magisterium for Islam. There are, however, works by Sunni authorities, works of enormous prestige which are foundational. Ibn Kathir is one such authority. With respect to apocalyptic theology in particular, Filiu refers to him as one of five 'Grand Masters of the Medieval Apocalypse.'[188]

'Imad al-Din Isma'il b. Kathir (700/1301-774/1373) was a prolific theologian, jurist, commentator, and *hadith* expert who spent most of his life and career in Mamluk-era Damascus.[189] Several of his instructors were scholars of great repute, none more so than the famous Hanbali Shaykh, Ibn Taymiyya (d.728/1328), whose theological paradigm and interpretive agenda indelibly marked our scholar. Ibn Kathir enjoyed several prestigious postings as a religious scholar and was engaged in the political life of his day, but also faced opposition and pressure on account of his adherence to his teacher Ibn Taymiyya on some controversial issues.

Ibn Kathir was prolific in his literary output, writing in defence of the *jihad* (against Crusaders on Cyprus) and producing works in *fiqh* and *hadith* studies. His most enduring legacy comes in his universal history (*al-Bidaya wa-al-Nihaya*) and his commentary, *Tafsir[i] al-Qur'an al-'Azim*.[190] Also important are his works in the *qisas* and *sira* categories, as well as the apocalyptic book, *Al-Nihaya fi-al-Fitan wa-al-Malahim*,[191] which may be subsumed in his universal history. Accolades accrued to Ibn Kathir early on (from his own *shaykhs* and, later, al-Suyuti) and continue in the modern era.[192] Ibn Kathir's works remain extremely popular and broadly available in Arabic and in multiple translations.[193] With respect to his Qur'an commentary, it may be said that no classical commentary has 'achieved more contemporary currency' than that of Ibn Kathir.[194]

Ibn Kathir is a leading representative of the Taymiyyan (*salafi*) school.[ii] The *salafi* approach to both religion and text has not everywhere and always enjoyed eminency, but this theological bent and hermeneutical method have been influential over the long run; they certainly are today. For traditional, conservative, or 'orthodox' Muslims, Ibn Kathir's credentials as a *mufassir* (commentator) are especially impeccable. His commentary is arguably the most popular one in Arabic today and is the flagship work of the *salafist* school.[195] Ibn Kathir is 'a constant point of reference for all of the sacred literature of the 20th century.'[196] Keeping our interest in the apocalypse in mind, his *Tafsir* is 'a splendid example of a combination of apocalyptic and exegesis that has seldom been rivalled.'[197] (As to his exclusively eschatological book, the *Nihaya*, it provides the core of our material on the Dajjal, with supplementation coming in from the *Tafsir*.)

---

[i] '*Tafsir*' is the most common Arabic term for 'commentary' [on the Qur'an].

[ii] More below.

Ibn Kathir's apocalyptic work appears against a specific cultural and historical backdrop and pursues some manifestly polemical aims. He also employs a specific methodology in his efforts to champion what he saw as essential orthodoxy against a field of threats and detractors. Under the influence of his famous master, Ibn Taymiyya, he deploys a *salafi* hermeneutic. Walid Saleh describes Ibn Kathir's *tafsir* as the first full, if partially successful, attempt at implementing Ibn Taymiyya's 'radical hermeneutic.'[198]

And what is this method and strategy? Simply put, the Qur'an is to be interpreted by recourse to the Qur'an and then the *sunna*, that is, *properly verified traditions* from the prophet and then his Companions or their Successors.[199] Critical is the notion that once the reported interpretations from the *salaf*, the pious two or three generations following Muhammad, are verified, no further authority comes into play. Philology, history, grammar, and so on, are effectively sidelined. So too are scholastic convention and even leading theological lights intervening between the time of the *salaf* and the interpreter himself. The radical, fundamentalist, or scripturalist interpreter freely evades the binding authority of even the most esteemed figures of Islamic intellectual history.[200] This interpretive mode was not always ascendant in the medieval era and beyond, but has established a clear dominance in conventional Islam since at least the late twentieth century.[201] In this scheme the early *hadith/*traditions in effect come to dominate the 'meaning of the Qur'an' and, thus, Muslim theology. The meaning of the 'Word of God' is basically equated with the 'sound' *hadiths* 'to the exclusion of any other possible hermeneutical approach to the Qur'an.'[202]

Ibn Kathir's Apocalypse and Sectarian Conflict

What were the factors that encouraged such a radical approach to Sunni interpretation? Well, as is so often the case, theology is hammered out amid the fray. The deployment of 'unassailable' *hadiths* could preserve the Sunni theological superstructure in the face of daunting challenges based on a more straightforward philological exegesis of some qur'anic passages. This challenge came in some cases from rationalist *kalam* scholars. A second serious challenge in the thirteenth and fourteenth centuries was the aggressive and increasingly popular Imami Shi'i ideology which was making inroads, even in nominally Sunni realms.[203] By way of reliance on only 'authorized and verified' *hadiths* (such as those typically found in the famous Six Books or in the *Musnad*), theology could be immunized against encroachment by dangerous pro-Shi'i materials.[204]

Armed with these tools and sharing the agenda of his Hanbali teacher, Ibn Kathir set out to buttress a pure (Sunni) Islam in the face of multiple deviancies; that is, to explain the Qur'an, not to mention a 'correct' theology of the last days, by way of recourse to the authoritative voice of the *salaf.* In terms of his commentary, he must be judged a massive success. Of course, the irony here is that his adherence to the *salafi* program was not to be quite so complete as later generations would idealize, and thus, even Ibn Kathir will come in for some *very mild* chastisement from contemporary conservative Muslim scholars.[205] For example the *Tafsir* editor, al-Arna'ut, commends our theologian for his adherence to *sunna*, avoidance of speculative divergences, and employing the prophetic *hadiths* to explicate the meaning of the text. Nonetheless, he mildly chides him for employing *some isra'iliyat*[206] and *hadiths* of dubious authority (without sufficient censure of them).[207] In other words, the complaint is that he did not carry out the purist *salafi* agenda, for which he is famous, with quite enough rigour.

In any case, Ibn Kathir put his considerable skills into a sizeable literary output guided by a hadith-driven, *salafist* agenda. Ibn Kathir and the theologians of like persuasion were waging a battle on behalf of Islamic purity against a host of perceived threats and various forms of corruption, degradation, and 'innovation' in the Muslim polity. Indeed, the so-called 'lesser signs' of the coming Hour entail schism, moral corruption, spiritual laxity, and so on. Vitally, these types of *fitan*, ubiquitous in latter-days prophecies, were very much the concern of the Taymiyyan movement in Ibn Kathir's own day.

In Ibn Kathir's 14th century setting, one might well imagine that with a host of pressing social-religious concerns (the Christians and Jews, the Shi'i movements, moral decline, and ideological challenges from philosophers, street mystics, and theologians) and with Crusaders still afloat in Cyprus, the present looked troubling to our *salafi* theologian—at least in comparison with an imagined 'original purity.' Gazing back past the epochal destruction wrought by the Mongols within living memory, the age of the prophet and Companions must have gained an ever more golden luster by way of contrast. Here there is a convergence between the tendencies of the apocalyptic *hadiths* and the *salafist* agenda. The exaltation of the golden age of the pious predecessors dovetails very nicely with eschatological warnings anchoring Ibn Kathir's *Nihaya*—warnings insisting that Muhammad's generation was the best of all, and insisting (with true apocalyptic pessimism) that all succeeding generations represent a continuous chain of decline![208] The worst is yet to come.

When compiling his apocalyptic material, Ibn Kathir in his commentary used a few qur'anic passages as a springboard from which to deploy *hadiths* which are the actual substance of the apocalypse. However, even with the limiting influence of the 'Taymiyyan hermeneutic,'[i] Ibn Kathir faced a great mass of apocalyptic material and the outsized chore of choosing, ordering, commenting occasionally, and harmonizing the *hadiths*, which were not innately coherent or sequential. This is especially true of his great book, the *Nihaya*; this work is notable in that it does, as a collection, present a roughly ordered picture of the last-days events, even though it is hardly a single running narrative. Beyond this literary task, though, lay the theological agenda of our scholastic master, fortifying Sunni orthodoxy against all competitors.

Again we recall the comments above about apocalyptic writing, historical setting, and religious polemics.[209] We have already mentioned the concern of Ibn Kathir and the 'Taymiyyan school' with defending true Islam – the golden mean[210] – against assaults and innovations from rationalist theologians (worse yet, skeptic or pantheistic philosophers) on the one hand, and charismatic Shi'ite partisans (including Druze and Nusayri groups) on the other. Internal threats included the corrupting influences of the minority communities of Jews and Christians; the appeal of mystics, street magicians and augurs, and dynamic Sufi gurus of dubious orthodoxy made matters even worse; the external threats to 'pure' Islam (and to the Mamluk state) ranged from Crusaders[ii] to Mongols to Turkish warlords. The deviances of these various groups might range from gnostic tendencies to incarnationism to antinomianism to pseudo-miracles performed by monks or mystics; these 'innovations' threatened the *umma* from within and

---

[i] Whereby only 'validated' *hadiths* from the pious ancestors should be admitted.

[ii] Offshore in Cyprus or further afield by this time.

from without.[i] Still a further cause of potential worry was the female element[ii] of society.[211] We do well to keep this host of perceived social threats and spiritual enemies in mind as we examine Ibn Kathir's picture of the Dajjal along with his henchmen, his claims, and his horrific deeds.

Another common norm of apocalyptic thought which well suited the theo-social agenda of the Taymiyyan cadre is its relentless application of a taxonomy of separation. In the confusing, dark, and morally distorted last days, the apocalyptist strives to 'unveil' the truth; to expose in stark terms a reality that has gone murky; to glaringly set off good from evil with no grey region in between. Just as in a *fatwa* from Ibn Taymiyya, the *hadith* stories in the *Nihaya* (such as those concerning the trials of the Dajjal) put great effort into differentiating 'the sheep and the goats.' The literary efforts of Ibn Taymiyya and his followers aim at the clarification and delineation of the 'in' and the 'out,' the 'true' and the 'false.' Jews, Christians, 'innovators,' and sectarians need to be branded and separated from the *umma, which* must be guarded against their perilous[iii] influence.[212] The apocalyptic warnings provide one more plank in that platform.

Various strands of the apocalyptic storyline are well suited to this theological, polemical, and political agenda. For example, a clear thrust of the Jesus and Mahdi traditions *à la* Ibn Kathir is to roundly chide and denounce both Christian and Shi'ite expectations about their last-days deliverers. Ibn Kathir's depiction of the promised Mahdi of 'approved' traditions is couched in a baldly anti-Shi'i framework.[213] As to the Christians, we have already noted the classic profile of a Jesus who doles out their come-uppance, who returns breaking crosses, killing swine, and putting an end to *dhimmi* communities. [214] With respect to the breaking of crosses, this coalesces well with the general Islamic antipathy to the notion of the crucifixion, an event said to be denied in Q 4.157. [215]

---

[i] As Muhammad had warned in *hadiths,* the threat always was one of imitating the ways of the Byzantines or Persians, Jews or Christians – and meeting their fate!

[ii] Ibn Taymiyya warns that much corrupting innovation comes from women, just as was the case with Israel.

[iii] The threat of contamination and assimilation is so real for Ibn Taymiyya that it is important even to impose external differences of habit, clothing, facial hair, and dress on the *dhimmis.*

It is hard to say how close to the End Ibn Kathir thought he was. While he does carry traditions that might seem to imply the Hour would arise around 1591 AD,[216] he also is quite careful to emphasize the uncertainty of any and all predictions of the End.[217] So, on the one hand, Ibn Kathir seeks to throttle any prognosticating excess. On the other hand, he held that prophetic portents of the end had already begun ticking off at the birth of Islam (including a previous massive fire in the Hijaz[218]). The End was looming, the countdown was on.

As the faithful looked ahead into the oncoming unknown, even the events of 'today' were fraught with peril, temptation, division, and *fitna* befitting the apocalyptic *hadiths*. Indeed, even the Dajjal, when he finally arose, was but the culmination of an ongoing deception: tradition had long warned of a multiple series of imposters (*dajjals*)[219] to come. Further, as we shall see, among the Antichrist's lures to *kufr* are *heretical claims, apparent miracles, feats, apparitions, and sundry tricks*, concerns immediately relevant to Sunni purists like Ibn Kathir himself.[220] Also, the Dajjal's followers in Ibn Kathir's book seem to be composed of the very social groups that, for the *salafis*, presented a real and present danger to Islamic purity. The Evil One's partisans range from Jews to women, from the ignorant rabble to wild, Turkic tribesmen. So, as Ibn Kathir wrote of the Last Day, one feels his eyes were quite firmly fixed on his own day, however near or far the actual End might be. And so we turn to one of the most important 'sign-figures' of the looming End, the false Messiah, the Dajjal, and to the profile he cuts in Ibn Kathir's apocalypse.

PART TWO

The Dajjal and His Nemesis the Messiah

Any profile of the Dajjal, the deceiver, the 'false Messiah,'[221] will entail some of the (Islamic) Jesus-traditions; their stories are intertwined. To simplify and flatten out the diverse and disparate notions present in the myriad of latter-days *hadiths* is no simple task. Nonetheless, we can tentatively identify a sequence of coming events in Ibn Kathir's apocalypse. A sequence selectively specifying the elements most relevant to our current study might look like this:

Muslim conquest of Constantinople (presumably under the command of the Mahdi) → rise of the Dajjal → the return of Jesus and defeat of Dajjal → the trial of Gog and Magog → Jesus' glorious reign → the remaining fantastic signs prior to the resurrection.

The well-known template of the return of Jesus makes its appearance not only in Ibn Kathir's explicitly apocalyptic book, but also in the *Tafsir*.[222] In *hadiths* Ibn Kathir forwards, Abu Hurayra affirms that Q 4.159 refers to a *future* death of Jesus after he returns, eliminating pigs, crosses, and the presence of *dhimmi* communities, and instituting a glorious Islamic age on the earth. Of critical importance in this process, of course, is the fact that Jesus leads the Muslim armies to victory and kills the Dajjal.[223]

Staying with this segment of the *Tafsir*, Ibn Kathir quotes Muslim 52.9.34, a famous tradition with noteworthy components. This tradition pertains to the conquest of Constantinople and then the arrival of Jesus to dispatch the Dajjal. In the assault on the city, the classic motif of 'the thirds' of the Muslim army arises (the deserters, the martyrs, and the conquerors). This narrowing into thirds only helps solidify and clarify the faithful remnant, a standard apocalyptic concern. The Antichrist[i] appears precisely at the picturesque moment of peace, when the victors have hung the swords on olive branches.[224] Jesus arrives at the time of prayer in Syria (Al-Sham), *and leads the Muslims in prayer* (!).[ii] In language that seems grossly literal, the Dajjal seems to dissolve upon sighting Jesus, but apparently just before his evil adversary melts wholly away, Jesus physically expunges the evil one. Jesus brandishes his spear with the enemy's blood on it.

Muslim 52.20.110 is also featured[225] and entails descriptors of the Dajjal, namely that he is young and curly-haired and resembles a certain Ibn Qatan. The descent of Jesus and attendant matters furnish some of the core classical motifs associated with the eschatological Jesus.[226] He comes down by the white minaret to the east of Damascus accompanied by two angels,[227] wearing two dyed sashes and his head moistened.[228] Also notable is the powerful breath of the Masih which is deadly to the unbeliever.[229] He dispatches the Dajjal at the gate of Lod.[230] Notably, this particular

---

[i] Curiously, in this version the false Messiah, Dajjal, is simply identified as Al-Masih, when he is first mentioned.

[ii] There are inherent tensions among the traditions as to the respective roles of the Mahdi and Jesus; Ibn Kathir seeks to resolve some of the problems in his apocalyptic *hadith*-compilation (the *Nihaya*). Usually Jesus is seen praying *behind the imam of the day* (the Mahdi?).

tradition extends the apocalyptic storyline *in a single hadith*, including the insertion of Gog and Magog into the sequence. Following this, God sends a purging rain, transforms a hyper-productive earth, and then finally takes the Muslim souls away by means of a pleasant wind. Only the wildly promiscuous wicked remain, and upon them the Hour dawns. In related reports,[231] after the 'rapture' of the faithful, an astonishing chain of happenings eventuates in the Judgment in which 999 per 1000 are sent to the Fire.[232]

As to the venue of Jesus' return, Ibn Kathir seems partial to a 'home court advantage,' subtly advocating the predictions set in Damascus in Syria at the eastern minaret at the time of the morning prayer.[233] In fact, he finds occasion, in speaking of the descent of Jesus, to posit the specific minaret of the Umayyad mosque to which the traditions seem to point; the Christians of his day already were humiliated in having to pay to restore the minaret and will fully and finally taste their just requites when, not *their* 'Jesus,' but 'Isa b. Maryam descends![234] Nonetheless, Ibn Kathir remains aware of respectable reports which seem to locate the descent of Jesus in Jerusalem (e.g., Ibn Majah, *Sunan* v.5, 36.33.4077 just below).[235] Jerusalem, of course, was already established as an 'eschatological city' in Middle Eastern religious thought.

Ibn Kathir presents a rather long *hadith* in his *Tafsir* which is taken from Ibn Majah's *Sunan*.[236] After mention of the two holy refuge cities of Mecca and Medina, the tradition shifts to the third shrine city, Jerusalem (بيت المقدس). It is here that most of the last faithful Muslims are making their stand with their righteous Imam. The familiar descent of Jesus ensues at the time of morning prayer, with Jesus insisting that the Imam lead. Immediately afterwards battle ensues with the Antichrist leading his throng of 70,000 Jews with ornamented swords and woven coverings.[237]

Jesus pursues the Enemy and catches up with him at Lod's eastern gate.[238] Stones, walls, beasts, and trees (all but the thorny *gharqada* tree of the Jews) will betray hidden Jews to the *mujahidun*.[239] There is not unanimity in the sources as to the location of Antichrist's demise (*Afiq*, Jerusalem, Lod); Ibn Kathir does carry the tradition on *Afiq* (a Palestinian location) as the site of the last stand,[240] but his dominant tendency is to place the final clash somewhere in the Holy Land's central zone (Jerusalem, Lod) rather than further north.

Then Jesus begins to rule (the Imam receiving no further mention). The basic characteristics of his reign (e.g., the abolishing of crosses and pigs) with the universal idyllic dominance of Islam are asserted. A 'millennial' style description of Jesus' rule foresees an end to all warfare and the dominance of agriculture in a super-fructified earth. In fact, the rule of Jesus sounds very much like that of the Mahdi in other traditions: 'The earth will be filled with peace just as a vessel is filled with water.'

A comparable battle-tradition[241] from Ibn Hanbal[242] orders the action in various triads (three strongholds for the Muslims, the Muslims breaking into three groupings,[243] three heavenly voices exhort the faithful, etc.). The Muslims in Palestine (Afiq pass) are nearly routed when Jesus [the 'Spirit of God'[244]] descends, and, after a leader (*amir*) leads the prayer, advances on the Dajjal who melts away as the Messiah spears him through.

Jesus and the Dajjal are fatally interlocking characters in the Muslim apocalypse. In the 'majority report' of Sunni traditions, Jesus is, of course, *the* vanquisher of this Archenemy. Naturally, the Messiah facing down the embodiment of evil is a famous biblical stencil (cf. Rev. 19-20).[245] An interesting factor in the Jesus-and-the-Dajjal traditions is the inversion or 'negative mirroring' between the two figures.[246] Jesus is sometimes described as curly haired and 'red-complected,' but notably the Dajjal is so described as well. While the handsome Jesus performs the circling of the Ka'ba with his hands on two companions, the Dajjal does the same with one companion. Below we note a tradition Ibn Kathir brings in which the Dajjal performs specifically Jesus-like miracles and another where he appears with two angels. Both of them also provide prosperity and abundance, of a sort. On the other hand, Dajjal is also said to be fat and with a bulging, blind eye (see below).[247] In the apocalyptic milieu, evil runs parallel to the good, but as a gross caricature.

The Dajjal's Associates

Frequently, the Dajjal's followers hail from marginal groups in Muslim communities.[248] As we shall see in greater detail, there is a strong (though not exclusive) strain in the stories emphasizing the Jewish connections of the Dajjal, perhaps even his Jewish identity. In a tradition just noted, from the *Musnad*,[249] the Dajjal brings with him 70,000 people wearing the garment called *sijan*.[250] In fact, most of those with him are Jews and women. It would seem that according to this worldview, the Dajjal's followers are corrupters/deniers of the truth ('Jews') or those easily taken in ('women').[251] One can well imagine Ibn Kathir, the elite scholar, writing with a concerned eye trained on the 'suspect' classes in Mamluk society. In this *hadith* the famous template of the eschatological battles (*malahim*) is included: rocks and trees speak, exposing the infidels to the Muslim warriors. In his parallel section of the *Nihaya*, Ibn Kathir adds other latter-day battle reports, including the attacks of the Turks[252] (whether or not the Dajjal is mentioned). In terms of Ibn Kathir's own environment, we may think of the fact that Turks—and even Tatar Mongols—are elsewhere[253] said to number in the Dajjal's forces. Ibn Kathir even entertained the notion that Gog and Magog are latter-day descendants of Turkic tribes.[254] Even more extraordinarily, as we shall see below, our theologian manages to connect the 'latter-day Turks' to the Jews.

Identifying the Dajjal

The bulk of our investigation so far has been structured around the appearances of the Dajjal in the *Tafsir*'s comments on Jesus, alongside some parallels from the apocalyptic book, the *Nihaya*. This gruesome figure is developed in more garish and extensive detail in the latter.[255] If we think of the Dajjal as one of the classic 'ten signs,' remarkably, he casts a shadow over far more than just ten percent of the *fitan* material in the *Nihaya*. In fact, by my estimate, when considering the traditions dealing with '*fitan wa-malahim*,'[i] the Dajjal figures significantly in about 50% of this material. The Dajjal was always an element in the apocalyptic tradition collections, but such a disproportionate emphasis in Ibn Kathir's book certainly deserves attention.

Whatever the speculation (or not) as to the Antichrist's appearance in 14th-century Damascus, for some, the threat of spiritual deception and theological 'innovation' was ever present. None epitomizes in his own person these sinister enticements to deviance more than the Dajjal. He is *fitna* incarnate, and as such, a pressing subject for our dogged defender of the *sunna*. At the same time, Ibn Kathir often seems eager to reign in uncontrolled speculation on this persona and his appearance.

---

[i] That is, the *realia* related to the approaching Hour—not the traditions about Judgment Day itself, nor about Heaven and Hell.

The *hadith* sources present the character and identity of the Dajjal in an interwoven tissue of narrative strands not easily harmonized. At times he is seen to be a quasi-historical man whose emergence might be imminent even in Muhammad's day; he may be likened to more than one ancient personality; or he may be some outlandish mythical being, currently chained up on a remote isle, set to burst out at any moment, or whenever the end-of-time arrives. Commonly, the Antichrist hails from the East, but that too can vary. In one case his eastern provenance is qualified in that he appears in the 'gap' zone between Iraq and Syria.[256] In many cases the Dajjal is said to come from Khurasan, while a few later Islamic revelations have him coming from the West or from mythical countries related to the Alexander Romance.[257]

The Dajjal is infamous for being one-eyed or having some sort of ocular issue.[258] At the very least, his *one* eye is repulsive and manifestly bulging 'like a floating grape.' Ibn Kathir seeks to harmonize and adjudicate between traditions which imply distinct irregularities with *both* the Dajjal's eyes. The eye defect is a reflection of a larger deficiency and shame. Indeed the entire description of this portentous character is intensely derisive— curly hair, ignoble parentage, a nasal twang, his head like a tree branch! Ibn Kathir alerts us to another report in which 'the other eye is like a prominent star.'[259] In describing this Archenemy, Ibn Kathir provides a series of *hadiths* taken from sources outside the so-called Six Books. [260] Although he labels some of them as 'fable' (خرافة)[261] he still bothers to report them, sometimes at length. He rehearses the disparate reports in which the Dajjal is either monstrously tall or else rather short; he also comes on a (apocalyptic) steed, an outsized donkey.[262] The donkey's stride may be as long as a three-day journey.[263] In one case Dajjal is a fearsome, tattooed warrior with his head in the clouds and legs in the sea.[264]

In the lengthy Ibn Majah *hadith*,[265] several criteria for exposing the Antichrist for the false power he is are offered to the listener:

1. The Dajjal will claim to be the Lord, when in fact the vision of God comes not before death.[266]

2. He is blind in one eye, whereas such an impediment is ludicrous with respect to God. (Whereas, 'Your Lord is not one-eyed.'[267])

3. The word *kafir* (infidel) will be seen on his forehead and understood by all Muslims, literate or not.[268]

Persons are sometimes graphically marked out as on the side of good or evil in the *hadiths*.[i] The physical markings of eye distortions and 'marks of unbelief' on the Dajjal's forehead identify the evil and serve to make it intensely plain.[ii] Once again, it is a stock-in-trade tendency of apocalyptic to dramatically clarify and distinguish the good from the evil in this dark and confusing world.[269]

Ibn Sayyad

Evident in even the 'authorized' books of *hadith* is the fact that in the prophet's own day, or at least among the earliest Muslim communities, there was a very tangible expectation of the Dajjal's soon emergence. A common apocalyptic template is the notion of Antichrist already present but not yet revealed;[270] this may be seen in the stories in which Muhammad is portrayed as wondering if the Dajjal is in an adjacent palm grove and in the Tamim al-Dari narratives below. There is evidence of rife speculation as to just who this malevolent character might be. The most persistent early guesswork about the Dajjal in the standard collections appears in the *hadiths* concerned with a certain Ibn Sayyad, apparently from the Jews of Medina.[271] Ibn Kathir brings a representative selection of the Ibn Sayyad stories and seeks to assess whether or not he was the Dajjal.

In one *hadith* series represented in the two *Sahih* collections, the prophet goes with 'Umar b. al-Khattab and others to meet Ibn Sayyad, who is apparently a young man, if not a boy.[272] In their confrontation the impertinent youth asks Muhammad to acknowledge *him* as the Apostle of God! The exchange is ambiguous. The prophet asks what the lad 'sees,' as though he were a soothsayer or *kahin*. Ibn Sayyad's sayings are cryptic and his confused response includes what might be apocalyptic symbolism.[273] (In some cases Ibn Sayyad envisions [Satan's] throne upon the waters—evil parodying good in the dark days of the End.[274]) 'Umar asks leave to dispatch the imp, but Muhammad tells him that if it is *he,* then the attack will be fruitless, and, if not, the killing would be without merit. The meeting ends without

---

[i] One may think of the stories of the corporeal 'seal of the prophets' on Muhammad's body. Also, one role of the beast, *Dabba* is to go through the earth marking out believer from infidel.

[ii] This may be yet another case of 'inverse-mirroring,' in that pious Muslims often carry the 'marks of frequent prayer' on their foreheads.

resolution, but there is a surprising degree of uncertainty shown on the prophet's part, and a marked tolerance of the youngster's impertinence.

Similar observations may be made with respect to another related Ibn Sayyad *hadith* type.[275] In this series again Ibn Sayyad acts strangely, perhaps like a mystic or *kahin*. He is here named Saf b. Sayyad.[276] Muhammad's surreptitious attempts to listen in on his mutterings are foiled by the boy's mother. Muhammad rues the missed chance to discover if Ibn Sayyad was indeed the Antichrist. The prophet does not appear in the most flattering light in these tales and is remarkably concerned about the potential danger Ibn Sayyad represents.[277]

Other variations on the story also involve verbal sparring between Muhammad and the lad (also called 'Abdallah), the prophet's angry denunciation of the mother, and the near-brawl with 'Umar (who is warned off because only Jesus would be up to the task 'if he is *the one*').[278] Common trends in these tails involve the Jewishness of the boy and his deformed features (eyes and teeth). In one version the report concludes with the refrain about the stones and trees betraying the Jews of the Dajjal.[279] The report tells us that in the future not one of these Jews who follow the Dajjal will be left alive by Jesus.

A recurrent thread in the Ibn Sayyad stories is his sometimes physical clashes with the future caliph, 'Umar. One story has Ibn Sayyad braying loudly like a donkey and 'Umar shattering his staff on the boy.[280] Later, 'Umar's sister, Hafsa, reprimands him for his action, reminding him that the Dajjal 'would emerge as a result of compounded anger.' Another frequently attested lesser sign of the last days is the incidence of '*harj*,'[281] usually translated as violence or gratuitous killing.[282]

Of course, the key question about Ibn Sayyad is, 'Was he the Dajjal?' Though the question might look like an irrelevance by Ibn Kathir's day, the problem was that many early traditions seemed to insist that he was. Apparently 'Umar's son and other early figures were so convinced.[283] Ibn Kathir also brings the tradition in which the prophet predicts the birth of the Dajjal, with the requisite strange physical features, to previously barren Jewish parents.[284] The interlocutors visit Ibn Sayyad's family and find that he exhibits eerie behaviour and 'his eyes sleep while his heart does not.' The conditions of the prophet's prediction seem precisely to be fulfilled in Ibn Sayyad. Even traditions which provide *prima facie* evidence exculpating Ibn Sayyad often end up injecting lingering doubt on the question. In one example (Muslim 52.19.90), Ibn Sayyad seems to admit some wistful fascination for the notion that *he could have been the one!*

Nonetheless, Ibn Kathir says, 'Some of the *'ulama'* say that some of the Companions considered him the Dajjal. But this is not so, for he was simply an ordinary man (رجلاً صغيراً).'[285] Ibn Kathir goes on to detail the *hadith* type[286] just mentioned in which Ibn Sayyad seeks to exonerate himself: *'Didn't the Apostle of God say that [the Dajjal] would not enter Medina, while I was born there? And that he would be childless, while I have children? And that he is an infidel, while I have believed?...'*[287] Still, there is a touch of contingency even in Ibn Kathir's confident pronouncements.[288] Ibn Kathir was obviously attuned to the notion of the avatars of the Dajjal, the multiple deceivers who according to *hadiths* would afflict the *umma*.[289] Typically, thirty of these 'liars' were expected.[290] In sum, our scholar's point apparently is that, as an ordinary man, Ibn Sayyad was clearly not *the* Dajjal, but he was, at the least, strange and worrisome, possibly even a 'minor dajjal.'

Tamim al-Dari

Ibn Kathir also presents various renditions[291] of the famous Tamim al-Dari report about the Dajjal.[292] This tale is remarkable in that it involves a report from Muhammad *on the authority of another,* a Christian convert called Tamim al-Dari. In this tale a band of seafarers arrives on a mysterious (Mediterranean?) island and is greeted by the strange Jassasa (spy?) of the Dajjal. There are multiple uncertainties in the story from the location of this island to the nature of the weird hair-covered creature, the Jassasa, companion to the Dajjal. To that point the Dajjal is safely chained in a monastery on the isle.[293]

The interchange between the seafarers and their fearsome interlocutor is pregnant with angst. He asks the Arabs a series of questions which apparently serve as indicators of the 'ripening of the *eschaton*.' He asks about telltale 'signs'[294] and the (soon) emergence of the prophet of the *ummiyyin*.[i] Cataclysm appears to

---

[i] The Arabic root involved here (*u-m-m*) commonly indicates illiteracy, and Muhammad is understood to have been illiterate in the traditional biography. However, many scholars assume that the original idea was not Muhammad's illiteracy but that he was 'the unlettered

be in the offing. For example, Lake Tiberias, he says, will soon be dry.[295] The sense of divinely ordered destiny is made clear in the Dajjal's saying: 'I am the Messiah. I am about to be permitted to emerge and then will... tramp about in the earth. For forty nights I will not leave any town untouched except Mecca and Tayba,[296] which are entirely forbidden me.'

In any case, Ibn Kathir asserts that Ibn Sayyad was not at all the Dajjal *who will emerge at the end of time,* again, leaving open the thought that he may be one of the multiple, minor 'dajjals.' It is just this Tamim al-Dari story that Ibn Kathir claims is the decisive criterion.[297] Our theologian then goes on to cite well-known traditions such as those asserting that the Antichrist will resemble Ibn Qatan[298] or describing his exaggerated power or the presence of the tell-tale sign on the forehead, readable by all believers.[299] Evidently, these *hadiths* represent further negations of the proposition that Ibn Sayyad might be the Dajjal. In fact, later on Ibn Kathir goes on to give a summary history of the minor dajjal, Ibn Sayyad, the Jewish convert to Islam, including mention of his deceptive speech and outrageous claims.[300]

'But as for the Greatest Dajjal, he is the one mentioned in the *hadith.*.. from Tamim al-Dari' with the tale of the Jassasa.[301] In the last days, after the Muslims conquer Constantinople he will be permitted to emerge... with 70,000 Isfahani Jews. In addition, 70,000 Tatars and a contingent from Khurasan follow. He comes first as a despot king, then claims prophethood (النبوة), and then lordship[302] (الربوبية). He takes all that lies before him, being kept only from the two *harams* of Mecca and Medina. Only the ignorant and the rabble of the riff-raff and commoners will follow him. It is the ones guided by God, his righteous servants, the upright party of God, who will oppose and reject him.

The problems associated with the Deceiver in Ibn Kathir's discourse are something of a schematic review of the societal ills that so consumed the stringent Sunni purist. We have in effect a diatribe against the commoners' religious praxis, spiritual seduction in some measure linked to charisma, the Jews, and even thunderings against the Mongols (Tatars).

---

prophet' in that he was sent to a people as yet without a scripture (i.e., 'Gentiles'). The word in this instance (*ummiyyin*) is plural.

Aside on the Jews

The Jewish connection to the Antichrist is a common theme. Overall, Ibn Kathir displays little patience for *any* of the non-Muslim communities.[303] We have already seen that the sources on the last days incline to an anti-Judaic slant.[304] Ibn Kathir is persistently derogatory in his handling of texts related to the Jews.[305] His techniques sometimes involve ingenious harmonizations, creative associations, and hermeneutical *tour-de-forces*. In one tradition on the defeat of Constantinople in the apocalyptic battles (*malahim*), some of the victorious fighters are described as 'sons of Isaac.' Acting as an exegetical contortionist, Ibn Kathir manages to turn this triumphant phalanx into Byzantines converted to Islam, not possibly Jews.[306]

In another case, seeking to sort out the welter of last days antagonists among the Antichrist's followers, Ibn Kathir again displays some original, if debatable, thinking. Our scholar draws attention to three basic *hadith* types: the 'stones-and-trees-betraying-the-Jews' tradition about the latter-days battles;[307] the tradition that in the last days the Muslims must fight the Turks;[308] and a tradition on the Dajjal emerging from Persian zones[309] with 70,000 followers with 'faces like beaten shields' (typically a descriptor of Turkic tribes).[310] Engaging in some ingenious *isnad* criticism, Ibn Kathir manages to merge the evidence so as to conclude that the 70,000 Turkic followers of the Dajjal are in fact Jews themselves![311]

The Dajjal's Miracles and the Lure of Unbelief

The conflict with the Dajjal, the test or *fitna* of this imposter, involves both terrifying threat as well as mesmerizing temptation. Signs, portents, and miracles attend this evil paragon, some of them fearsome, some of them apparently delightful. One example is the propensity of time to alter,[312] a phenomenon also found in Christian and Jewish apocalypses. The Dajjal is said to remain for 40 years, though years of a peculiar sort. One year is said to equal half a (normal) year, one year is said to be like a month, and a month like a week. Time flies, indeed.[313] Ibn Kathir is predictably literalist in his understanding of this mysterious flow of time,[314] at one point calculating that the reign works out to a year and two and a half months.[315] Ibn Kathir views the supernatural time-bending as a further divinely inspired *fitna*, a test to lead the faithless astray and to firm up the believer.[316]

The Dajjal is, of course, the arch-persecutor of the faithful. In a field well-known for its vivid and surreal imagery, one violent template is particularly notable—the trial in which the Antichrist slaughters a faithful Muslim who witnesses against him, only for this person to be raised by God and protected from the Enemy thereafter.[317] At times the tale is reported in such a way as to emphasize God's sovereign power over even such a horrific event.[318] (Throughout the literature, speculations on the identity of this model believer range from the elusive al-Khidr to Elijah, but our stalwart theologian does not endorse such speculations.[319]) In any case, the Dajjal's devastation is so absolute that only the holy cities of Mecca and Medina are left unscathed, thanks to the fearsome angelic warriors guarding the approaches with drawn swords.[320] The 'purity theme' arises as a triple-quake[321] shakes Medina and expels the hypocrites from her midst.[322]

As is so typical in the apocalyptic milieu, evil parodies the good while in fact embodying its polar opposite. Thus, this false god offers death and life, prosperity or destruction, as does God himself. He offers heaven and hell (جنة ونار), but in his case these are in fact the opposite entities. In a certain incident, one of the ever-fickle Bedouin will be swayed by the Dajjal's sorcery by which he seems to raise to life long-dead parents.[323] He will also send wasting and famine upon tribes that reject him and great rain and abundance on those that acknowledge him.

The Imposter's wonders, in conjunction with his excessive claims, represent an attack on the 'pure Islamic monotheism' and a siren call to *kufr*. Ibn Kathir offers an extended report from Nu'aym, a report not paralleled in the Six Books.[324] Here the Enemy claims the qur'anic title, 'Lord of the Worlds' (رب العالمين), and states that the sun progresses at his permission (الشمس تجري بإذني). He goes on to perform the wonder of slowing the sun's progress; this explains the slowing or warping of time in the Antichrist's day. It also serves as another instance of the mimicking of divine authority, for indeed, just before the *true* cosmic finale, the sun will rise from the west. He also appears to restore lost animals, relatives, and loved ones to people, though these are in reality devils he conjures. As usual, he is prevented from entering the sanctuary of Mecca. However, the hypocrites of both holy cities flow out to follow him. Also included are the motifs of the man slaughtered and raised and inanimate objects exposing the Dajjal's henchmen. His lavish provisions receive much attention in this tradition. He brings with him mountains of lamb, cooked meats that never cool, green gardens, fire, and smoke, and flowing rivers.

The interaction of Jesus and the Dajjal here is colorful.[325] The Antichrist is headed toward Jerusalem but the divinely ordained showdown occurs at the gate of Lod where we find the descended Jesus. In this case, there is a tussle over the matter of the prayers, but, surprisingly, the involved parties are Jesus and the Dajjal, who for all his heresy seems still to pose as a Muslim. After rowing over the issue of who leads the prayer, Jesus says, 'O enemy of God, you have claimed that you are the Lord of the Worlds. Why then do you pray?'[326] (It is hard not to see christological conflict with the Christians reflected here.[327])

There is another tale brought by Ibn Kathir which is interesting in that it describes the Dajjal's use of both supernatural power and a cunning incremental strategy in his program to deceive the masses.[328] Early on he apparently fights *for* Islam, but eventually, he claims prophethood, which alarms those possessed of understanding, so these separate from him. He then exceeds all bounds claiming to be Allah.[i] For this, God deforms his eyes and cuts his ears.[329] At this point *any* with faith the size of a mustard seed will separate from him. His followers are mainly Jews, Zoroastrians, and Christians—the 'foreign polytheists.' This story also climaxes with his evil feat of slaughtering and raising an individual: He claims to be divine, giving and taking life.

It is not surprising that in the prophecy the 'intellectual elite' discern the deception first. The list of those taken in or otherwise spiritually corrupted is not surprising either. In other cases women are pointedly described as susceptible to the Dajjal's magnetism; to keep his women (wife, daughter, sister) from their attraction to the Dajjal a man will have to tie them up![330] The *fitna* of the Dajjal's miracles represents a threat to the purity of religion and to the unity of the *umma*.

The Dajjal is a sort of latter-days 'final exam,' something of a litmus test by which spiritual realities are unveiled. He is a perfect apocalyptic agent, a double-edged threat. Using signs and wonders, benefits and blandishments, he manipulates people into acknowledging him, or he threatens and attacks those who resist.

---

[i] The pattern here might well be, from Ibn Kathir's perspective, a warning against 'charismatic mystic' or Imami innovation away from 'pure' Sunni Islam.

On these terms an esoteric tradition carried by Ibn Kathir (*Nihaya*, 70-71) is instructive: As in other stories, the Dajjal proffers what would seem to be visible renditions of Paradise and Hell, except that these realities are actually inverted with him. He is deformed and one-eyed, and the word *kafir* is visible on his face.

With him are two angels from among the angels, resembling two prophets from among the prophets...[331] One of them is on [the Dajjal's] right and the other is on his left. That is a *fitna*. The Dajjal will say, 'Am I not your Lord? Do I not give life and cause death?' One of the angels will say to him, 'You lied.' None of the people will hear him except his companion [angel] who will say to him 'You are right.' The people will hear the angel and think that he believes the Dajjal. That is a *fitna*.[332]

The story ends with the Dajjal prevented from entry to Medina and destroyed *by God* in Syria at the mountain pass of Afiq. This somewhat awkward tale[333] does communicate very graphically the seductive threat of evil and deception in the apocalyptic era. Even an angel may seem to corroborate the Antichrist. He is clearly an inverse of the Messiah.[334] On the other hand, the very fact of angelic presence serves to underline the divine authority underlying all the anticipated events of those days.

On the Reality of the Dajjal's Miracles

A major element of the trial of the Dajjal is the terrifying power he appears to wield to the benefit or harm of those he would seduce. The Antichrist is seen to produce strange signs and wonders or to be attended by such.[335] Bukhari 9.88.244, if not intended metaphorically, implies that Dajjal will supernaturally manipulate nature or at least that bizarre phenomena will accompany him—i.e. watery, cold fire and fiery water. In other versions he is offering, simply, false versions of Paradise and Hell (Muslim 52.20.109). In Muslim 52.20.110 he appears to have power over the elements—bringing fertility or drought to the earth. Venturing beyond the tightest boundaries of the conventional *hadiths*, Ibn Kathir brings one story that, while 'legendary' (خرافة), captures the existential choice represented by the Antichrist:

> With him are two rivers. One of them is as fire burning brightly in the eyes of the beholder and the other is whitewater. So whoever among you comes across him should immerse his eyes and drink from the river of fire which is with him, for it is actually cold water. As for the other, it is *fitna*.[336]

Several times Ibn Kathir warns the reader of the Dajjal's tempting offer of 'water that is fire and fire that is cold water.'[337] He goes on to remind us of the abundance[338] that comes to those who follow the Dajjal, and the loss and deprivation of those who resist him. There is also, as we saw, the recurrent stencil of a young man killed and revived by the vile Imposter.[339] The blessing and prosperity of the messianic age parallels and contrasts with the lure of apparent wealth and prosperity under the Dajjal (e.g. Bukhari 9.88.238 and Muslim 52.20.110).[340] The universe of the Antichrist is ethically inverse, but only the truly faithful will see through the parody.

The dramatic, almost divine, quality of the wonders wrought by the Dajjal creates theological tensions for those simultaneously scholarly, pious, and literalist. With respect to the powers of the Antichrist, Ibn Kathir notes that various scholars from traditionalists to Mu'tazilites have held that his activity is pure conjuring tricks with no supernatural power at work at all.[341] Ibn Kathir will not go that far, and castigates those of his theological opponents whose arguments he invalidates *because they fail to base themselves squarely on the sound, authorized, multiply attested hadiths from the prophet.*[342]

In presenting Islam as the middle way, Ibn Kathir's Taymiyyan outlook forwards a strong *salafi* theology, a robust literalist hermeneutic, and rational argumentation.[343] Ibn Kathir in dealing with the Dajjal seeks to *steer between* superstition and gullibility on the one hand, and rationalistic unbelief[i] on the other.[344] According to him, the manifest supernatural acts of the Antichrist's day are *divine* tests or *fitan*: God tests his servants through the Dajjal '*by means of the manifest miracles he makes with him.*'[345] In the apocalyptic future God leads many astray by these tests and also guides many by them [Q 7.155, 178; 74.31]. Dajjal will display deficiency, depravity, and iniquity, while bringing miraculous deeds with him. For the most part, these signs and marvels of Dajjal's day must be taken at face value. The sign of unbelief between Dajjal's eyes is proven to be 'a tangible inscription, not (something) metaphorical, as some of the people say.'[346]

---

[i] For his part, Ibn Taymiyya both denounced charlatans and magicians *and* believed in the reality of supernatural feats. For Ibn Taymiyya, the practitioners of corrupt wonder-working (sometimes guilty of *shirk*) are typically Christians, then Sufis and Shi'is too, not to mention the general populace, women, and Tatars taken in by charlatan entertainers.

So, with respect to the miracles of the Dajjal, Ibn Kathir is a dogged literalist, or at least nearly so. At times his statements seem to set up undecipherable tensions. He affirms the reality of many of the miracles, but also writes some of them off as illusions and tricks.[347] In one place this seems to be his assessment of the killing and raising of the young Muslim.[348] The Dajjal's divinely permitted powers are not to be doubted, and yet much of what he does *is* mere trickery and cunning. Ibn Kathir does not come down entirely clearly on which acts are which.

How Severe a Test is the Dajjal?

In a lengthy tradition we now know well[349] (as in many others) the prophet warns the listeners that the coming *fitna* of the Dajjal *will be the worst experienced in all human history since the days of Adam.* Muhammad offers his people knowledge about the Antichrist which no prophet has yet disclosed.[350] In case any Muslim should face the assault of the Dajjal, the prophet charges him to find safety in reciting the opening of Surat al-Kahf, the 18th chapter of the Qur'an, which will be coolness and security for him as the fire was for Abraham.[351] This protective function of Sura 18 is a well-established rubric. The notion of the greatness of the Dajjal's *fitna* and the possibility that Muhammad will still be around when the Imposter emerges are also common refrains.[352]

A tradition from Jabir b. 'Abdallah[353] parades some of the stock patterns we are beginning to expect: Medina will be a sanctuary, but its *mostly female* (!) 'hypocrites' will stream out to the Dajjal from it. He has an army of 70,000 Jews. He is one-eyed (or deformed of eye), though Allah is not. Then the prophet warns his people, 'There has not been and will not be a *fitna* greater than that of the Dajjal until the rise of the Hour!'[354] On the other hand, Ibn Kathir also presents a series of *hadiths* which are somewhat ambiguous with respect to the question of how dire a threat Muhammad thought the Dajjal was.[355] On balance, the horror of the tribulation of the Dajjal is taken to be of ultimate degree.[356]

As many traditions attest, if Antichrist arises in Muhammad's day, the prophet himself will deal with the threat; if not, God will take care of it while the Muslims themselves contend.[357] This great '*fitna*' fulfils a very important, preordained, purpose: it tests and *purifies* the faithful. According to Ibn Kathir, 'He is [but] a human made by God to be a test of mankind in the last time: **He leads many astray by it, and guides many by it. He does not lead any**

astray by it except the transgressors [Q 2.26b].'[358]   Despite the miraculous powers, signs, and provisions, Dajjal is a 'light' or 'easy' thing for God, fully subsumed under his inexorable sovereignty.[359]

The Imminence and Relevance of the Dajjal for Ibn Kathir

Even in Ibn Kathir's 14th-century setting, the issue of Dajjal's identity and presence remained relevant, whether as commentary on the issues of the day or as a continuing literal threat. Though many prophetic reports on the apparently soon rise of the Dajjal[360] originate *at least* half a millennium before the days of our theologian, Ibn Kathir manages both to incorporate and yet neutralize such sayings.[361] He draws in a mass of traditions with inherent tensions, and yet finds enough centripetal force to hold them together. Thus, the vexed issue of Dajjal's identity and the role of Ibn Sayyad is ultimately resolved by the possibility of a climaxing sequence of Antichrists. The Evil One's powers seem overwhelming in many of the traditions; nonetheless, he too remains subject to divine *qadar.* A series of *dajjals will* arise, and the prophet has extensively forewarned about the coming ultimate one.

Did Ibn Kathir think that the Dajjal's emergence was imminent? Well, ambiguities and tension must color the answer—much as with the larger issue of the imminence of the End for him (see above in Part One). Certainly, the Dajjal was entirely *relevant.* The Antichrist's relevance for our theologian subsists in multiple levels. First, he is doggedly real, actual, and even human, however bizarre. He is yet to come, *perhaps* even quite soon. There is no fixing of dates, however. Second, in another sense he *has* come and keeps coming in various avatars and guises, the prophesied minor *dajjals.* Finally, at yet another level, the Dajjal is in part an overarching symbol for Evil: In the theological-social battles Ibn Kathir was waging, even by writing his apocalypse, the Dajjal symbolized a contemporaneous adversary.

The 'unveiling' of apocalyptic transcends mere future-fascination: *the present* is to be understood in light of this revelation.[362] Ibn Kathir was a stalwart champion of 'true' Islam, an Islam fated in prophetic tradition to become once again 'a stranger.' From this vantage point, the threat represented by the Antichrist was in fact more than academic; it was imminent.

The Dajjal Shaped Gap in the Qur'an

Why is the Dajjal not mentioned clearly in the Qur'an?[363] Ibn Kathir asks:

> One wonders what is the wisdom in the fact that the Dajjal—with all his evil, depravity, wide impact of his activity, and claims to Lordship; all the while manifesting deceit and falsehood; and given that all the prophets have warned about him—is not mentioned in the Qur'an, nor does it warn about him, clarify his name, or underline his lies and obstinacy.[364]

We shall have to greatly abbreviate our Mamluk theologian's rather involved and interesting argumentation. His answer is in three parts. The first two responses pertain to the exegesis of two qur'anic passages. Space will only allow us a glance at one of them (the other is Q 4.157-159, allegedly about Jesus' expected post-parousia death). Ibn Kathir cites Q 6.158: *On the day when some of the signs of your Lord shall come, its faith shall not profit a soul which did not believe before, or earn good through its faith* (Shakir). Citing Tirmidhi[365] to the effect that these signs, after the rise of which faith avails not, are the Dajjal, the Dabba, and the sun rising in the west, Ibn Kathir tells us that the Qur'an *does after all* point to the Antichrist when it mentions these 'signs.'

Ibn Kathir's third response to the dilemma is to explain that Dajjal is not named in the Qur'an 'out of spite for his claim to divinity.'[366] Though Dajjal's threat was beneath God's explicit mention, the apostles and prophets effectively mediated this knowledge. Ibn Kathir anticipates the objection that Pharaoh also made extreme claims of deceit and slander and yet is mentioned in the Qur'an (79.24; 28.38). His answer is that the matter of Pharaoh is a past affair and his deceit is well-known to every believer and rational person. The matter of the Dajjal, however, is a fixed but future event mention of which was left out of the Qur'an, 'for his deception is too obvious to point out and to warn against...'[367]

Ibn Kathir sees the issue of the Dajjal as clear and obvious, comparable to the clarity attendant on the choice of Abu Bakr as caliph after Muhammad (so obvious that the prophet did not need to leave a testament concerning the succession).[368] Similarly, Muhammad's appearance itself was clear and self-confirmatory, not requiring further corroboration beyond the reception of faithful hearts.[369] The blasphemy and corruption of the Dajjal are to be so severe, Ibn Kathir explains, that God left off mentioning him in the Book because believers would readily discern his error and only increase in faith.[370] In fact, precisely this stance will be modeled by the one the Dajjal will kill and then revive. That man will say: 'By God, I have only increased in insight about you! You are the one-eyed liar that the Apostle of God told us about.'[371]

Ibn Kathir's explanations are creative enough, but not altogether effective. It is perhaps predictable that in defending his explanation of the Dajjal's absence in the Qur'an, his first two arguments must revert inevitably to the *hadiths*. There is a certain irony here: Everyone knows that the Antichrist figures prominently in tradition (*hadiths*), but the question is, why he is a 'no-show' in the Holy Book itself? Ibn Kathir attempts to answer this by finding elusive evidence for him in the Qur'an after all. But to produce any such evidence whatsoever, recourse must be had, once again, to the *hadiths* (and even there to insist on some fairly tenuous connections). We are back where we started.

With respect to the third argument, Ibn Kathir may be credited with trying to present a coherent theological rationale for the seeming omission of this major figure from holy scripture. It is not obvious, however, that he has decisively resolved the problems. The argumentation connected to Pharaoh is not particularly satisfying. With respect to the idea that some realities are so inherently compelling that no scriptural prefiguration need be given, one marvels at a seeming implication of this logic, namely that there was no need of prior prophetic notice about the coming of Muhammad.[i] As far as the succession of the first caliph, the choice of Abu Bakr may have been 'obvious' to the community, but evidently not 'obvious' enough to have prevented a lasting fracture in the Muslim *umma*. Finally, if the Dajjal's perfidy and blasphemy are indeed so obvious as to require so little attention in the Qur'an, then the energy and ink spent on him in the tradition collections, not to mention Ibn Kathir's own book, also present something of an incongruity to say the least.

Ibn Kathir and Today's Apocalyptic

Here we can offer only some brief suggestions regarding the ongoing impact of Ibn Kathir's apocalyptic. One point is the ready

---

i Ibn Kathir has not made this claim; nonetheless, his logic at least raises the question.

availability today of his relevant works in Arabic, and also, in some cases, translations or at least abridgments. Ibn Kathir's influence can be felt in the chronologizing, harmonizing, and streamlining of tensions in the latter-days storyline.[i] We think, for instance, of the situating of the descent of Jesus in Damascus, the general agreement on a sequence of Mahdi and then Jesus, the expectation of the Dajjal's demise in the environs of Jerusalem or Lod, and so on. For all the unfettered freedom on display in the modern Arabic apocalypses, Ibn Kathir's *implied* narrative from the *Nihaya* emerges as fairly standard.

Another possible sign of Ibn Kathir's influence lies in the fact that most popularizers of the Apocalypse denounce rationalist denial of the miracles or wonders of the Dajjal story, as did Ibn Kathir.[372] Again, citing Tottoli, Ibn Kathir has become 'a constant point of reference' for Muslim writers. Ibn Kathir is, not surprisingly, one of the common authorities in modern writing on the Dajjal.[373] The prophetic traditions, especially from the 'authorized' tomes, are usually the assumed or nominal basis for the modern works; they certainly were foundational for Ibn Kathir's latter-days theology.

On the other hand, many current Arabic writers on the Apocalypse still feel quite free to continue their apocalyptic trawling further afield in 'stranger waters.' (Further, most contemporary apocalyptists tend to expend very little energy on examining or even reporting *isnads*. This is obviously far from Ibn Kathir's own methodology.[374]) D. Cook points out that, in the profuse field of today's popular Arabic apocalypses, the writers rather quickly tend to move past their foundations in 'certified' *hadiths* to employ prognostications sourced in imagination, anti-Semitic conspiracy theory, UFO theory, popular Christian eschatology, or elsewhere.[375] For example, the modern apocalyptic writer Sa'id Ayyub may be said to have 'overlaid [a] Christian framework on the Muslim sources... and made the Muslims win.'[376] In other words, the contemporary popularizers have frequent recourse to what Ibn Kathir would likely denounce as *isra'iliyat*. Among the classic

---

[i] No claim is being made that Ibn Kathir is the *only* influence in this trend, rather that he is among the most prominent theological voices in the classical stream feeding Muslim apocalyptic thought.

authorities, Ibn Kathir is possibly the most beloved in the modern apocalypse, but his reputation has not ensured strict emulation.[i]

In contrast, to the implicit and *subtextual* linkage of classical apocalyptic to the issues of the surrounding culture, contemporary writers frequently link their apocalypses *in explicit detail* to our own day. Under the pressures of globalization or other concerns and influences, the contemporary apocalyptic speculator has broken free of the constraints of traditional sources and writing conventions in the effort to make the apocalyptic *hadiths* relevant.[377] So, in popular portrayals the Dajjal is creatively made to rampage through today's headlines as readily as he wreaks destruction in the pages of ancient tradition. Not only is modern writing on the End of Days qualitatively different to the classical with respect to the Dajjal, but there is also a quantitative difference; though this Antichrist has long provided a focus for all things oppositional or loathsome to Sunni Islam,[378] the current fascination with him is remarkable, perhaps even dominant.[379]

Similar notes of convergence and divergence may be seen when it comes to the place of the Jews in Ibn Kathir's apocalypse and that of the modern popular writers in Arabic. The anti-Judaic inclinations, we have seen, are well embedded in the stories, and these are exploited, embellished, and added to a host of anti-Jewish elements in the contemporary writers. Nonetheless, in Ibn Kathir's work there is nothing like the *central role* that anti-Jewish themes and Jerusalem/Palestine play in the modern writers.[380] The different degree of emphasis is easily enough explained by the constraints of the sources Ibn Kathir used[ii] and the differing historical circumstances. Commenting on the modern Muslim authors, David Cook points out that since the trauma of the Six Day War previous explanatory frameworks have proved insufficient for the apocalyptist; the Jews' victory had to be explained by recourse to seeing them as 'agent or even avatar of the Antichrist,' a theme copiously developed.[381] Once again, Ibn Kathir emerges as a stimulating but not absolute influence on our day.

When it comes to the theologically perplexing question of why the Dajjal does not appear in the Qur'an, the basic substance of Ibn

---

[i] Another example would be the penchant of some modern writers to 'date-fix' the End, an activity of which our scholar roundly disapproved.

[ii] Obviously, anti-Semitic tracts like the Protocols of the Elders of Zion could not figure for Ibn Kathir as they do for some modern Muslim apocalyptists.

Kathir's answers are frequently repeated by popular authors today. His arguments appear to have left their imprint, *though he is not always formally credited.* According to Tottoli, when today's authors cite classical authorities for their explanations of this problem, the favorite source is Ibn Hajar al-'Asqalani (d. 852/1448).[382] (It is clear that Ibn Hajar himself was influenced by Ibn Kathir, at the very least in his historical writing.[383])

In sum, when it comes to Islam and apocalyptic today, much remains the same, and much continues to change. That is, Ibn Kathir continues to enjoy great prestige as a representative of the classical consensus; nonetheless, apocalyptic remains stubbornly resistant to scholarly taming. The Muslim apocalypse continues to be self-renewing. There is within apocalyptic an uncanny potential to maintain the tension between the persistence of the present world and the promise of imminent resolution.[384] Ibn Kathir is himself a brilliant exemplar of that tension and has helped to preserve the credibility of apocalyptic theology for the dominant Muslim schools of thought for generations.

Final Thoughts

The Dajjal is a siren call, a parody of good, and especially of Jesus. He can be threatening by his deception or by his terrible force, in equal measures. But he is also a caricatured persona with respect to his obvious and clear evil. In many respects he is a cipher for the threat of evil 'from within.'[385] Dajjal may be seen as emblematic of an era of 'irreligion and infidelity,' a time like the End, a time like 'these times'—those terrible days of faithlessness foretold in the traditions in which a man *wakes as a Muslim and is an infidel by evening.*[386]

As with many other characters, *themes,* and plotlines, the story of the Dajjal can often be set alongside elements of Christian eschatology, revealing areas of overlap as well as more or less direct contradiction. Pieces of the various Christian and Muslim renditions of the End may be read as inversions or counterpoints. This is hardly surprising in that the monotheist faiths have their foundation in shared cultures, topography, and textual authority and yet developed in sometimes overt and tense contestation.

On the other hand, for all the shared cultural, religious, and textual resources of the Christian and Muslim latter-day schemas, the reader who crosses the boundary from one eschatological metanarrative into the other will soon feel, not simply that a line has been crossed, but, rather, that she has fallen down a 'rabbit hole.' Certainly many profiles, patterns, and names will at first appear familiar (messiahs, antimessiahs, Gog and Magog, climactic battles, holy cities, angels, and so on). But the nominal overlap is actually more obscuring than enlightening. Similar terms and even familiar storylines are ultimately embedded in radically different universes of discourse. With the story of the Muslim Antichrist this becomes patently plain: the move from Christian to Muslim apocalyptic is not simply a trek into an adjacent county; it is a transfer into another world.

From Death to the Judgement: Jurist and Sufi Perspectives from Arabic and Malay Contexts

Peter Riddell[i]

The British Muslim writer Yahya Birt, a white convert to Islam, made an analysis of conversions to Islam taking place in Scotland, drawing on the 2001 British census results. He reached some interesting conclusions which apply well beyond the Scottish context:

> ... out of all the minority religions and the main Christian denominations, Islam is the religion people are least likely to leave or convert to... In other words, it is the least attractive to others and yet paradoxically the most resilient...[387]

We will not take up the issue of conversion to Islam in this paper. But Birt's comment about Muslims being bound to their faith raises important issues. Why is Islam so successful at holding its numbers? Apostasy laws are no doubt a major factor. But fear of punishment after death is no doubt also a factor.

The theme of the fear of God's punishment is frequently articulated by Islamic scholars at various levels. Consider the following opening of a sermon by the Indonesian cleric and prolific author H.A. Mustofa:

> O Muslims. We should always be God-fearing. In other words, we should always follow His commands and prohibitions. Furthermore, to be God-fearing engenders a fear of death which can stimulate fear of punishment in the grave, as well as a hope for God's assistance with all complications.[388]

The prominent 20th century Indonesian writer, philosopher and politician Hamka (full name Haji Abdul Malik Karim Amrullah, d. 1981) casts a more positive spin, but at the same time he stresses the importance of staying focused on the afterlife during earthly existence:

---

[i] Professor Peter Riddell is Vice Principal Academic at the Melbourne School of Theology, where he also serves as Director of the CSIOF. He is also a Professorial Research Associate at SOAS, University of London, and previously lectured at the Australian National University, the Institut Pertanian Bogor (Indonesia), SOAS and the London School of Theology, where he was awarded a Chair in Islamic Studies in 2003. He has published widely on Islamic Studies and Christian-Muslim Relations.

... death is not obliteration; it is not disappearance and termination. Death is only a change to the nature of living, from the perishable to the eternal, from the world to the hereafter. As long as we live in the world we should not lose sight of this.[389]

Islamic sacred scripture has much to say about *al-akhira* — the afterlife. In fact, a concern with eschatological themes is primary to Islamic doctrine. If Christian doctrine points towards the death and resurrection of Christ as the watershed event in human salvation history, Islam points towards the Day of Judgement as the principal motivating factor for human belief and behaviour in the temporal world.

In this paper we will address the issue of eschatology in its broadest sense, not merely focusing upon the final judgement, but rather considering Islamic perspectives on death, the tomb, resurrection and the last day. We will place particular attention on the writings of Southeast Asian Islamic scholars, to supplement our engagement with the primary scriptures of Islam. We will also consider how the various Islamic scholarly comments encountered shape Muslim attitudes to adherents of other faiths, especially Jews and Christians.

The Call of the Sacred Texts

A survey of the qur'anic text reveals a huge number of verses which remind both the believer and the unbeliever of impending judgement, reward and punishment. The following verses from *Sura 90* provide an example, explaining that a combination of works and faith will earn God's favour and avoid the terrors of Hell:

> 12. And what will explain to thee the path that is steep?
> 13. (It is) freeing the bondman;
> 14. Or the giving of food in a day of privation
> 15. To the orphan with claims of relationship,
> 16. Or to the indigent in the dust.
> 17. Then will he be of those who believe, and enjoin patience, and enjoin deeds of kindness and compassion.
> 18. Such are the Companions of the Right Hand.
> 19. But those who reject Our Signs, they are the Companions of the Left Hand.
> 20. On them will be Fire vaulted over.

As is so often the case, the Qur'an serves to provide a doctrinal framework which is expanded in great detail by the prophetic

Traditions. The Qur'an sounds the warning of punishment for unbelievers and the promise of reward for the believers, but the Hadith accounts explain in detail the form that this punishment and reward will take.

The relatively late canonisation of the prophetic Traditions vis-à-vis the compilation of the qur'anic text has caused many non-Muslim scholars to conclude that the Traditions were developed in large part as a response to a perceived lack in qur'anic detail. Such a view asserts that emerging Islamic theology required a detailed doctrine of the Hereafter, so Traditions were invented, and in order to increase their authority, they were associated with Muhammad. It is in this context that Seale writes that 'as Islamic *Sunna* ('tradition') grew and expanded in the centuries that followed Muhammad's death, new horrors were added which the Prophet never conceived[i] ... [such as] the interrogation in the grave and the torments that follow.'[390]

Death and the Grave

Scholars on the Experience of Death

The Hanafi jurist Abu al-Layth al-Samarqandi (d. 983) quotes the famous early Jewish convert to Islam, Ka'b al-Ahbar, as describing the process of death in the following terms: 'Dying is like a thorny tree being pushed into a man's insides, so that every thorn takes hold of a vein therein, and then is dragged out by a man mighty of strength, so that what is rent is rent and what remains remains.'[391]

Further on al-Samarqandi quotes at length a prophetic tradition which has Muhammad describing the events surrounding death in the following terms:

> When a man who is a true believer is drawing near to the next world and is about to be cut off from this world, there descend to him angels whose faces are white as the sun, bringing with them a shroud from Paradise and celestial aromatics, and take their seat just within his vision. Then the Angel of Death arrives, takes a seat at his head and says: 'O thou tranquil soul, come forth to Allah's favour and forgiveness.' Then ... it comes forth, flowing as easily as a drop from a water-skin... But when an unbeliever is drawing near to the next world and being cut off from this world, there descend to him from heaven angels whose faces are black, bringing with them hair-cloth,

---

[i] Ed: See Amanda Parker's chapter on the 'torments of the grave.'

and take their seats just within his vision. Then the Angel of Death arrives, takes a seat at his head and says: 'O thou pernicious soul, come forth to Allah's discontent and wrath.' Thereupon his soul is scattered through all his members and [the angel] drags it forth like the dragging of an iron spit through moist wool, tearing the veins and the sinews.[392]

Note should be taken of the use of colours to express contrast, where white signifies good and black signifies evil. It is also important to note the difference between Ka'b's view that all suffer during the death experience, while al-Samarqandi reports that only the evil-doers suffer during the process of death.

Let us consider this in more detail via a literary work originating in the Malay-Indonesian world.

'Abd Ra'uf of Singkel

The Aceh-based Sufi 'Abd Ra'uf of Singkel (ca. 1615 - ca. 1693) is arguably the most important Islamic scholar from the Malay world to have lived during the formative stages of Malay Islam. He made a detailed record of his nineteen-year study visit (1642-1661) to the various centres of Islamic learning in the Arabian Peninsula. His prolific literary output, in wide-ranging fields of Islamic learning, provided succeeding generations of Malay students of Islam with copious materials for study.

One of his shorter works which bears directly on the subject of this paper is *Lubb al-kashf wa al-bayan lima yarahu al-muhtadar bi al-'iyan*[393] (Essential Exposition and Clarification on the Visionary Experience of the Dying and what Gladdens him) which describes the experience of the dying. 'Abd al-Ra'uf wrote this as a reflection on a Jawi text he encountered, which he described as being based on *Kitab al-tadhkira bi-umur al-akhira* by Abu Abdullah al-Qurtubi, a prominent Malikite scholar of Hadith and exegesis who was born in Spain and died in Upper Egypt in 1272.[394]

Lubb al-kashf begins with the following words: 'When a person is at the point of death he experiences several visions.' These visions tempt the dying person to abandon Islam and to turn to other faiths. *Lubb al-kashf* proceeds to address the matter of faiths 'of the Book', namely Christianity and Judaism, which it presents clearly as having strayed from the true path. The Christians and Jews are presented, along with Satan, as those who tempt the dying to abandon Islam during the dying process.

> When a vision of black appears to him, which is Satan, then he should utter [the creed] 'There is no God but Allah and Muhammad is the prophet of Allah, He, He, He.' When a vision of red appears to him, which represents the Christians, then he should utter 'There is no God but Allah and Muhammad is the prophet of Allah, He, He, He.' When a vision of yellow appears to him, which represents the Jews, then he should utter 'There is no God but Allah and Muhammad is the prophet of Allah, He, He, He.' When a vision of white appears to him, which represents the vision of our prophet Muhammad the messenger of Allah, then he should utter 'By the will of Allah he was one of the true believers'.

Note again the use of colours here: black = evil, or Satan; red = Christians; yellow = Jews; white = goodness. In this context it is relevant that in 1250 a decree by the final authorities of the Abbasid Muslim empire based in Baghdad determined that Jews and Christians found in public without distinctive badges or belts were to be executed. In 1301 the colour yellow was allocated to the distinctive markings of the Jews, while blue was allocated to Christians living within Muslim domains.[395] This may well explain the context of al-Qurtubi, the ultimate source of the above quote.

In *Lubb al-kashf,* demons are portrayed as disguising themselves as relatives of the dying in an attempt to lure the believer away from Islam. This co-locating of Christianity and Judaism with demonic forces has a powerful impact:

> When a servant of Allah is at the point of death, two devils sit next to him, one on his right and one on his left. The devil on his right takes the form of his father, and says to him: 'O my child, I truly love and cherish you. Please die in the Christian faith, as it is the best of religions.' The devil on his left takes the form of his mother, and says to him: 'O my child, my womb was your shelter, my milk was your nourishment and my lap was your place of repose. Please die in the Jewish faith, as it is the best of religions.'

Furthermore, *Lubb al-kashf* is strongly determinist in orientation, as is evident in the following quote:

> Thereupon Allah inclines whoever He wishes towards faiths which have gone astray... Whenever Allah wishes to show one of His servants the true path and to affirm him through statement of the Divine Unity, the angel of mercy comes to him - some scholars identify him as Gabriel - and he drives away from that person all the devils, and he wipes his face...

Though only a short work, *Lubb al-kashf*'s significance should not be underestimated. Firstly, it engages with matters of common concern to individuals regarding the experience of death. Secondly, it acts as a vehicle for the transmission of teachings by a major Islamic scholar from the late Abbasid period, whom it identifies for the edification of its readers. Thirdly, it sows seeds which shape the attitudes of its Muslim readers to adherents of Christianity and Judaism.

The Experience of the Grave

Upon death, the deceased faces the process of assessment in the grave. The Indonesian scholar Hamka writes as follows: 'It seems that before experiencing paradise or hell, one must pass through the period in the grave. Because this is a reflection of what will be experienced later.' Hamka draws heavily on Hadith accounts for his discussion, and refers to the counting of good and bad deeds of each departed person:

> Although a person acknowledges faith [in Allah], nevertheless the calculation of the sins and errors which he committed during his life will be taken into account. Exception and relief will only be applied after that calculation, measuring the relative weight of his good and bad deeds.[396]

The Hadith accounts graphically capture details absent from the Qur'an, such as the following account attributed to Ibn 'Abbas:

> Bukhari 1.4.215: 'Once the Prophet while passing through one of the grave-yards of Medina or Mecca heard the voices of two persons who were being tortured in their graves. The Prophet said, 'These two persons are being tortured not for a major sin (to avoid).' The Prophet then added, 'Yes (they are being tortured for a major sin). Indeed, one of them never saved himself from being soiled with his urine while the other used to go about with calumnies (to make enmity between friends).' The Prophet then asked for a green leaf of a date-palm tree, broke it into two pieces and put one on each grave. On being asked why he had done so, he replied, 'I hope that their torture might be lessened, till these get dried."

Also Muhammad is reported as praying on the grave:

> Muslim, Book 004, Hadith 2087: Anas reported that the Apostle of Allah (may peace be upon him) observed prayer on the grave.

This kind of report provides the basis for Muslims in diverse cultural contexts to pray for their departed loved ones on the grave, that the testing not be severe.

Comments by Scholars

Such details in the Hadith, and associated inconsistencies, are transferred to the classical writings which often attempt to reconcile scriptural inconsistencies by developing systematic doctrine. Such an attempt occurs in the *Testament of Abu Hanifa* (d. 767), where the great Baghdad-based father of the Hanafi law school maps out what he sees as an orthodox doctrine of what happens in the grave.

> Article 18: We confess that the punishment in the tomb shall without fail take place.
>
> Article 19: We confess that, in view of the Traditions on the subject, the interrogation by Munkar and Nakir is a reality.[397]

The angels Munkar and Nakir are specifically tasked by Allah to examine the deceased in the grave. Abu Hanifa's need to affirm their interrogation, and that the punishment in the tomb did take place, points to a debate among classical Islamic theologians surrounding these events. The late 11th century Maturidi theologian al-Nasafi (d. 1114) reported that the Mu'tazila, the early school of theologians who prioritised reason and rational thought in shaping their understanding of Islam, did not accept that these events took place, though al-Nasafi himself was in agreement with Abu Hanifa.

> The Mu'tazilites… teach that neither intelligence nor analogy can accept the reality of the torments of the tomb, or the questioning of Munkar and Nakir… The truly orthodox people teach that the torments of the tomb and the questioning by Munkar and Nakir are realities, and that the pressure of the grave is a reality, whether a man be a believer or an unbeliever, obedient or reprobate. If he is an unbeliever his torment in the tomb continues till the Resurrection Day, but he gets relief from the torment on Fridays and during the month of Ramadan because of the sacred character of these periods… Believers fall into two classes. If [the deceased] has been obedient there will be no torment in the tomb for him… If he has been disobedient he will suffer both the torment and the pressure of the grave, but the torment will be cut off on Fridays…[398]

The Damascus-based Hanbali jurist Ibn Qudama (d. 1223) similarly took an anti-Mu'tazila line on these issues. In the following passage he affirms the priority of faith in revelation over reason, in a way which points to his Hanbalite allegiances, and underlines a literalist interpretation of Qur'an and Hadith references to the punishment in the tomb:

> Faith also requires belief in the reality of punishment in the tomb and the squeezing which will really take place and that Munkar and Nakir, the two angels, will come to the people in the grave asking about their Lord and their helper and prophet.[399]

Torments of the tomb are particularly graphically described in the Hadith collections. Believers are provided with silk and musk, and their tomb becomes a 'verdant garden'. Unbelievers are given sackcloth and live coals, and their tombs are crawling with seven-headed snakes.[400]

The great 11th century peripatetic theologian, philosopher, jurist and Sufi Abu Hamid al-Ghazali (d. 1111) provides graphic accounts of discourses in the grave, and unpacks some of the detail in the following terms:

> We are dealing with the unseen world. The snakes and scorpions of the tomb are not of the same species as the snakes and scorpions of our lower world; they belong to a different species and are perceived by a different sense of sight... suffering may be of the mind, as is the case when one dreams that he has been stung and cries out in his sleep... the mind, unlike the body, suffers no change at death and the deceased retains consciousness; he may therefore suffer pain or enjoy felicity, as the case may be.[401]

The modern Indonesian cleric H.A. Mustofa, citing al-Samarqandi, says in one of his sermons that anyone wishing to avoid the torments of the grave should do four things and avoid four things. The four things to do are observing the five daily prayers, giving charity generously, frequent reading of the Qur'an, and frequently pronouncing God's praises. The four things to avoid are lying, perfidy, bearing false witness, and immodesty. Mustofa depicts the grave as the entry point to one of two outcomes, echoing Hamka's statement that the grave is a reflection of the end of times:

> Remember that the grave is like a garden of the gardens of Paradise or a chasm of the chasms of Hell. And the grave itself declares each day: 'I am a house of darkness! I am a place of loneliness! I am the abode of maggots!'[402]

Likewise, Hamka distinguishes two kinds of experience of the grave, with the good reaping the benefits of their pious earthly existence:

> For sinners the realm of the grave will be lengthy in duration. But for those who feel that their lives have been more weighted towards good, the duration will not be long. What does fast and slow mean in this context? What does measurement in days and years mean? Is it not the case that in our present lives, for someone who cannot get to sleep, one night feels like twelve hours. And for someone who sleeps well, one night only seems like a passing moment?[403]

Popular stories on the experience of the grave

With such graphic detail available in the primary texts and scholarly literature, it is not surprising that the account of the experience of the grave in those sources is developed in creative ways in more popular literature. One example among many concerns a popular story about a conversation between the prophet Isa and a skull which is found in many locations across the Muslim world.

The account of the story which we will draw upon is found in the *Serat Centhini*, which originates from the Indonesian island of Java. The barebones of the account are as follows:

- There is a meeting between *nabi* Isa/Jesus and a former king's skull, during which Jesus asks questions about the skull's provenance and story.
- In response, the skull relates details about the end of its life: its final illness, process of death, and meeting with the angel of death, followed by burial and accounting for its deeds. Because of misdeeds, the skull relates to Jesus that it was clubbed by two angels (Munkar and Nakir), the Earth opened beneath it and it plunged into hell's fires.
- In hell, the body saw a vision of chairs for the prophets Ibrahim, Muhammad, Musa and Isa, and also saw angels torturing an old man.
- Clara Brakel-Papenhuyzen summarises the next stage graphically: 'Names of the seven fiery hells, each filled with a specific category of sinners. The latter's punishments are described: many souls are squeezed into a box filled with huge fires and boiling molten metals. The skull-king is entwined and bitten by a big snake, assisted by masses of poisonous

centipedes and scorpions. This goes on for thousands of years.'[404]

- As the story continues, it transpires that the skull had worshipped the idol of a cow during its life. Isa suggests that the skull pray to God in order to be resurrected to life, upon which the skull should live the life of a righteous believer.
- The skull is indeed resurrected and lives a virtuous life for a further 800 years.

These kinds of popular stories are important for many reasons, not least because they give substance to the notion of ordinary Muslims fearing God's punishment after death. With horrors such as those presented in this story, it is little wonder that Islam is the religion people are least likely to leave, for fear of earning divine retribution.

The Final Judgement

Qur'anic comment

Qur'an 81:1-18, taken from one of the earliest Meccan Suras, provides a graphic window into the events of the last day:

> 1. When the sun (with its spacious light) is folded up;
> 2. When the stars fall, losing their lustre;
> 3. When the mountains vanish (like a mirage);
> 4. When the she-camels, ten months with young, are left untended;
> 5. When the wild beasts are herded together (in the human habitations);
> 6. When the oceans boil over with a swell;
> 7. When the souls are sorted out, (being joined, like with like);
> 8. When the female (infant), buried alive, is questioned -
> 9. For what crime she was killed;
> 10. When the scrolls are laid open;
> 11. When the world on High is unveiled;
> 12. When the Blazing Fire is kindled to fierce heat;
> 13. And when the Garden is brought near;-
> 14. (Then) shall each soul know what it has put forward.
> 15. So verily I call to witness the planets - that recede,
> 16. Go straight, or hide;
> 17. And the Night as it dissipates;
> 18. And the Dawn as it breathes away the darkness

This will be a day of great torment, according to H.A. Mustofa:

> Remember that after [the grave] comes a day (hour) which is more dire, a day when small children will rapidly grow up, adults will be like drunkards and pregnant women will abort. And you will see people appear drunk, not through drinking alcohol, but rather through the dire and terrifying punishment of God.[405]

The three verses contained in Q18:47-49 are important for understanding the methodology of the Judgement to be employed by God on the Day of Resurrection:

> 47. One Day We shall remove the mountains, and thou wilt see the earth as a level stretch, and We shall gather them, all together, nor shall We leave out any one of them.
> 48. And they will be marshalled before thy Lord in ranks, 'Now have ye come to Us as We created you first: aye, ye thought We shall not fulfil the appointment made to you to meet':
> 49. And the Book will be placed; and thou wilt see the sinful in great terror because of what is therein; they will say, 'Ah! woe to us! what a Book is this! It leaves out nothing small or great, but takes account thereof!' They will find all that they did, placed before them: And not one will thy Lord treat with injustice.

The Cambridge Malay Commentary

The library of the University of Cambridge holds in its manuscript collection the only extant copy of an early Malay commentary on *Surat al-Kahf,* the eighteenth chapter of the Qur'an. This is one of the very oldest Malay language manuscripts extant, having been put into writing around 1600.

The author of the Cambridge Malay commentary was determined to present rich narrative in support of his exegetical goals. And the way to do this, on the subject of the final Judgement, was to engage with Hadith reports. In commenting on Q18:47-49, the anonymous author draws heavily on the prophetic Traditions.

We will focus on verse 48, which specifies that on the Day of Judgement, all people will be aligned in rows before God, awaiting judgement. The Qur'an is not explicit regarding the physical presentation of the people, but the commentaries, based on the Hadith, affirm that all will be naked. Clearly the Malay commentator was intrigued by this, as in his own social environment (and indeed today) people would have felt ashamed to be naked in front of other people.

In commenting on this verse, the Malay commentator selects a Hadith account, ultimately attributable to 'Aishah, which reassures the reader that on the final Day a sense of personal privacy will be far from people's minds. The qur'anic text appears in parentheses with the commentary interspersed outside the parentheses:

> And they will be marshalled) by the angels, O Muhammad, (before thy Lord), and they will be (in ranks), and they will see that there is no-one for protection. ('Now) a decree pronounced for the unbelievers who deny the Day of Judgement: (have ye come to Us) on this day naked, with nothing to your name (as We created you first) when you came from the earth alone, without any clothes or wealth. (Aye, ye thought We shall not fulfil the appointment made to you to meet') which was said to you by the prophets. And We will resurrect you from the grave, assemble you in the field of Mahshar, cause you to be fearful, and criticise your actions.

> An account from 'Aishah, may God be pleased with her: one day I asked the Prophet of God peace be upon him: 'Prophet of God! How will the people appear who are resurrected from the grave on the Day of Judgement, when they are assembled in the field of Mahshar?' The Prophet of God peace be upon him said: 'All those resurrected from the grave to the field of Mahshar will be naked.' So I said: 'Will all the women be naked too, O Prophet of God?' The Prophet of God replied: 'All the women will be completely naked.' So I asked: 'O Prophet of God! Won't all the women feel ashamed?' The Prophet of God replied: 'The events at the time will be so important, that no-one will be concerned with other people, nor will anyone even notice other people. Each will be concerned with themselves; no-one will feel any curiosity towards other people.'[406]

The details of the punishment

One of the key classical texts dealing with the Hereafter and the Judgement is al-Samarqandi's previously mentioned *Tanbih al-ghafilin* (The Arousement of the Heedless). This work has as its core a conjoining of Hadith accounts on various themes connected with the Hereafter, and as a result it presents the most graphic, gruesome portrayal of the terrors of Hell, as well as the physical delights of Paradise.

God is portrayed as a calculating, vengeful God, who goes to considerable lengths to impose the most painful punishment on the unbelievers in Hell:

> The Fire was stoked for a thousand years till it became red. Then it was stoked for a thousand years till it became white. Then it was stoked for a thousand more years till it became black, so that it is black as the darkest night.[407]

Such is the fate awaiting those in the Hereafter who do not make the right choices in the temporal world. However, al-Samarqandi not only paints a portrait of the punishments awaiting the doomed, but also provides the ingredients for living a life pleasing to God in this world:

> It has been said that the most excellent of men is he who is found in possession of five good qualities, the first being that he abounds in worship of his Lord, the second is that it be evident that he is serviceable to people, the third is that folk have no fear of being harmed by him, the fourth is that he does not put his hope on what is in men's hands, and the fifth is that he makes preparation for death.[408]

Al-Samarqandi's work is interspersed with qur'anic verses in places, but the small qur'anic input is far outweighed in influence by Hadith accounts. The overriding tone of the work is therefore graphic in ugliness or opulence, depending on whether Hell or Paradise is being portrayed respectively.

Hamka on non-Muslims and the reward of Paradise

In his work *Pelajaran Agama Islam* (Studying Islam) Hamka devotes chapter seven to the topic 'Belief in the Last Day'. His broad ranging discussion includes an important discussion of the issue of salvation and non-Muslims.[409] He responds to a question from an East Javanese village Muslim:

> In the Qur'an, Sura 2 verse 62, it says that apart from believers, there are also Jews, Christians and Sabeans who benefit from God's rewards, because they have faith in Allah and the Last Day and do good works. The clarification I seek is as follows: which Jews, Christians and Sabeans are referred to here?

Hamka seems to initially respond in irenic terms:

> The reference in this verse to Jews, Christians and Sabeans means those Jews, Christians and Sabeans in all periods since the time of the revelation of that verse fourteen centuries ago, right up until our present times. Those who are believers at the outset remain believers for all time, right up until our present time and beyond.

However, as his response develops, a significant measure of exclusivism becomes evident:

> If there is among those some who only acknowledge the prophethood of Moses, without recognising the prophethood of Jesus and Muhammad, as is the case with Jews of today, their faith is

certainly not acceptable. If they only believe in Jesus, and resolutely refuse to recognise the prophethood of Muhammad, their faith is certainly not acceptable.

Hamka goes on to polemically criticise those Jews and Christians who do not accept the prophetic status of Muhammad and the Qur'an as revelation. He accuses them of being motivated by envy: 'Envy is the reason that they are not willing to recognise that which is within their own sacred texts, which foretold that a last Prophet would come to perfect the divine law of the earlier prophets...'

He proposes that Islamic mission to Jews and Christians is the answer, stressing that compulsion is not appropriate. He concludes by articulating the conditions upon which Jews and Christians can taste the rewards of Paradise: 'And the door to enter Islam will remain open to them until the very Day of Resurrection'.

Here, once again, Jews and Christians fare badly in the writing of Islamic scholars, except in cases where they are willing to accept the prophethood of Muhammad.

There is a wealth of other detail presented in the both Qur'an and Hadith accounts about the final Judgement. This leads to a number of areas of inconsistency. Consider the following pair of accounts taken from the Hadith collection by the traditionist Muslim:

> The Messenger of Allah (peace_be_upon_him) observed: Three are the (persons) with whom Allah would neither speak on the Day of Resurrection, nor would look at them nor would absolve them, and there is a painful chastisement for them. The Messenger of Allah (peace_be_upon_him) repeated it three times. Abu Dharr remarked: They failed and they lost; who are these persons, Messenger of Allah? Upon this he (the Prophet) observed: They are: the dragger of lower garment, the recounter of obligation, the seller of goods by false oath.[410]

> The Messenger of Allah (peace_be_upon_him) observed: Three (are the persons) with whom Allah would neither speak nor would He absolve them on the Day of Resurrection. Abu Mu'awiyah added: He would not look at them and there is grievous torment for them: the aged adulterer, the liar king and the proud destitute.[411]

Furthermore, scholars debate whether it will be a bodily or spiritual resurrection for each person; the author of the Cambridge Malay commentary on Sura 18 evidently regarded it as a bodily resurrection.

The duration of the punishment

Another area of debate relates to the duration of the punishment. Islamic scholars have disagreed about whether punishment in Hell is eternal for the unbelievers, or whether those guilty of grave sin will be brought out of Hell after a time through intercession.

The classical Persian commentator 'Abd Allah ibn 'Umar al-Baydawi (d. 1286) reports some scholars as considering that 'the good deed of the unbeliever ... will bring about some lessening of punishment...'[412] However, the earlier Baghdad-based Mu'tazilite commentator Abu al-Qasim Mahmud ibn Umar Zamakhshari (d. 1144) is not inclined to such a view:

> ... it is certain that the 'inhabitants of paradise'... and those of the hell-fire will remain there forever without exception... The inhabitants of the hell-fire will not always remain only in the punishment of the fire; rather, they will also be punished through severe frost and in other ways...[413]

In this he shows his undoubted sympathies for the views of the Mu'tazila, for whom the eternal punishment of sinners was a key plank in their belief. Such disagreement among the classical scholars reflects the diverse viewpoints presented in both Qur'an and Hadith accounts regarding the events associated with the final Judgement.

Nurcholish Madjid on the duration of punishment

The prominent Indonesian scholar Nurcholish Madjid (d. 2005), a beacon of liberal Islamic thought, comments on this:

> When the Day of Resurrection has arrived, nobody will speak except by His permission. Mankind will be divided into two groups: the suffering and the joyous. As for the suffering, they will remain in Hell where they will moan incessantly. They will remain there forever, while the sky and earth exist, except if your Lord wishes otherwise. Because your Lord certainly carries out whatever He wishes. As for the joyous, they will be in Paradise, remaining there eternally, while the sky and earth exist, except if your Lord wishes otherwise, as a limitless mercy.[414]

While at one level Madjid might appear to align himself with the Mu'tazila in declaring that those sent to Hell remain there forever, nevertheless, he leaves the door open for that alternative viewpoint by inclusion of the crucial phrase 'except if your Lord wishes otherwise.' This phrase places his views within the boundaries of orthodoxy.

Modern Day Radicals

It is appropriate to conclude with a brief word on modern Islamist radicals, given how pertinent this discussion is to much which drives them. Several characteristics of modern day radicals stand out: a fascination with death; a flourishing ideology of messianism and the ad hoc appearance of mahdi-like figures (Osama Bin Laden received mahdi-like acclamation from some quarters); the often-repeated statement in radical pronouncements that death as a martyr circumvents all the horrors of the grave and the final day that others must endure.

In the above context, consider the 9/11 hijacker letter, written by lead hijacker Mohammad Atta to inspire other members of his group the night before their destruction of the World Trade Centre in New York:

> you are doing an act that Allah loves and is content with. Because there will be a day by the permission of Allah that you will spend it with pure women in paradise. Smile in the face of adversity all young men for you are going forth to the everlasting paradise... Know that the paradises have been ornamented for you with the most beautiful of its ornaments and the women of paradise are calling upon you to come forth oh you friend of Allah and she has worn the best of it's [sic] ornaments... When the hour of zero comes, breathe deeply and open your chest welcoming death in the way of Allah. Always remember that you end your life with prayer and that you begin with it before the target and let the last part of your speech be, 'There is No God but Allah and Muhammad is his messenger.' And after it, if God is willing, the meeting in the high paradise.[415]

Conclusion

We have seen that there are three key stages in the way Muslims understand eschatology: death, the experience of the grave, the Day of Judgement and thereafter. Throughout the texts we have referred to there appears a fundamental two-fold opposition: believers versus non-believers, the righteous versus the unrighteous.

There are profoundly different experiences of the three key stages for each of these groups. The righteous benefit from a relatively benign experience of death; life in the grave is pleasant; eventual judgement leads to eternal bliss. However, the unrighteous experience an agonising death; life in the grave is full of horrors; eventual judgement leads to eternal punishment.

Some details are debated among Muslim scholars. Does the grave torment actually occur? Is it physical or spiritual? Is the resurrection corporeal or spiritual? Are Muslim sinners sent to Hell forever or are they brought out after some time?

Regarding non-Muslims, the texts consulted did not cast them in a particularly favourable light. They fall very clearly into the non-believer side of the twofold equation. They are equated with demons in *Lubb al-kashf* by 'Abd al-Ra'uf of Singkel, where they are associated with falsehood and deception. Hamka is somewhat more accommodating, in terms of Christian and Jewish access to rewards of the Judgement, but only on condition that Christians and Jews recognise Muhammad's prophethood and the Qur'an as the word of Allah.

This poses a challenge for Christians and Jews interacting with Muslims. Such themes are pervasive, trickling down to the Muslim masses, as seen by the question from the East Javanese villager which Hamka responded to. Christian-Muslim dialogue sessions in Western contexts might seek to address such negative portrayals of Christians and Jews, but the greater challenge lies in getting a more positive portrayal of Christians and Jews to be embraced by Islamic scholars in the far-flung corners of the Muslim world.

This can only be achieved with the assistance and support of leading Muslim thinkers. Furthermore, it will require a fundamentally new hermeneutic by Islamic scholars, supported by a large dose of courage on their part, in the face of resurgent radicalism which draws on a very literalist reading of the Islamic sacred texts.

Part Two:

Specific Perspectives on Islamic Eschatology

Shia Eschatology in Contemporary Islamic Politics

Anthony McRoy[i]

Introduction

In Islam, politics and religion are not practically separated in the way the US Constitution demands, nor is there the same *conceptual* distinction. Muhammad was as much a Ruler as a Preacher, and the *Shari'ah* addresses civil and as well as what Western legal systems would see as purely religious issues. That being the case, we should not be surprised that Islamic eschatology has a strong political aspect. Since politics also involves military issues, we should neither be surprised that issues of *jihad* are also present in Islamic prophecy. Specifically in Shia eschatology these two factors concern the coming of the Mahdi and to a lesser extent of Jesus. Belief in these comings has influenced Shia politics in Iran, Lebanon, Iraq and elsewhere. Most pertinently at the present hour, it is intimately connected to the (possible) role of Shia eschatology in regards to the Iranian nuclear programme. This paper will therefore examine the role of Shia eschatology in politics.

The Background to the Mahdi concept

The Mahdi as an eschatological figure is not explicitly present in the Qur'an, but is common to Sunni and Shia Hadith collections. That the idea is emphasised in both traditions in all likelihood points to an early eschatological expectation arising as a result of the theological and constitutional crisis that arose following the death of Muhammad and most probably after the death of Ali, the First Imam of Shia belief. The severing of Muslim unity, the dynastic conflicts that characterised the Ummayad and Abbasid eras, and the perception among many Muslims that the current political order was illegitimate would doubtless have enhanced eschatological expectation of a divinely-sent deliverer who would restore Islam to its pristine condition. Such conditions are often perceived to have continued and indeed degenerated in the

---

[i] Dr Anthony McRoy is a dual UK and Eire citizen, and is married with grown-up children. He lectures in Islamic Studies at the Wales Evangelical School of Theology. He is the author of *From Rushdie to 7/7*, and has contributed to various books and conferences, both domestic and international, on Biblical, Islamic and Muslim world issues. He has also contributed to various media presentations.

centuries since then, notably after the collapse of the Ottoman Khilafah (Caliphate) in 1924 and with the voracious progress of Western cultural and political dominion since the First World War. Khomeini saw a continuity of declension after the death of Ali (AD 661) to the contemporary era, and used it as evidence for his theory of the *Vilayet-i Faqih* ('Guardianship of the Jurist'):

> After the death of the Most Noble Messenger (s), the obstinate enemies of the faith, the Umayyads (God's curses be upon them), did not permit the Islamic state to attain stability with the rule of 'Ali ibn Abi Tālib ('a). They did not allow a form of government to exist that was pleasing to God, Exalted and Almighty, and to His Most Noble Messenger (s). They transformed the entire basis of government, and their policies were, for the most part, contradictory to Islam. The form of government of the Umayyads and the Abbasids, and the political and administrative policies they pursued, were anti-Islamic. The form of government was thoroughly perverted by being transformed into a monarchy... this non-Islamic form of government has persisted to the present day...[416]

The Shia view the eschatological Mahdi as the *ultimate* Defender of the Oppressed. Significantly, Muhammad's grandson Hussein is said to have made his way to Iraq in response to an agonised plea by the people of Kufa in 680 AD:[i] 'This is a letter to Husayn bin Ali from his Muslim and faithful supporters. Be quick and hurry up, for the people are waiting for you, and they do not look towards anyone other than you. Hurry up. Hurry up. We repeat: Make haste. Make haste.'[417] The usual Shia exclamation upon reference to the Mahdi is 'May Allah hasten his coming (or return)'. The people of Kufa urgently desired the coming of an Imam who would establish 'justice' and deliver them from 'oppression', and it was this which Hussein promised in his reply to them:

> You have written that you do not have an Imam and asked me to come to you so that Allah may perhaps draw you together on truth and guidance through me... I swear by my life that a true Imam and leader is only he who takes decisions according to the Qur'an, establishes justice, promotes the Divine religion and dedicates himself to the path of Allah.[418]

Early in Shia history, hopes for a 'defender' sent by Allah to deliver the righteous *Umma* from oppressive rulers came to centre on the Mahdi:

---

[i] Ed: Hussein was cut down on this journey by troops of the Umayyad state.

Narrated by Abu Sa'id al-Khudri:

I heard the Prophet declare from the pulpit: 'The Mahdi ... will fill the earth with justice and equity as it is filled with tyranny and injustice.' (*Bihar al-anwar,* Vol. 51, p. 74)

Identification of the Mahdi as the ultimate 'defender' immediately demonstrates a difference with those who have looked to *ordinary* human figures. The Mahdi, in contrast, is a *supernatural* character, and for the Shia, his manifestation to the world is supernatural and thus God-given:

Ja'far as-Sadiq

... Abu Khalid al-Kabuli ... said:

Ali b. al-Husain... told me: '...I see your master, rising above the hill of your Najaf destined for Kufa, with three hundred and some odd over ten men, Jibraeel on his right, Mikaeel on his left, Israfil ahead of him, and with him (is) the Prophet's standard, unfurled... (*Bihar al-anwar,* Vol. 52, p. 327).

The fact that the Mahdi is supernaturally manifested in *Iraq* (i.e. attended by angels), aiming to reach Kufa just as Hussein did, provides a further connection with the martyred Imam Hussein. The land where an Imam – specifically 'the Lord of the Martyrs' (in Shia terminology) was slain, will be the land where the last Imam – al-Mahdi – will manifest himself[i] to complete the work begun by Hussein in confronting tyranny: 'I am the seal of successors. And through me shall Allah, the Mighty and Glorious, drive away the calamities from my progeny and my Shias.' (*Bihar,* v. 52, p. 30). So, just as the journey to Kufa was the scene for what Shia believe to be the greatest tragedy in their history, the ultimate journey to Kufa is viewed as the scene for the final triumph of the Mahdi over what Shia denounce as 'oppression'. This is confirmed by a saying attributed to Imam Mahdi himself and by a tradition of Imam Reza:

Imam Mahdi said, 'I pray for any believer who remembers the sufferings of my martyred grandfather, al-Husain, and then prays for my relief (*al-Faraj*)'[419]

...O Son of Shabib! If you wish to cry for anything or anyone, cry for al-Husain Ibn Ali (PBUH) for he was slaughtered like a sheep... Certainly, the seven heavens and earths cried because of the murder of al-Husain (PBUH). Four thousand Angels descended on earth to

---

[i] Ed: The Mahdi is often thought to manifest himself in Mecca in Sunni sources.

aid him, but (when they were allowed to reach there) they found him martyred. So they remained at his grave, disheveled and dusty, and will remain there until the rising of al-Qa'im (Imam al-Mahdi (PBUH)), whereupon they will aid him. Their slogan will be, 'Vengeance for the blood of al-Husain.'...[420]

The *Ziyarat Al-Nahiya al-Muqaddasa*, traditionally ascribed to the Twelfth Imam (i.e. the Mahdi), emphasises the identification of the Mahdi with opposition to the oppression that Imam Hussein resisted:

> Salutations from the one, who, had he been present with you in that plain, would have shielded you from the sharpness of the swords with his body and sacrificed his last breath for you... But ... as I could not fight those who fought you, and was not able to show hostility to those who showed hostility to you I will, therefore, lament you morning and evening, and will weep blood in place of tears, out of my anguish for you and my sorrow for all that befell you...

It can be seen that Shia eschatology looks *backward* as well as forward. In Shia theology, the victory of the Mahdi sets right what they see as the great wrong of Karbala. The sacrifice of one Imam sets the scene for the triumph of another – the last.

Alid lineage as a central factor in Shia eschatology and politics

The central distinction between Sunni and Shia Islam concerns the succession to Muhammad – as governing Amir, rather than Prophet. According to Shi'ism, the community is not to be led by communally-elected Caliphs, but by divinely-designated Imams:

> In Shi'i usage... *the term acquires a specialized sense as the person placed* in charge of all the political and religious affairs of the Islamic nation. More precisely, the *Imam* is a person appointed by God and nominated first by the Prophet and then by each succeeding Imam, through explicit designation *to lead the Muslim community, to interpret* and safeguard both religion and law (*shari'ah*) and to guide the community in all its concerns.[421]

The Shia believe that the first Imam was Muhammad's son-in-law Ali.[422] All his successors should be of his family – the *Ahl-ul-Bayt*:

> Muhammad ibn Yahya has narrated from Ahmad ibn Muhammad ibn 'Isa and Muhammad ibn abu 'Abd Allah and Muhammad ibn al-Husayn from Sahl ibn Ziyad all from al-Hassan ibn al-'Abbas ibn al-Jarish from abu Ja'far al-Thani who has said the following.

'Amir al-Mu'minin Ali said to ibn 'Abbas, 'Layla al-Qadr (the night of destiny) comes every year and in that night the command for the whole year descends down. To receive that command are the Leaders with Divine Authority after the Messenger of Allah.'

Ibn 'Abbas then asked, 'Who are they?' He said, 'I and the eleven persons from my descendants who all are Imams, (Muhaddathun) such persons to whom angels speak'.' (*Usul al-Kafi* Hadith 1373, Ch. 125, h 11)

Shia traditions also present the election of Abu Bakr as the first Caliph in 632 as being essentially an illegitimate usurpation and *coup d'état* – indeed, since Ali is held to be divinely-selected as the successor to Muhammad, as an act of apostasy:

Through the same chain of narrators the following is narrated.

'...Ali took the hand of Abu Bakr and showed the Holy Prophet (s.a) to him, who said to him, 'O Abu Bakr, believe in Ali and in the eleven Imams from his descendants. They are all like me except prophethood. Repent before Allah because of what you are involved in. You have no right in it.'

The narrator has said that then he went and was not seen around.' (*Usul al-Kafi* Hadith 1375, Ch. 126, h 13)

It follows from this that religio-political authority in Shia Islam is held to lie with the Imams who are Alids. Therefore, in Shia theology, all Sunni rulers are usurpers. The same holds true for all non-Muslim political authority, not just in terms of the religious identity of the persons involved, but also of their constitutional structure – it must be according to Shari'ah, and led by Alids. Even Shia rulers who do not meet these criteria are guilty of apostasy. Hence, the Shia position on the Mahdi actually looks back even beyond the martyrdom of Imam Hussein to the supposed usurpation of power by Abu Bakr and his supporters against Ali. Essentially, in the Shia vision, as the Mahdi returns to rule the earth, after subduing it with the help of Jesus, power is where it is meant to be – with the Alids, not with the Sunni usurpers, or anyone else for that matter.

The central concept of the Mahdi is that of being 'the Rightly-Guided' One. In Islamic terms this refers to someone whose character and conduct, unlike the dictatorship and corruption that has often been the defining quality of many Muslim rulers down to the present, reflect the Sunnah, or model, of the Prophet. In short, the picture that is presented is that of the ideal Islamic governing

Amir, in many ways a mirror-image of Muhammad. This factor is evidenced by the Shia tradition that the Mahdi will be an Alid descendant of Muhammad:

> Narrated by 'Abd'ullah ibn Mas'ud,
>
> who heard Rasul'ullah … say:
>
> 'The world will not come to an end until a man from my family who will be called al-Mahdi, emerges to rule upon my community.' (*Bihar al-anwar*, Vol. 51, p. 75.)
>
> Narrated by Umm Salama:
>
> The Prophet says: 'Mahdi will be among my progeny, among the children of Fatima.' (*Bihar al-anwar*, Vol. 51, p. 75)

The majority Shi'ite group, the Twelvers, explicitly identify the Mahdi as the Twelfth Imam - Muhammad ibn al-Hasan al-Mahdi, born 869 AD, who went into the 'lesser occultation' in 874, during which time he communicated by a succession of four deputies, and the 'greater occultation' in 941, since when there has been no direct communication: 'The Shi'a believe that he is the son of Imam Hasan al-'Askari. He was born in 255 (A.H). His occultation began in the year 260 (A.H). He is still alive, but protected by God in the state of occultation till preparations are made for his reappearance.'[423]

The absence of direct communication from the Twelfth Imam did not make the position of the Shahs in Iran, notably the last monarch Mohammed Reza Pahlavi, any easier. Since the revolutionary forces led by Khomeini in 1978-79 claimed to be acting in the name of the Twelfth Imam, this in itself undermined the Shah – the son of an army officer (Reza Khan) who staged a successful military coup, and who rather grandly spoke of Cyrus the Great as his 'ancestor' during the 2,500th celebration of Iranian monarchy in 1971 at Persepolis, rather than any genuine descent from Hussein.[424] Moreover, apart from other factors, Khomeini – and many other revolutionaries – could claim to be Alid *sayyeds,* descendants of the Prophet, and thus linked to the Mahdi in terms of lineage – which placed the Pahlavi dynasty at a distinct disadvantage. It also placed Sunni rulers, such as Saddam Hussein in Iraq, or the Al-Khalifah dynasty in Bahrain, dominating and, in Shia estimation, oppressing Shi'ite majorities, in a precarious position.

The Revolutionary Challenge of the Mahdi to 'corrupt' and 'unjust' regimes according to Shi'ism

The whole point of the existence of the Mahdi is to end what Shia see as sinful governance in the world, assisted in some sense by Jesus:

> Narrated by 'Ali b. Abi Talib:
>
> ... the Prophet... replied: 'God will conclude His religion through him [the Mahdi], just as He began it with us...' (*Bihar al-anwar*, Vol. 51, p. 84)
>
> Narrated by Abu Sa'id al-Khudaris:
>
> I heard the Prophet declare from the pulpit: 'The Mahdi ... will fill the earth with justice and equity as it is filled with tyranny and injustice.' (*Bihar al-anwar*, Vol. 51, p. 74)
>
> It is reported that the Prophet ('s) said, 'Among my progeny is the Mahdi. When he emerges, Jesus the son of Mary will descend to help him, then Jesus will send him ahead and pray behind him.' (*Bihar al-anwar*, Vol. 14, p. 349)

After the death of the four deputies of the Hidden Imam, a crisis of legitimacy arose. Could there be any legitimate Islamic governance in the absence of the Twelfth Imam? Khomeini's theory of the *Vilayet-i Faqih* was an attempt to resolve this issue. Essentially, a popularly elected government in conjunction with guidance by the *ulema* rules in trust for the Mahdi – what might be called a regency authority until the Twelfth Imam is manifested in Iraq.[425] Shi'ism places a particular emphasis on justice and in resisting oppressors: 'This emphasis on divine justice has influenced not only the theoretical aspect of Shi'ism, for the Shi'a regard justice as so fundamental an aspect of Islam that they have often called for its implementation in society.'[426] Hence, the absence of *Shari'ah* governance, the prevalence of injustice and despotism are conditions that the Mahdi is held to remove.

It should be noted that in the first aspect, Shia eschatological hopes for the Mahdi relate to the *internal* situation of Muslims – that is, he is someone who will deliver them from oppressive rulers who *themselves* claim to be Muslims, as opposed to confronting non-

Muslim political forces.[i] In historical times this had particular reference to Sunni rulers who oppressed the Shia on theological grounds, whereas in the contemporary era it is the perceived threat that large Shia communities pose to Sunni rulers that has caused *communal* inspired oppression, as with Saddam Hussein in Iraq or the Al-Khalifah dynasty in Bahrain – both minority Sunni regimes ruling over Shia majorities. Both theological and communal factors (and the presence of oil) have influenced the Wahhabi discrimination against Shia in Saudi Arabia's Eastern Province.

The exceptional aspect of the 1979 Islamic Revolution in Iran is that it was conducted against a ruler from the Shia community. However, it still fitted the pattern of opposition to *internal* 'oppressors'. In this respect we can see a link between the jihad of Hussein against the Sunni aspirant Yazid on the one hand, and Mahdist expectation on the other. Hussein went to Karbala to confront illegitimate rule, sacrificing himself in the process. This self-sacrifice was not immediately successful in toppling the tyrannical government, but Mahdist expectation held that a descendant of the Prophet (a *sayyid*) would be ultimately responsible for overthrowing oppressive regimes.

Thus, we can say that for the Shi'a, the Mahdi is effectively a *revolutionary* figure opposed to 'unjust' regimes. The 1979 Revolution aimed at establishing legitimate rule according to Shia Islam – i.e. in the name of the Twelfth Imam - by overthrowing the Shah, viewed as an oppressor. One hadith from the Twelfth Imam states: 'And surely on my re-appearance, whenever I reappear, there will be no allegiance in my neck of any of the oppressive tyrants' *(Bihar al-anwar,* v.53, p 181). Perhaps the 1979 Revolution should be called 'the Mahdi's Revolution'. Hence, Shia eschatological expectations influence their political response to what they see as oppression.

The Mahdi as the giver of comfort and encouragement for Shia

The general experience of the Shia throughout much of their history is that they have been the victims of oppression. At times this has been *political* in the sense of various regimes that have engaged in state repression, such as that of the Pahlavi dynasty,

---

[i] Ed: In the Sunni sources, there is some sense (often implicit) that the Mahdi will be leading the Muslims against outsiders, perhaps against 'Constantinople.'

other times it has been at the hands of *sectarian* Sunnis. Frequently, in relation to the Lebanese-Israeli struggle in the 1980s and 90s this led to incidents causing them to equate the Israeli occupation with 'oppression'. At such times it is important to understand the *psychological* factor involved in Mahdist expectation, which has several facets.

Firstly, Shia believe that despite the Occultation of the Twelfth Imam, he is still present to aid them in their struggles. For example, the Hadith asserts that just as the sun continues to shine and enable us to live even when the clouds prevent seeing it, so does the Mahdi aid his followers: 'As for deriving benefit from me in my occultation is like deriving benefit from the sun when it hides behind the clouds' (*Bihar al-anwar*, v. 53, p. 181). A classic statement of the Mahdi's role in providing both psychological comfort and practical guardianship is found in this hadith:

> Abu Muhammad al-Qasim ibn al-'Ala'... has narrated from 'Ad al-'Aziz ibn Muslim the following.

> '...The Imam is as a comforting friend, a very kind father, a real brother, and a tender-hearted mother of a small child, a refuge for people in disastrous conditions...' (*Usul al-Kafi* Hadith 504, Ch. 15, h1)

Secondly, there is the issue of eschatological *hope*. However intense the oppression, however extensive the suffering, Shia have always been buoyed and upheld by the succour given by the expectation of the Imam's return. They believe that his coming will dispel and vanquish tyranny; in short, they will be on the winning side.

Thirdly, it must be remembered that when Shia mourn and weep, especially over Hussein, they are engaged in a *practical* act of eschatological expectation. In regard to the annual Ashura festival, Shia have the hope of Paradise through shedding tears, and especially noteworthy is the tradition from Imam Sadiq that promises this for anyone weeping over *any* oppressed believer.[427] A classic practical example is seen in the 1979 Iranian Revolution, where every martyr's funeral became a political demonstration that intensified the jihad against the Shah. Khomeini stated 'Lamentation of the martyrs, means preservation and perpetuation of the Movement. It is narrated that he who cries (at Imam Hosein's martyrdom) ...will be admitted to the Heaven. Such a person who appears sad, whose face shows his affectation by tears, is actually helping to preserve the uprising and movement of Imam Hosein (a.s.).'[428] Thus, the tears of the mourners were also tears of comfort and joy that their loved ones had ascended to Paradise as martyrs.

Fourthly, even though the Mahdi is believed to be yet in Occultation, Shia seek his practical help – not just comfort, but for *invigoration* to *resistance*. The *Ziyarat al-Ashura* contains this statement: 'O Abu 'Abdullah... I am at war with those who make war with you, till the Day of Judgement', emphasising the permanence and immediacy of defensive jihad against oppression. Then the supplication is given which links the petitioner with the hope of the Mahdi: 'I pray to Allah ... to grant me an opportunity to be with a victorious Imam, from the family of Muhammad...' This demonstrates the *practical* inspiration and comfort that the Mahdi is said to give his followers: he *prepares* them for jihad.

In Lebanon during the Israeli occupation of the south Shia morale remained high, buoyed as they were by looking back to Karbala and forward to the Mahdi's appearance, since their tears were simultaneously sorrow for the loss of a loved one, after the manner of Hussein, but also joy at the martyr's immediate entry into Paradise. They held that just as the Mahdi would avenge the blood of Hussein with the blood of Oppressors, so the Lebanese Shia could avenge the blood of their progeny with the blood of the enemy. The example of the Mahdi and his *Ziyarat* was therefore instrumental in bringing about the victory of both Khomeini's revolution against the rule of the Shah in Iran and the Hezbollah jihad against the Israeli occupation.

The internal foe in Lebanon which the Shia fought - the Israeli occupation - was different than in Iran. Here it was externally-based, but was 'internal' in the sense of occupying the land. Hezbollah fused together the example of Imam Hussein in martyrdom with eschatological expectation of the Mahdi, and according to its statements, developed the concept of *sought-out* martyrdom as a military tactic, as its statement declares:

> Hezbollah also used one of its own special types of resistance against
> the Zionist enemy that is the suicide attacks. These attacks dealt
> great losses to the enemy on all thinkable levels such as militarily
> and mentally. The attacks also raised the moral [i.e. morale] across
> the whole Islamic nation.[429]

Sheikh Naim Qassem, Hezbollah Deputy Secretary General, made the explicit link with Hussein:

We have learned through Imam al-Hussein that the love of martyrdom is part of the love for God. We have learned to glorify jihad for the sake of Islam. Generations after al-Hussein's resurgence in Karbala, we still learn from the magnificent accomplishments that materialized through his martyrdom. His vision was not momentary or restricted to the battle: it was directed at the future of Islam and of Muslims.[430]

However, what is almost totally neglected in Western study of the movement is the role of *the Mahdi* in inspiring Hezbollah; Qassem referred to eschatological promises concerning Jerusalem:

The role of those who persevere and resist in and around the Dome of The Rock in Jerusalem is mentioned in the accounts of the Prophet (PBUH)

One sect of my people shall uphold their religion, conquer their enemy, and will never be harmed by any assailant except that which befalls them of distress and hardship, and they will remain as such until God's order comes unto them.

When asked where this party is, the Prophet (PBUH) said: 'In Beit-ul Maqdis (Jerusalem) and under its wings.' Tradition also speaks of the appearance of the Twelfth Imam, Imam al-Mahdi (PBUH), who will work to purify Jerusalem. Accounts quoted from the Prophet (PBUH) state:

A man of my people treading on my path and tradition shall emerge. God shall bestow heavenly grace on him, and the land shall offer its benediction. He will disseminate justice on the land that would by then be a haven for tyranny. He works for seven years on this nation. He reaches Beit-ul Maqdis (Jerusalem).

Therefore, there is no separation between the religious duty of liberating Palestine and the Godly promise of victory.[431]

It can be seen that Hezbollah's jihad proceeded on the dual basis of the example of Imam Hussein and the promise of the Mahdi's appearance. Moreover, Hezbollah clearly saw their jihad as preparing for the coming of the Mahdi: 'If we are confident that our actions but pave the way for Imam al-Mahdi's emergence – he who will bring evenhandedness and justice after the reign of tyranny and despotism, then the future is quite promising.'[432] Therefore, in Hezbollah's view, its jihad was both a microcosm of the jihad of Hussein, with the Israeli government and its forces playing the role of Yazid, but also a microcosm and a model of the future jihad of the Mahdi against the Dajjal (Antichrist) and, with the Israeli occupation forces seen as precursors of that ultimate oppressor. Thus, Hezbollah's 'steadfastness' – which the movement viewed as an effective victory - over the Israeli bombardment in 2006 was seen as the triumphant jihad of the Mahdi.[i]

It is also worth considering that when the Iraqi Shia leader Muqtada al-Sadr formed his militia which opposed the US-UK occupation of Iraq and Sunni groups like Al-Qaida which waged a vicious sectarian war against Iraqi Shia, he named it *Jaish al-Mahdi* – the Mahdi Army.[433] They saw themselves as 'a real army in the service of Islam'.[434] Given the history of Shia oppression under Saddam and the prophecy of the Mahdi's emergence in Iraq, the choice of name indicated both an act of pride and an indication of eschatological expectation.

The preparation for the jihad of the Mahdi

We earlier noted Shomali's reference to the need for Shia to make 'preparations for his reappearance'. This has direct pertinence to the issue of Iranian nuclear policy, a matter of great controversy at the time of writing. Obviously, there is no absolute evidence on Iranian nuclear ambitions. Iran claims that it only wants a peaceful nuclear industry; the West is suspicious that its real intentions are a nuclear arsenal – which it could use against its neighbours or the West. There is also the fear that it could supply guerrilla groups with nuclear military technology. In the course of this issue there have been journalistic accusations that Iran desires to use nuclear arms in a precipitate war against its foes to bring about an apocalypse which will result in the coming of the Mahdi. Perhaps the misunderstanding has arisen from the comments by various Iranian politicians and clergy about 'preparing' for the return of Mahdi. So what does this 'preparation' entail? *It is at this point we leave description for speculative analysis, with several possibilities.*

Firstly, there is the Iranian denial that they do indeed want a nuclear arsenal. Secondly, even if we do not take such a denial seriously, there may be ordinary reasons for such an aspiration. Iran is the only country since 1945 to suffer a war in which WMDs

---

[i] Ed.: It might then be observed that on purely theological grounds one might question whether Hezbollah could ultimately limit its conflict with Israel to the mere objective of securing only Lebanon from Israeli 'oppression.' They are the Mahdi's advance guard in the struggle which must finally aim at Jerusalem itself.

have been used against it – by Saddam in the Iran-Iraq war, 1980-88 – and it may be the case that Iran wants to deter any future use of such weapons against it from any quarter.[435] Thirdly, and linked to the previous point, Iran faces two nuclear arsenals on either flank – the Israeli arsenal in the west, Pakistan's on the east. Its relations with the former are perpetually hostile; with the latter, intermittently so. It should also be considered that Pakistan backed the Taliban regime in Afghanistan, a regime that persecuted Shia (specifically the Hazara community), and killed Iranian diplomats, nearly provoking a war.[436] Should Pakistan ever fall to a Talibanesque regime, Iran would doubtless feel vulnerable against a nuclear-armed Sunni sectarian power – unless it possessed its own nuclear deterrent. Finally, it should be considered that the history of US relations with nuclear-armed Russia and China – and indeed, India, Pakistan and even North Korea – suggests that *realpolitik* would compel Washington to regard Iran with more respect at a peer level, something important for Eastern cultural issues of honour and 'face'.[i]

None of these considerations are specifically *religious*, let alone eschatological; rather, they are, to a great extent, the pragmatic considerations of defence policy. However, the issue before us is the influence of *Shia eschatology* upon politics – and claims that Iran wants to provoke a nuclear apocalypse to bring about the return of the Mahdi. Since it is the Shia Hadith which provides data about the Mahdi, we should look *there* to see if this is viable. The first point to note is that the coming of the Mahdi is no ordinary event; it is supernatural, and this character means that any attempt to fake it would be difficult. Three angels – Gabriel, Michael and Israfil - attend the Mahdi in full public view when he emerges in Iraq (q.v.). According to the Shia Hadith, angels are viewed as having wings.[437] In *Al-Amali* (27.3), Jibraeel is presented as having six hundred wings, which would make any attempt at fabrication a Herculean task. This should caution commentators against rash exclamations concerning Iranian policy today. Secondly, we should note also that the appearance of the Mahdi occurs in *Iraq*, not Iran. Hence, any attempt by Iran to fabricate the coming is undermined by this fact. Thirdly, the Shia believe that since the entry into world

---

[i] Ed.: These Iranian perspectives are surely important and not to be overlooked, whether or not one accepts *wholesale* a Shi'i/Iranian self-perception as innocent victim and/or righteous responder to aggression.

of the Hidden Imam is held to be both dramatic and miraculous and according to the hadith, no one knows the time of his coming.[438]

This is relevant to the present situation. If no one but Allah knows the time of the Mahdi's manifestation, then the occasion of his appearance is purely supernatural – it will come out of the blue, so to speak. The realia of these Hadith caution us as to the likelihood that these latter-days events could be fabricated by any government. Similar questions attend the idea that the Mahdi's return could be provoked by a nuclear war, since that would imply that people knew the actual timing of the reappearance – it would immediately follow an apocalyptic conflict. Moreover, we should remember that the argument on Iranian nuclear ambitions centres on *theological* issues – what the Iranian government, as a Shia body, believes. As Shia, they would believe that if they attempt to fabricate the reappearance of the Mahdi, they will be destroyed (by Allah):

> Another companion by the name of 'Abd al-Rahman b. Kathir was with Imam Sadiq when Mahzam Asadi came to visit the Imam and asked him: 'When will the Qa'im from the family of the Prophet rise and establish the just government that you are expecting, for it has been delayed? When shall this be realised?' The Imam replied: 'Those who fix the time of the appearance are certainly telling a lie. Those who become hasty in this matter will definitely destroy themselves. Those who are patient will be delivered and will return to us.' (*Bihar al-anwar*, Vol. 52, p. 103.)

It is also important to consider that nowhere in Shia traditions do we encounter the idea that the Hidden Imam reappears after a conflagration started by the Shia. There are certain events which are said to precede or accompany his manifestation, many outside human manufacture. For example, one sign is a unique eclipse:

> Shaykh Saduq says: Narrated to us Muhammad bin Hasan (r.a.): Narrated to us Husain bin Hasan Aban from Husain bin Saeed from Nadhr bin Suwaid from Yahya Halabi from Hakam Hannat from Muhammad bin Hammam from Ward from Abi Ja'far (a.s.) that he said:

> 'Two signs will be seen before the reappearance: there will be a lunar eclipse for five days and there will be solar eclipse for fifteen days. Such a phenomenon has not taken place since the arrival of Adam (a.s.) on the earth...'[439]

Another sign will be a terrible flood in Kufa (Iraq):

Ghaibat Tusi: It is narrated from Ahmad bin Ali Raazi from Muhammad bin Ishaq Muqri from Maqani from Bukkar from Ibrahim bin Muhammad from Ja'far bin Saad Asadi from his father from Imam Ja'far Sadiq (a.s.) that he said:

'In the year of the reappearance, there will be such a terrible flood in the Euphrates that even the lanes of Kufa will be inundated.'[440]

There are other signs, but suffice to say that in none of them do we find any intimation that the appearance of the Mahdi could be caused by his followers – the Shia – starting an apocalyptic war.[i] So are there any traditions indicating how Shia should actually prepare for his coming, and what does 'preparation' mean?

Firstly, Shia believe that there should be some political revolution that lays the basis for his rule: 'The Messenger of Allah ...has said: 'A group of people will rise up from the East and will prepare the groundwork for the government of al-Mahdi.' (*Bihar-al Anwar, Volume 51, p. 87*)' Doubtless, the Iranian government would ascribe the 1979 revolution as the fulfilment of this. When Khomeini issued his work *Hokumat-i-Islami*, it included this call to people to 'Prepare yourselves to be useful to Islam; act as the army for the Imām of the Age in order to be able to serve him in spreading the rule of justice.'[441] He continued: 'The Imams ... not only fought against tyrannical rulers, oppressive governments, and corrupt courts themselves; they also summoned the Muslims to wage jihad against those enemies.'[442] On that basis, Khomeini gave the call to overthrow the Shah: 'Islam is the school of *jihad*, the religion of struggle; let them ... transform themselves into a powerful force, so that they may overthrow the tyrannical regime imperialism has imposed on us ...'[443] Thus we may term the Iranian Revolution as the victorious revolution of the Mahdi, which the Shia revolutionaries believed prepared the way for his appearance by laying the political groundwork – a microsm of what the Twelfth Imam is held to accomplish at his coming.

---

[i] Ed.: All these observations should make us pause before drawing an easy straight line from Mahdist doctrine to an Iranian president 'pushing the red button.' This is not to say, however, what could or could not happen in the unpredictable world where religion, politics, and economics all intersect. Further, apocalyptic theology is often malleable and subject to reinterpretation. The Shi'i Imami tradition may tend to limit wild eschatological speculation more than some other religious streams do, and an awareness of the 'standard' traditions and interpretations of Shi'i eschatology *is* essential here; even so, knowledge of such traditions cannot be held to be an absolute fail-safe guide as to how any of these texts might ever be used in the future.

Secondly, the Mahdi's coming also involves *military* readiness: Imam Sadiq said: 'Prepare yourselves for the revolution of our Qa'im, even if it means to gather an arrow [for fighting God's enemies].' (*Bihar al-anwar*, Vol. 52, p. 366).[444] It follows that the Shia must have weapons *ready* for the jihad of the Mahdi. Obviously, arrows are scarcely effective weapons today, so their contemporary equivalent must be considered – guns and bombs, especially nuclear weapons. The Shia Hadith suggests that the swords of the Mahdi's forces are of a special kind:

> Regarding a group of supporters of al-Mahdi (*'atfs*), Imam as-Sadiq (*'a*) said: 'The supporters of al-Mahdi (*'a*) have swords made of iron, but this is different from common iron. If one of them would strike a mountain with his sword, the mountain will be divided into two. With such soldiers and equipment, Hadrat al-Qa'im (*'atfs*) will wage war...' (*Bihar al-Anwar*, vol. 27, pp. 41; vol. 54, p. 334.)

These 'swords', unless they are miraculous, may be equated with modern nuclear weapons, which possess the destructive force outlined in this tradition. Whatever the interpretation, it can be seen that the 'preparedness' involved does not involve the actual *employment* of weapons, but rather their *possession* by the Shia, for use at the Mahdi's command *after* his appearance. That is, if there is an eschatological reason for any genuine desire of Iran to possess nuclear weapons, it is to have them ready for their use by the Twelfth Imam, in fulfilment of the commands in the Hadith.[i]

The third point to consider is that a major feature of Islamic eschatology is the emphasis on the Antichrist - *Al-Masih Al Dajjal* ('the Deceiver-Christ'). There are many and various traditions about this, and we can only examine those pertinent to our theme:

> Khaythama reported that Abu Ja'far said, '...O Khaythama! There will come a time for the people when they will not know who is Allah and His unity until Dajjàl appears and Jesus the son of Mary, may peace and blessings be with both of them, descends from the sky, and Allah will kill Dajjàl by his hands and a man that is from our House will pray with the people. Do you not know that Jesus will pray behind us,

---

[i] Ed.: It bears restating that what is presented here is an assessment based on mainstream Shi'i theological texts; we cannot, of course, account for any possible mutations in how these texts might some day be deployed. Further, there are multiple influences and interests that ultimately feed both human and sate behaviors. No claim should be made that these particular theological texts are the *only* influences meriting consideration in the current geo-political scenario. They certainly are one of the important influences, however.

although he is a prophet? Beware that we are better than him.'
(*Bihar al-anwar*, 24, 328, 46)

It is reported that, 'Jesus ('a) will descend, wearing two saffron colored robes.' According to another tradition, 'Jesus the son of Mary will descend to a hill of the Sacred Earth that is named Ithbaní [or Ithbayt]. Two yellow dresses are on him and the hair of his head is anointed and there is a lance (arm) in his hand by which he kills Dajjàl. He comes to Jerusalem while the people pray the afternoon prayer and Imàm is in front of them. Imàm comes back, but Jesus prefers him and prays behind him according to the revealed law of Muhammad. Then he will kill the swine, break the crosses, destroy the churches and temples and kill the Christians unless they believe in him.' (*'Umdah*, 430)

It is reported from Abu 'Abd Allah from his fathers that Hasan the son of 'Alí ('a) said when disputing with the king of Byzantium, 'The life of Jesus in the world was thirty-three years. Then Allah raised him to heaven and he will descend to the earth in Damascus, and it is he who will kill the Antichrist (Dajjàl).' (*Bihar al-anwar*, 14, 247, 27)

To return to the issue of illegitimate government, from the Shia perspective, those rulers not obeying God's will in the constitutional and cultural spheres are held to have apostatised from Islam. It is on this basis we can view the revolutionary actions of the Mahdi and the Messiah in Islam. The Mahdi is held to come to establish a true Islamic government and society; at his coming, he faces the crystallisation of anti-Islamic forces in the shape of the Dajjal, both as an individual and, in some modern Islamic discourse, a religio-political system, uniting apostate Muslims with other non-Muslim elements. The Shia Hadith presents their encounter as necessarily *confrontational*. In order to establish the ideal Islamic State and society, the Mahdi must fight the power of the Antichrist. It is clear from Shia hadiths that the Mahdi engages in jihad and judgement of God's foes.[445]

Moreover, whether the Dajjal is a system, an individual or both, he (and/or 'it') is not destroyed directly by the *Mahdi*. Rather, as Shia *ahadith* testify, this task belongs to the *Messiah* – Jesus, who slays the Antichrist with a lance.[446] This immediately points to the *supernatural* character of the engagement. In Shi'ite narrations, the coming of both the Mahdi and Jesus are miraculous, the former being accompanied by angels and visible in character, the latter descending from Paradise to Damascus. The visibility (rather than secrecy) of the events and angelic presence accompanying them underline the supernatural character of the Mahdist/Messianic judgment and jihad, rather than ordinary human actions. Everyone in the world will be able to recognise these events. It follows that the Mahdi's responsibility of vanquishing injustice from the world through military means is inextricably linked to the Second Coming of Jesus.

The final point concerns Shia jurisprudence on jihad. Shi'ite theology recognises two distinctions in military *jihad,* with a qualification on the authority to call to military action: 'There are two types of jihad: *ibtida'i* (to be begun by Muslims) and *defa'i* (defensive). In the view of Shi'ite jurisprudence, *ibteda'i jihad* can only take shape under the direction of the Holy Prophet or one of the twelve immaculate and perfect Imams, otherwise it is forbidden.'[447] In short, only the Imam of the Age can order offensive jihad. The 'Imam of the Age' in the contemporary period is the Twelfth Imam – the Mahdi. According to Shia theology, only *he* may give the command to offensive jihad. No Iranian or Iraqi ruler can give it, nor even the consensus of Shia *ulema.* This is important to recognise in the present context of concern about Iran's purported 'nuclear ambitions'. Whatever the truth of that matter may be, Western calculations ought to incorporate Shi'i jihad theory into the equation. On the face of it, Iran, as the Islamic Republic, would be barred (theologically speaking) from using nuclear weapons to *conquer* America – until the Mahdi returns and orders such. At best, Iran could only (again, theologically speaking) employ them if *attacked* by American nuclear bombs – i.e. in *defensive* jihad. Only the Twelfth Imam as the Mahdi can give the order for *offensive* jihad. To be sure, an awareness of human nature and the vicissitudes of realpolitik might provide other reasons for resisting even the potential proliferation of further nuclear weapons in the Middle East.[i] Nonetheless, from the above study it should be clear that speculation about Iranian nuclear ambitions have thus far proceeded without due attention to the actual character of the coming of the Mahdi in Shia eschatology.

---

[i] Ed.: It might be quite easy to provide examples of leaders, both secular and religious, who have found ways to construe whatever potential conflict as 'vital to national interests' and as 'requiring preemptive action,' or to construe a given adversary as a 'real and present threat' or as the 'real' aggressor; in so doing some have launched 'defensive' conflicts which to most outside observers look markedly offensive.

Conclusion

This paper has shown that Shia eschatology – especially in relation to Mahdist expectation – has played a major role in the Iranian Revolution, and in Lebanese and Iraqi militia activity. The nature of this role is to provide instruction – i.e. to resist 'oppressors' – psychological comfort and encouragement, and prophetic hope. Ultimately, Shia eschatology has a profoundly political character in that it rejects all non-Shia authority – including that by Sunnis – as effectively usurpation, and its aim is to put right what Shi'ism believes went wrong after the death of Muhammad. A major facet of Shia eschatology is the need for Shi'ites to prepare both politically and militarily for the coming of the Mahdi, and if the Iranian government is indeed intent on producing nuclear weapons in relation to this event, we should comprehend it in these terms. Thus, according to Shia eschatology, the time for non-Shia to worry about a possible nuclear *offensive* jihad by Shi'ites is if we see someone arising in Iraq attended by angels, later assisted by someone descending from Paradise to Syria.

Ahmadiyya Perspectives on the Last Day: the writings of Mirza Ghulam Ahmad (1835-1908)

Steven Masood[i]

Jama'at Ahmadiyya, also known as the Ahmadiyya Movement, is an Islamic reformist movement founded in India at the end of the 19th century. The founder was Mirza Ghulam Ahmad (1835 – 1908). Adherents are referred to as Ahmadis or Ahmadi Muslims. After the death of the founder, the movement split on the question of leadership. The small dissident group later came to be known as the *Ahmadiyya Anjuman Ishaat-e-Islam Lahore.*[448]

Ghulam Ahmad based his claims on the idea of *tajdid*, the advent of a leader known as *Mahdi* and the Islamic doctrine known as the *Nuzul al-Masih (*the descent of Jesus*)*. The idea of *tajdid* (renewal or reformation) is not found in the Qur'an but is based on traditions. For example, Muhammad is reported to have said, 'Surely, Allah will raise at the head of every century, one who will revive religion for the entire *umma'*.[449] Thus many revered personalities in Islam have been acknowledged as being *mujaddid* (reformers) of their respective ages.

Also mentioned among the traditions is the prophesied advent of a special messianic figure, the Imam *Mahdi* (the guided one), connected by descent with Jesus. The idea of Imam Mahdi in Islam is akin to being a counterpart to the Christian Messiah. He takes the form of an eschatological restorer of the faith. Since the Mahdi as restorer is sometimes identified with the returning of Jesus,[450] Mirza Ghulam Ahmad claimed himself as the fulfilment of not only the *mujaddid* of the 14th century in the Islamic calendar, but also claimed to be *Mahdi* and Jesus.

Both Muslims and Christians believe in the return of the same Jesus who ascended into heaven. Ghulam Ahmad rejected not only the ascension of Jesus but also his coming back in person. He believed

---

[i] Dr Steven Masood is a Christian from a sectarian Muslim background. He has a MTh and PhD from the London School of Theology, with theses for both addressing subjects related to Islam and Christianity. Apart from teaching, Steven delivers seminars, speaks at conferences and churches on various subjects including Christian approaches to Muslims. He is a widely published author of both scholarly and popular works. Further information on Steven is available at www.JesusToMuslims.org

that Jesus died a natural death.[451] He argued that the belief of the descent of Jesus contained 'a metaphorical meaning bearing the news of a person in the likeness of Christ'.[452] To pave the way for himself to be the coming of Jesus in the last days, Ghulam Ahmad claimed that Jesus died like any other mortal, and the future descent envisaged was not the same person, nor was it a literal descent. To 'prove' his own coming in the spirit of Jesus, he referred to the example of John the Baptist in the Gospel account where Jesus said that John the Baptist 'is Elijah who was to come' (Matthew 11:14, also 17:13).[453]

While the majority of Muslims in the Sunni, Shi'a and Sufi walks of life await the coming of the Mahdi and the return of Jesus before the Last Day, the followers of Ghulam Ahmad believe that the coming of the Mahdi and the return of Jesus have already been fulfilled. The Ahmadiyya movement differs from mainline Islamic interpretations of the qur'anic verses and the *Ahadith* references about the signs of the Last Day, as well as the events that will take place before and on that day.

Just as the life of an individual has an end and the life of a nation has an end, so the life of this entire physical world has an end. According to Ahmadiyya teachings, the end of the physical world is called the 'Day of Judgment' because each person shall then become fully conscious of the effects of his or her deeds in this life, and have a 'body' (so to speak) made out of his or her own deeds. The Day of Judgement will bring the spiritual world into full manifestation in place of the present physical one. It is on the Day of Judgment that everyone will fully be awakened and raised to the higher spiritual life.

Immediately upon death, a person begins to feel an awakening to the higher life, made from his deeds in the present life. However, this is only a partial realization. On the Day of Judgment, this entire universe will come to an end. Then the dead will be resurrected and accounts taken of their deeds. People with good records will be rewarded and welcomed into heaven while those with bad records will be punished and cast into hell. The concept of hell in Ahmadiyya thought is more of a reformatory, where people will spend limited time before eventually entering heaven, which will last forever.[454]

It would seem on the surface that the Ahmadiyya movement follows the orthodox idea of belief in Islam concerning the Last

Day, but one very soon finds that it has its own unique interpretations of the passages of the Qur'an and traditions concerning the signs and the happening of events.

The coming of a leader

Sura 18:98-99 is generally treated by Muslim exegetes as describing the events that will lead to the Day of Judgement,[455] but Ahmadiyya add that it also contains the news of the coming of a special teacher (referring to the leader of the movement: Ghulam Ahmad).

According to the interpretation, this leader would come at a time when God will allow every sect to strive for a limited time in order to make its religion and faith overcome the others. Ghulam Ahmad is said to have claimed that the qur'anic passage stated: 'Each sect will strive to make its religion supreme. They will [still] be engaged in this battle when *Sur* (the trumpet) will be blown at the command of God. Then we [God] will unite all factions under one faith' (i.e. Ahmadiyya Islam).[456]

Ghulam Ahmad went further on in his exegesis to argue that the above qur'anic passage meant that

> when the Christian religion and its rule would hold sway over the world ... [then] in such an age the heavenly trumpet will be blown to unite all nations under the religion of Islam, that is, that the heavenly system will be established in accordance with the *Sunna* of God; a heavenly reformer will come. ... God's major purpose in this is to shatter the glory of the cross ... to prove thereby that [a doctrine of] raising mortals to [the status of] divinity is a folly.[457]

Gog and Magog

Muslim exegetes agree that Sura 21:96-97 refers to Gog and Magog (*Ya'juj wa Ma'juj*), who will appear in the period between the second coming of Jesus and the Day of Judgement.[458] It is interesting to note that when Ibn Mas'ud inquired about Gog and Magog, Muhammad replied, 'Gog and Magog are two nations'.[459]

Several exegetes suggest that Gog and Magog are the descendants of Japheth the son of Noah.[460] The Ahmadiyya movement, in line with Ghulam Ahmad's teaching, believes that Gog and Magog are 'the English and the Russians'.[461] It is during their powerful struggle that the promise of the coming of the *Mahdi* and the second coming of Jesus would occur, albeit in spirit. Referring to himself, Ghulam Ahmad claimed that as John the Baptist was Elijah in spirit, so he had come in the spirit of Jesus as the '*Muhammadi Masih*'. Referring to the above passage from the Qur'an, Ghulam Ahmad wrote:

> The sum of these verses is that in the latter days, many religions will spread in the world and there will be many sects. Then two nations will emerge, whose faith will be Christianity, and who will attain to supremacy of every kind. So when you see that the Christian religion and Christian governments have spread throughout the world, know that the time of the promise is near. [462]

The shaking of the earth

While Muslims see Sura 99 as one of the qur'anic chapters containing eschatological material, for the Ahmadiyya movement this chapter serves as evidence for the coming of their leader as the Mahdi and Messiah into the world. Ghulam Ahmad himself taught that the prediction in this passage was not about real earthquakes but about the mannerisms of people: 'A great change will come over the people of the world and they will give themselves up to selfishness and worldliness.'[463]

He wrote that when the Qur'an states that the earth will bring forth all its burdens (Sura 99:2), it means 'worldly knowledge, worldly cunning, worldly scheming, and all the other worldly qualities in human nature will become manifest'.[464] He also claimed that the earthquake meant that the earth would display its *special characteristics*:

> Many of its properties will be known through physical and agricultural science; mines will be dug and cultivation will become extensive...the earth will become productive and every kind of implement will be invented; so much so that 'man will say: what is the matter?', why are new branches of knowledge, new kinds of technology, and new inventions coming into being? Then the earth, i. e. the hearts of men, will tell their story, that all these new things happening are not from them; it is a type of revelation from God, for it is not possible that man by his own efforts be able to produce such wonderful knowledge.'[465]

Sura 81:1-2 states, 'When the sun is folded up; when the stars become murky.' The traditional interpretation is that the whole

Sura concerns the Day of Resurrection, not only these two verses. Elsewhere in traditions on this subject Sura 82 and 84 are added.

Ibn Umar is stated to have heard Muhammad say, 'Anyone who would like to know about the Day of Resurrection in a way as though it is occurring before his [own] eyes should recite, "When the sun is folded up; when the sky is cleft asunder; when the sky is rent asunder."'[466] According to the Ahmadiyya however, the *sun* in this passage is Muhammad himself, who is also called *Sirajan Muniran* and *Nur*. The stars are the religious leaders.[467]

Ghulam Ahmad stated that the passage referred to a time when an intense darkness of ignorance and sinfulness would envelope the earth. The religious leaders would no longer possess the light of sincerity. They would not care for the teachings of Muhammad and his office.[468] The spiritual understanding of the religious leaders would be lost and worldly knowledge would be gained.

Referring to verse 3 of Sura 81, Ghulam Ahmad stated that the passage showed how mountains would be turned into places to dwell, and routes would be constructed through mountains for pedestrians, vehicles and for trains.[469] He claimed that the recent appearance of these facilities indicated that the time of the *Promised Messiah* had now arrived.[470] According to Ghulam Ahmad, the Qur'an stated that a time was coming when riding camels for long journeys would be abandoned. He believed the prophecy marked the time in which he himself was living.

Referring to the word *ishar* in verse 4, he said that 'it means a pregnant camel, which is of great value in the eyes of the Arabs'.[471] Classical commentators do present such an interpretation, but state that in fact the example refers to the situation of people who would not care anymore for their wealth and status because of the destruction around them.[472] Denying that it referred to the Day of Judgement, Ghulam Ahmad wrote:

> Doomsday is not the time when a male and female camel could mate, and a pregnancy would ensue. This is, in fact, a reference to the invention of the railway train with the mention of a pregnant camel providing a strong argument that an event in this world is referred to, preventing one's mind from inferring a reference to the Hereafter.[473]

Referring to the passage, 'When the wild ones are gathered together' (Sura 81:5), Ghulam Ahmad claimed that it meant primitive nations would someday become civilised.[474] He said, 'Due to the spread of worldly knowledge and technology, no difference will remain between the high and the low.'[475] He went on to suggest the passage meant that people of low caste would one day 'hold power and government.'[476]

Ghulam Ahmad said that both Sura 81:6, which states, 'When the oceans boil over with swell (*sujjirat*)' and Sura 82:3, which says, 'When the oceans are suffered to burst forth (*fujjirat*)' refer to the extensive network of large rivers and canals that has been dug up for cultivation.[477] From the passage, 'When souls are joined together' (Sura 81:7), he deduced a relation between nations and countries:

> The meaning is that in the last days, due to the opening up of roads and the setting up of postal and telegraph services, relations among human beings will increase. One nation will meet another; links and trade connections will extend far and wide, and ties of friendship will increase between distant countries.[478]

Most exegetes of the Qur'an said that some Arabs buried their daughters alive before the advent of Islam. With this context in mind, they say that Sura 81:8-9 predicts that such people will be punished on the Day of Judgement by the testimonies of the victims.[479] Ghulam Ahmad however found in the verse a reference to the wickedness prevailing in contemporary India.[480] It is not clear if he was referring to the Hindu custom of *Suttee*, according to which a widow throws herself on to her husband's funeral pyre to be burnt alive with his dead body. (The practice was banned by the British Raj in 1829.)

Similarly, Ghulam Ahmad read into the passage 'when the scrolls are spread' (Sura 81:10) a reference to the modern means of publication and distribution of books. He wrote: 'This [verse] refers to the printing press and the postal services that will be commonplace in the last days'.[481] Following the same method of exegesis, he argued that the passage 'When the sky is unveiled' (Sura 81:10) refers to the gifts and signs from heaven relating to his own coming.[482]

When referring to similar verses in 84:1 and 82:1, however, he said the sky would not 'burst' nor lose its power; rather, the verses refer to the spiritual situation of the people. In other words, for a while before the coming of the Promised one, 'Blessings will not descend from heaven and, in consequence, the world will be filled with darkness and obscurity.'[483]

Ghulam Ahmad accused Christians of being the cause of this darkness. Then, he claimed the qur'anic words 'When messengers are appointed' to be about himself. He alleged that God would appoint a messenger; 'i.e. the sending of the *mujaddid,* whose advent was promised by the Holy Messenger, would take place in response to the darkness [spread by] the Christians.'[484]

He went further, saying that from these verses 'it is very clear that they contain the prophecy that, in the last days, the Christian faith will spread widely in the world and people will resolve to efface Islam from the earth. So far as it is possible for them, they omit not even the smallest step in their support of their religion. Then God will turn to the aid of the faith of Islam.'[485] He thought that the above signs were given to prove that he himself had come. He wrote the following to support his idea, and claimed it was divinely inspired:

> What has happened to you people that you follow a way against God and reject what has been decided and decreed? Indeed our time is the last days and is like the time of Jesus, which was the last age for the Israelites. As Jesus was the sign [of destruction] for the Jews, so I am the sign of the hour during which every living being will be judged.
>
> Indeed most of these signs are written in the Qur'an: the camels are abandoned; scrolls and books are published. There was the eclipse of both the moon and the sun during the month of Ramadan; canals have been dug and ways have been opened [for travel]. People from far places are meeting each other . . . So it proves that this age is indeed the last days of which the Qur'an speaks . . . This is the time when the last of the *Khulafa'* will be appointed in the *umma* of our Prophet, the best of all. This has certainly been fulfilled . . . Is there anyone else who you see and claim that he is the promised Messiah and may have brought greater signs than mine?[486]

Al-akhira: the hereafter

Belief in the hereafter and judgement are the last of the basic articles of faith in Islam.[487] Terms like *al-Akhira* are used to specify life after death. In line with general understanding, Ghulam Ahmad believed that the afterlife is a reflection of this world. The basis of any entrance to life after death is laid in our present-day life on earth. The promise of paradise for the good and hell for the wicked begins here. He stated that limitations on our knowledge while here on earth allow only a few people to realise this principle.[488]

However, everything will be manifested in the hereafter because human perception will then be clearer.

The Qur'an states that 'some faces will be bright while others will be gloomy' (Sura 3:106) in the hereafter. Elsewhere it uses the metaphor of blindness for spiritual decay. For example, it states, 'He who is blind in this life shall be blind in the hereafter and even more astray' (Sura 17:73). Ghulam Ahmad believed that spiritual blindness would be felt physically in the hereafter.

In his exegesis of Sura 79:37-41, Ghulam Ahmad wrote that the consequences of this life would be borne in the hereafter, after which a further improvement will occur. All matters that are spiritual in this world will be personified in a physical way in the hereafter. Those who follow God's commandments and keep away from evil, and those who follow the reverse path, begin their respective journeys into paradise or hell while still living in this world.[489]

The Qur'an states that those who believe and do good deeds will own gardens with streams in Heaven (Sura 2:26). By way of exegesis, Ghulam Ahmad said that just as a garden would not flourish without water, so one might not enjoy God's garden of paradise in the hereafter if he has not performed *a'mal al-saliha*, the righteous work in this life.[490]

Alam al-Barzakh

Alam al-Barzakh is the state of existence that occurs between a person's physical death and the Day of Resurrection.[i] The word *barzakh* is used in this sense in the Qur'an in Sura 23:100. This word has also been used in the sense of an obstacle or a hindrance (Sura 25:53; 55:20).

According to Ghulam Ahmad, everyone is given a new body after death, as required to consciously live a higher life as well as to perceive spiritual delights and torments. The dead person is revived with this new form of body, invisible to people still living in the present world. Human faculties are revived in such a way that the new body experiences many visions; all the realities of the hereafter become visible to it. This new body is made by light or

---

[i] Ed: See Amanda Parker's chapter earlier in this volume.

darkness, according to the actions of the person during their life before death.[491]

While in this state of *barzakh*, the true state of a person's beliefs and prior actions are manifested, be they righteous or unrighteous, whether they were hidden while in the physical world or not. Wrongdoers suffer not only a physical torment, but also a torment of despair. They are made to taste the evil consequences of their deeds.[492] Nevertheless, their souls in the hereafter experience a continuous growth. Each succeeding spiritual condition will be so far above the preceding one that it would seem as if the preceding condition had died.[493]

At times, Ghulam Ahmad followed 'the allegorical way' when explaining the hereafter, and said that after death 'a window is opened from where the righteous person can see and enjoy the breezes of paradise,' while the wicked person bears 'the burning steam of hell'. This later state persists until the Day of Judgement. The size of the 'window' then corresponds to the grade or quality of faith together with the actions of the person while he lived in the physical world. [494]

In responding to a question on the subject, Ghulam Ahmad said that the departure of the soul from the body, or the relationship of the soul to the body and the grave, is a matter that cannot be perceived by the physical eye nor can they be determined by mere reason. Whatever is known about the soul, including its state and its relationships, is gathered from the Ahadith. He added that to understand all this in detail, one should be bestowed by God with the gift of *kashf* (vision). As for himself, he wrote:

> I can affirm from personal experience that the soul has a relationship
> with the grave, so it is possible to hold conversations with the dead.
> The soul also has a relationship with heaven, where it is assigned a
> station . . . This is a proven truth.[495]

Elsewhere, in response to a query regarding the possibility for some after death to not be restricted by the state of *barzakh*, Ghulam Ahmad said that the truth underlying this relation of being in two states, in heaven and in *barzakh*, is only revealed in our world in this life to those who possess the faculty of seeing visions. They see those who dwell in the graves and can even hold conversations with *them. He said that the necessary information linking the grave with* heaven can be found in the Traditions.[496] He added that 'the dead' can hear the sound of footsteps and respond to our greetings.

Before Ghulam Ahmad articulated his perspectives, the great Indian scholar Ahmad Sirhindi (1564-1624) had also commented on *barzakh,* saying the dead person finds himself in a state that is not the opposite of his temporal life. One may feel in the grave, but this sense does not depend on the possibility of movement. Sirhindi stated that the link between the body and the soul is not severed in *barzakh* but is rather diminished.[497]

Such exegesis suggests that in the hereafter, people (both evildoers and the righteous) are allowed to retain a sense of connection with both the spiritual and the physical worlds. The evildoer remains only to suffer punishment, because he has not brought his righteous deeds with him as 'sustenance'. However, those who love God do not suffer because they carry or 'inherit' their 'sustenance' (Sura 20:75).[498]

In a similar teaching, Ghulam Ahmad said that some wicked people after death not only receive the burning 'steam' of hell, but also are in fact thrown into the utter misery of hell itself as a result of their extreme disobedience to God. Nevertheless, such people do not taste the full reward of hell before the Day of Resurrection.[499]

Progression of status within barzakh

After death, a person exists either in a sort of paradise or in the torment of hell. The struggle continues even after death to achieve paradise on the Last Day. In *barzakh,* a person progresses from one step to the next, a righteous man towards the full blessing of paradise while the wicked may step towards a lower punishment or even toward a complete release from it.[500]

Ghulam Ahmad gave an example of this progress: A person dies in a lower state of his belief and righteousness. A small hole is opened for him in the grave in order to receive a glimpse of God's blessings while he waits for the Day of Judgement. If he has left some righteous progeny, who prays earnestly for his forgiveness and explicitly gives charity to the poor, then the window opens ever wider on a daily basis, as these good actions intercede on his behalf. Alternatively, if the dead person was adjacent to a man of God in his life, and the man of God prays earnestly for him to receive forgiveness, such an intercession will change the circumstances of the dead person. Again, perhaps the dying man leaves behind a project for the benefit of the public. God indeed will look at such a person favourably. The more people benefit from his project, the more the dead person receives God's blessings.[501]

This idea of progress means that a dead person may receive the benefit of charity given by living people and good acts sent by their relatives. In support of his doctrine, Ghulam Ahmad quoted a Hadith where God said, 'Indeed my mercy exceeds my wrath.'[502] He concluded that a time comes when the window becomes a wide gate, when the person has progressed so far that he enters paradise like the *shahid* (martyrs) and *siddiq* (righteous).[503] To demonstrate God's love and mercy for his creation and especially for human beings, Ghulam Ahmad wrote, 'There exist so many ways to enter paradise that, before the Day of Judgement, almost all *mu'minun* (believers) will enter paradise completely.'[504]

Alam al-Qiyama (resurrection) and al-jaza' (reward)

The state of *barzakh* is followed by a state of existence called *qiyama,* resurrection. Ghulam Ahmad believed that there would be a corporeal resurrection one day known as the Last Day, *al-Yaum al-Akhira*. Resurrected people will face the perfect manifestation of God, with whom every person will become acquainted.[505] This stage occurs sometime after the annihilation of the bodies (*Hashr al-ajsad*), but before the final Judgement and full entry to the Most Glorious Paradise (*Jannat-i Uzma*) or the Greatest Hell (*Jahannam-i Kubra*).[506]

According to Ghulam Ahmad, the consequences of faith and disbelief that are felt spiritually in this world will be demonstrated physically in front of a person. That stage will be seen in terms of a personified creation. The 'scales of deeds' will be determined and 'the narrow bridge' will be seen, at which time many spiritual matters will acquire a physical form.[507] People will enter the third and final stage after the Day of Judgement. Although there are stages before the day of reward and punishment, which both the wicked and the righteous must undergo, reward is the final stage. We taste the full prosperity (*sa'adat*) or the full misery (*shaqawat*).[508]

Following the Islamic traditions, Ghulam Ahmad believed in *al-sirat* (the way, also translated as 'the bridge'), which will pass right over hell like a bridge, and over which we will be told to cross.

Bukhari mentions Muhammad as saying, 'I shall be the first amongst the Apostles to cross [the bridge] with my followers.'[509] According to Ghulam Ahmad, those in the world who did not follow the straight path of God will not be able to cross the bridge safely without falling. Conversely, those who followed the straight path of God in this world will have trained themselves for that day. In Ghulam Ahmad's view, the Qur'an said that righteous people would cross the bridge 'like lightning' as they proceed toward, and thence reach paradise. God's promise will also have been fulfilled (Sura 43:68). Any person who did not follow the straight path in this world would not be able to cross the bridge and would fall into the fire, as stated in the Qur'an (Sura 27:90).[510]

The nature of paradise

The Qur'an declares that the bliss of paradise is kept hidden from us, and no sign or indication of it can be found in this world (Sura 32:15). Similarly, Muhammad is stated to have said that no eyes have seen it nor has any ear heard of it, nor can the minds form any conception of it.[511]

We are told elsewhere that there will be springs and rivers of milk. There will be rivers of wine, full of delight for those who drink, and rivers of pure honey (Sura 47:16). The fellowship of heavenly females called *hur* and young males called *ghilman* will also be there (Sura 44:51-54; 52:17-20; 55:70-72; 56:10-24, 35-38).

Ghulam Ahmad insisted that these bounties will be different to anything we have seen before. They will have nothing in common with anything in this world except their name. He wrote that those who considered paradise to be a collection of worldly bodies had wholly misunderstood the Qur'an.[512] He said the qur'anic language was wholly parabolic:

> The water of life, which a person possessing insight drinks spiritually in this world, will appear like a river in the life to come. The spiritual milk, of which he drinks spiritually like a suckling babe in this world, will be seen physically in paradise. The wine of the love of God, with which he is spiritually inebriated in the world, will be made manifest in paradise in streams. Every dweller in paradise will display a spiritual condition [which will be] the rivers and gardens [he will possess]; and on that day, God himself will emerge from behind the veils for the dwellers of paradise. In short, spiritual conditions will be no longer hidden but will become physically visible.[513]

Ghulam Ahmad said that the fruits of heaven would not be physical but will be 'a new creation'.[514] It is a divine mystery that the spiritual condition will appear to be like wine and 'good deeds done in this world will look like pure and clean streams.'[515] Only to those 'who possess spiritual insight is this mystery opened through visions. Wise people arrive at its reality through other signs.'[516] He claimed that the personification of spiritual matters in a physical form is mentioned in the Qur'an, one example being where the glorification of God is personified as a fruit-bearing tree.[517]

Both the Qur'an and the collections of Ahadith mention heavenly women in their discussion about the bounties and status of the dwellers in paradise. In addition to the general term *zawj*, which means a wife or a partner, the term *Hur* is also used. Both terms appear in discussions of the rewards for believers in paradise. For example, the Qur'an says of believers in paradise that 'they will recline on thrones arranged in lines and we [God] shall join them to companions with beautiful eyes.'[518]

A great number of Ahadith are found in the collections of Traditions about the state of believers in paradise. Muhammad is stated to have said, 'The state of even the lowliest person in paradise will be that he will have eighty thousand servants and seventy-two wives (*zawja*). A tent will be pitched for him. It will be made of pearls and rubies. The extent of its size will be equal to the distance between Jabiya and Sana'.'[519] When asked how the heavenly man would be able to cope with seventy-two women,[i] Muhammad is said to have replied, 'he shall be endowed with the powers of a hundred men.'[520]

While Ghulam Ahmad did not go into detail concerning such an idea of paradise, the Ahmadiyya exegesis of having 'women' partners in heaven is said to be allegorical. Muhammad Ali, the leader of the dissident Ahmadiyya group, wrote that both men and women of this world will have access to paradise, and perhaps it is these women who will be changed into *hur,* or perhaps the blessings are merely described as women because 'the reward spoken of here has special reference to the purity and beauty of character, and if there is an emblem of purity and beauty, it is womanhood, not manhood.'[521] About *ghilman* and *wildan,* he

[i] Ed: See Moyra Dale's chapter on women and Islamic eschatology.

wrote that perhaps they are 'the young children who have died in childhood.'[522]

Continuous progress in paradise

Concerning Sura 66:8, Ghulam Ahmad and his followers believe that all inhabitants of paradise will experience unlimited progress. They will each attain perfection, but will soon behold another target of perfection to achieve. They will consider their previous perfection as having been deficient and will ask God for a further level of perfection. When they attain this new perfection, they will behold the third and so on, always desiring a greater stage of perfection.[523]

The nature of hell and eventual salvation of all

Hell is described in the Qur'an with seven different names. The most frequently occurring is *jahanam*. Hell is the blazing fire. It is a place of great depth and degradation (Sura 104:8). Like paradise, hell is also completely unlike this physical world. Hell and the things in it are mentioned in physical terms but will not belong to this physical world.[524]

It is with such an understanding, and in line with Ghulam Ahmad's other views, that the Ahmadiyya believe that hell represents the consequence of evil deeds. They also consider it a place of remedy, perhaps akin to the idea of purgatory. Its chastisement is not only for torture but also for purification. Hell is a kind of hospital; sooner or later all the inmates are released. It is a place for the purging of the human soul of its shortcomings. It is a means of betterment, of purification such that people may receive another chance, albeit in another world.[525]

Ahmadiyya belief is that while paradise is everlasting, hell is not.[526] To them, the qur'anic reference which declares that those condemned to hell are to dwell there 'forever' is metaphorical. Ghulam Ahmad claimed, 'It is unreasonable and contrary to the perfect attributes of God, the glorified and exalted.'[527] He went on to say that at some time, God's 'attributes of mercy and grace will be manifested' and 'all will be taken out of hell' eventually.[528]

It is significant to note how the doctrine of an eternal hell has been juxtaposed with an idea of temporary punishment, and has been mentioned not only in the traditions of Islam but was and still is a major doctrine shared by many of those affiliated with *Tasawwuf* (Sufism). The great early mystic Abd al-Qidir al-Jilani (d. 1166)[529] is stated to have said that when hell is extinguished, there will spring up *jirjir* (watercress, *jirjir*: a large thick bean plant) in its place.[530]

The great Andalusian scholar Ibn Arabi (1165-1240) too spoke about the mercy of God and his forgiving all people. He believed that the punishment of those condemned to hell will stop eventually. He wrote, 'and as for the people of the Fire, they will indeed eventually attain tranquillity.'[531]

Ahmad Sirhindi, on the other hand, rejected such interpretations. He disagreed with Ibn Arabi by saying that 'the writer of *Fusus*... has not come to know that the extending of mercy towards believers and infidels is only in this world, but in the hereafter even the odour of mercy will not reach the unbelievers; as God says, none will be without hope except the unbelievers.'[532] Sirhindi went on to say that the idea of a temporary instead of eternal punishment for unbelievers was based on Ibn Arabi's own vision (*kashf*). He argued that Ibn Arabi's 'vision is against the consensus of the Muslims,' such a view could not be trusted or counted [as authentic].'[533]

Despite these views, Sirhindi was willing to concede that for a Muslim who 'has even a jot of faith [in God]' that 'there is hope that its effect will be to release him from eternal captivity.'[534] However, Sirhindi reiterated, 'I say that anyone who is an absolute unbeliever, eternal punishment is his destiny.'[535]

Despite such an interpretation from someone known as the *mujaddid alf thani* (renewer of the second millennium), Ghulam Ahmad and his followers claim that the mercy of God will eventually release everyone. They quote Muhammad as saying, 'A time will come when there will be none left in hell and the morning breeze will be striking against its doors.'[536]

Women and Islamic Eschatology

Moyra Dale[i]

A discussion of eschatology in the context of Muslim women needs to look not only to the writings in official religious texts, but also to the popular understanding of Muslim women in everyday life – what shapes their hopes and expectations? Hence the material in this chapter draws on conversations with Muslim women in a variety of contexts, as well as on religious texts and writings about them. In particular I make reference to the teaching in a women's mosque programme in a Middle Eastern city, where I was a participant observer over three years.

Belief in Eschatology, in the final Day of Judgement, and life after, is fundamental in Islam, as one of the basic articles of faith. Qur'anic verses promise equal rewards for equal obedience to men and to women.

> Verily the Muslims men and women, the believers men and women, the men and the women who are obedient, the men and women who are truthful, the men and the women who are patient, the men and the women who are humble, the men and the women who give alms, the men and the women who fast, the men and the women who guard their chastity and the men and the women who remember Allah much with their hearts and tongues, Allah has prepared for them forgiveness and a great reward. (*Al-Ahzab* 33:35: see also *Al-Nahl* 16:97 and *An-Nisa'* 4:124).

But in fact gender shapes daily life practices of faith, customs around death, and the expectation of what lies beyond it. Common *hadith* associate women with the afterlife both positively and negatively. Muhammad's view of hell is often quoted, where he saw that 'the majority of people in Hell are women.' In contrast the tradition that 'paradise is under the feet of the mother' is cited to show the place of honour that women have within Islam.

---

[i] Dr Moyra Dale has worked in education in the Middle East for two decades, in English teaching, adult literacy and teacher training. This research draws on involvement in a women's programme in a Sunni mosque in the Middle East over three years. It was stimulated by conversations with Muslim friends and seeing the changing patterns of women's religious practices in society.

In death and after death, what is the place of women, and what do they hope for?

Funerary Rites

Death is the ultimate rite of passage, and customs around death are indicative of the worldview underlying life in any cultural context.

At death, women wash the bodies of women. However it is traditionally men who take the body to the grave while women stay behind. From the upstairs women's section of a Middle Eastern mosque, I watched while sixty or seventy men stood behind a coffin, draped in black, in the main part of the mosque below. A man at the front made a short speech about the woman and then led the men in intercession for forgiveness of her sins. Some of the women in the upstairs room with me joined quietly in the intercession, facing in the direction of prayer, until the men finished and lifted the coffin up, taking it out. One of the leaders of the women's programme explained to me that women don't go to the burial because they 'may cry loudly, and this will express an objection to the act of God.'

Throughout the Middle East Muslim women are generally prohibited from burials due to the 'fact' that women are more emotional, so they 'must not attend funerals, offer vows at graves, or weep demonstrably in response to death.'[537] Similarly at feasts, it is usually men who go in the morning to the cemetery to offer prayers at family graves.[538] Emotional expression may be seen as challenging God's will: and Leaman suggests that offering vows at graves may be committing *shirk*.[539] A Pakistani woman explained that women are prohibited from graves because the spirits of the dead can see people naked. This variety of reasons offered for a common exclusion supports Labidi's claim that it derives from 'an underlying vision that women are a danger to both the religious and political order.'[540]

More positively, women, by reciting the Qur'an, seek to bring its *baraka* or power to situations of both illness and death. So Roushdy-Hammady records Turkish immigrant women, responsible for physical and spiritual needs of the sick, learning the Qur'an in order to be able to read aloud at a patient's bedside and also during funerary rituals.[541] In the Caucasus, the female *mulla* has the role of reciting qur'anic verses in Arabic at funerals, as well as singing laments.[542] The teacher at a Middle Eastern mosque encouraged her female audience to visit a bereaved member of the programme, both for comfort, and to 'seal' the Qur'an (bring blessing by reciting it completely). As more and more women, not just leaders, are memorizing the Qur'an, they are able to mediate this power / blessing.

In the Grave

During the time in the grave between death and the resurrection and final judgement, also known as *barzakh*[543] (*Al-Mu'minun* 23:100),[i] the individual faces punishment, the 'torment in the tomb' (*'adhab al-qabr*). *Ghafir* 40:46: 'The fire, they are exposed to it, morning and afternoon,' is also cited in support of this belief. So Muslim personal prayer commonly includes petitions for protection from the suffering of the grave.[544] I have heard this popular belief in conversation with Muslim women who have described to me the privations faced by wrongdoers, citing the state of exhumed bodies as evidence.[545] Only those who do great good deeds or martyrs (and possibly those who die on Friday or of a stomach disease) are spared the trial and torment of the grave.[546] Tradition suggests that this belief originated with women: it was a Jewish woman's conversation with 'Aisha which first introduced the idea of suffering in the grave to Muhammad,[547] and so into Islam.

Judgement Day

After the time of purgatory, or purification with suffering, comes judgement on the Last Day. Smith comments that many of the portents of cataclysmic disorder indicating the imminence of Judgement[548] Day have to do with women. These signs include women outnumbering men, a man obeying his wife (instead of his mother), women joining the workforce, women of child-bearing age not having children, a slave-woman giving birth to her master, women walking 'clothed yet naked', and female singers becoming popular.[549] Some contemporary commentators point to fulfillment of some of these signs now as a demonstration of social disintegration.[550]

---

[i] Ed: See Amanda Parker's chapter earlier in this volume.

Women are overwhelmingly (and negatively) implicated in signs leading to Judgement Day. However the Day itself is one of justice for the baby girls buried alive in pre-Islamic times (*al-Takwiir* 81:8-9). Beyond that, there is little female-specific reference in writings on Judgement Day: and I encountered little reference to the Day in women's discussions.

Heaven or Hell

What awaits Muslim women after Judgement Day? The damming *hadith* that they make up the majority of the inhabitants of hell hangs over them.[i] Bukhari records it a number of times: the fullest account reads:

> Narrated Abu Said Al-Khudri: Once Allah's Apostle went out to the *Musalla* (to offer the prayer) of *'Id-al-Adha* or *Al-Fitr* prayer. Then he passed by the women and said, 'O women! Give alms, as I have seen that the majority of the dwellers of hell-fire were you (women).' They asked, 'Why is it so, O Allah's Apostle?' He replied, 'You curse frequently and are ungrateful to your husbands. I have not seen anyone more deficient in intelligence and religion than you. A cautious sensible man could be led astray by some of you.' The women asked, 'O Allah's Apostle! What is deficient in our intelligence and religion?' He said, 'Is not the evidence of two women equal to the witness of one man?' They replied in the affirmative. He said, 'This is the deficiency in her intelligence. Isn't it true that a woman can neither pray nor fast during her menses?' The women replied in the affirmative. He said, 'This is the deficiency in her religion.'[551]

The most frequently cited reason in the *hadith* for women's prevalence in hell is their ungratefulness to their husbands. On this account, women's destination in heaven or hell is determined primarily according to their attitude of gratefulness or otherwise to their husband. Commenting on this *hadith,* Jad describes disobedience and ungratefulness to the husband as major sins.[552] A reciprocal *hadith* links women's entry to paradise with how their husbands regard them:

> At-Tirmithi (*sic*) reported from Umm Salamah, the mother of the believers that Allah's Messenger said: 'Any woman whose husband dies while he is pleased, happy and satisfied with her (acts, attitudes and behavior) will enter *Jannah* (Paradise).'[553]

---

[i] Hadith citations in this paper, unless otherwise referenced, are taken from www.searchtruth.com.

The Qur'an adds weight to the link between women's access to Paradise, and their husbands' attitudes, in *Al-Saffat* 37:22, where those who have done wrong are led 'with their companions' to the Fire, and *Al-Zukhruf* 43:70, where wives are given entrance to Paradise with their believing husbands. In particular the fate of the wife of Noah and wife of Lot is offered as a warning to (Muhammad's) disobedient wives (*Al-Tahrim* 66:10); not even being the wife of a prophet avails the recalcitrant. However Stowasser offers a more positive reading: 'Contemporary conservative Muslim women's literature also uses the story of Noah's wife to prove that Islam ... gives the woman complete freedom in the matter of her faith. Once she has chosen, she becomes responsible for her choice.'[554]

Heaven

On what basis do Muslim women hope to enter heaven?

Through Her Own Efforts

Merits

The most commonly cited determinant for entering heaven or hell is on the basis of the individual's good or bad deeds. Mu'tazilites argued for a simple balance on the scales of merits and demerits (from *Yunis* 10:61, also *Al-Zalzalah* 99:7-8, *Al-Anbiya'* 21:47, *Saba'* 34:3). More hopefully, *Al-Nisa'* 4:40 becomes the basis for teaching that the believer's good deeds will be multiplied by God, while each bad deed counts only for one. Some Muslim women have told me that one good deed is equal to ten bad deeds.[555] Other accounts suggest double, or from ten to seven hundred times more weight given to good deeds than bad.[556] Thus God's mercy is demonstrated with regard to good deeds and his justice in relation to bad deeds.[557]

However even beyond a simple balance of merits, on this basis God's mercy is proportionately more available to men than women, as Muslim women are always behind men in the opportunity to earn merits. The preceding *hadith* suggests that women are deficient in intelligence as measured by qur'anic stipulations of weight of testimony: and in religion due to their inability to acquire merits through performing the required *salat* prayer or fasting for at the very least a quarter of every month of their lives between about fifteen and fifty years of age.

Praying in the congregation is worth twenty-five times more than the prayer offered alone.[558] However while men are required to pray in the mosque, women (with slaves, boys and sick people) are not required to attend,[559] but pray at home. Mawdudi cites Muhammad telling a woman who wanted to pray under his leadership, that:

> Your offering prayer in a corner is better than your offering it in your closet: and your offering the prayer in your closet is better than your offering it in the courtyard of your house; and your offering the prayer in the courtyard is better than your offering it in the neighbouring mosque; and your offering it in the neighbouring mosque is better than your offering it in the biggest mosque of the town. (Reported by Imam Ahmad and Tabari.) [560]

While women adduce these *hadith* as evidence of God's mercy for women, so that they are not required to undertake arduous duties of piety during their menstruation, or to spend all their time getting dressed to go out to the mosque and return home and get changed again (note that this assumes women at home and not in the workforce), I have not yet encountered an explanation for the imbalance in acquiring merits.

Memorizing the Qur'an

However other activities, not gender-specific, can tip the scales towards a more positive balance. Memorizing the Qur'an confers special merit towards the hereafter. Young girls learning the Qur'an by heart in a mosque summer programme were told that every letter learned is a good deed. At a party celebrating those who had memorized the Qur'an, the chorus sings,

> Raise your voices and congratulate her,
> She memorized the entire Qur'an.
> Raise your voices and applaud,
> What you will get is more valuable than the world's treasures,
> In heaven you will be crowned,[561]

The leader of the programme told me, 'A person's status in paradise is according to how much of the Qur'an they have memorised: if they have memorised it all, they will gain the highest standing, if they memorised half, a medium rank, if they memorised a small portion, then they will be of small status.'

As Muslim women today are memorizing the Qur'an in increasing numbers, it offers them not only increased engagement with their faith in this life, but enhanced merits towards, or status in, the coming life.

Daughters and Mothers

A balance to the *hadith* which make entry to paradise for women conditional on them pleasing or being adequately grateful to their husbands (above) can be found in the *hadith* which offers protection from hellfire to the person who has two daughters and is generous to them.[562] A version of this was taught to the women at the mosque programme: 'If you raise a girl and marry her well, you'll enter into Paradise.' Far more frequently cited is the *hadith* that Paradise is under the feet of mothers. The actual *hadith* from Al-Tirmidhi reads:

> A man once consulted the Prophet Muhammad about taking part in a military campaign. The Prophet asked the man if his mother was still living. When told that she was alive, the Prophet said: '(Then) stay with her, for Paradise is at her feet.'[563]

So the *Sheikhah* taught (on Mother's Day), 'Islam raises (the mother) to a place that men don't dream of. If there were only this one *hadith*- is this found among any other nation? A child can't enter paradise unless he honours his mother. This is raising women, her rights, freedom of women.' Nevertheless even though it is so widely quoted, this *hadith* is not included in the most authoritative collections, and is generally regarded as weak.

Good deeds which count towards heaven are then deeds of pious practice, family relations, and qur'anic memorization.

Predestination and God's Mercy

However the balance of good and bad deeds, of merits and punishment, are not the only determiners in this gamble for eternity, but interact with God's mercy, and with *qadr* (predestination), the sixth item of Muslim belief.[i] A leader in the women's mosque programme explained the latter to me in terms of God's knowledge rather than human powerlessness in the face of preordained fate:

---

[i] Ed: The first five are belef in One God, angels, revealed books, prophets, and the Day of Judgement.

Allah, the Almighty, wrote the destinations of all people before He created them because His knowledge is not limited and he knows what will happen in the future. He wrote our destinations because He knows, not because He obliges (us to do it). People are created free to choose any deed they want. Our knowledge, as humans, is limited to the past and present, but His knowledge is not limited and he knows the past, the present and the future from the time of Adam P.B.U.H. until the Day of Judgement.

More than impotence in the hands of fate, a constant awareness of wrongdoing and dependence on God's mercy was apparent in conversations with Muslim friends. So too *dhikr* prayers at the mosque programme were deeply imbued with the worshippers' sense of needing God's forgiveness. Although the doctrine of innate sinfulness is foreign to Islam, God's mercy is His most repeated attribute. A popular *dhikr* prayer was, 'I was among the oppressors, and You are the most Merciful of the Merciful,' reflecting the qur'anic teaching that doing wrong is wronging oneself,[564] rather than God. Here there is no mention of sin against God, or of others hurt by sin, or notion of an inherent state of sinfulness. It is easy for an omnipotent God to forgive: because He has not been sinned against (for sin hurts the sinner rather than God), there is no cost to Him involved. In this understanding of the transaction between Forgiver and the forgiven, there is no obligation to forgive, and neither any cost. However merits help place the believer in the position to receive God's mercy. God's loving-kindness is to those who love him, not those who disobey him (*Al-'Imran* 3:32, 57). The *Sheikhah* taught the women, 'If we are merciful, God will be merciful with us. ... Anyone else who does good will receive a reward in this world and the next.'

The Ash'arite argument against a simple equation between merits and punishments draws (as did the Mu'tazilites) on *Al-Zalzalah* 99:7-8 and similar verses, but through Bukhari's related *hadith:*

> Narrated Anas: The Prophet said, 'Whoever said "None has the right to be worshipped but Allah" and has in his heart good (faith) equal to the weight of a barley grain will be taken out of hell. And whoever said: "None has the right to be worshipped but Allah" and has in his heart good (faith) equal to the weight of a wheat grain will be taken out of hell. And whoever said, "None has the right to be worshipped but Allah" and has in his heart good (faith) equal to the weight of an atom will be taken out of hell.'[565]

Hence God may condemn the believer to a limited period in hell and then she will be taken out to Paradise, or may completely pardon her – provided she has not committed the unforgiveable sin of *shirk*, associating with God. *Maryam* 19:71 indicates that all Muslims will 'pass over' hell. This leads Gardet to suggest '*jahannam*' as a higher zone of heaven in which members of the Muslim community who have committed grave sins will be punished for a time, and which 'will be wiped out when the last repentant sinner among the believers leaves it to enter paradise.'[566] However, against this, *al-Taubah* 9:68, in parallel with 9:72, suggests hell as a lasting destination.

The eternal destination of Muslims is then determined not solely on the balance of merits and demerits, but also by God's abundant but arbitrary mercy. While his sovereignty precludes any claim on his mercy (his mercy is a mediated gift, rather than in the context of a relationship),[567] it may be influenced by the petitioner's repentance (*tawbah*), and also by the intercession (*shifa'ah*) of Muhammad.[568]

Intercession of Muhammad

Teaching on *Ghafir* 40:3 in the weekly morning mosque lecture, the *Sheikhah* told her students, 'There must not be an intermediary between me and God. ... God is closer to you than any intermediary, he is the most merciful of the merciful.' Similarly, the Saudi-produced edition of the Qur'an interjects in its translation of Al-Baqarah 2:186, 'I respond to the invocations of the supplicant when he calls on Me [God] (*without any mediator or intercessor*).'[569] However Muhammad occupies a privileged place between his followers and God, particularly with regard to the next life: 'Key of Paradise' is one of the titles given to him.[570] Teaching on *Al-Zumar* 39:17-19, the *Sheikhah* told her listeners, 'There doesn't need to be someone between you and God;' but this was not exclusive of Muhammad's intercessory role. While his intervention was not effective for those wrongdoers already destined for the fire, it could still help 'if someone has mistakes and sins, but also does good deeds, (then) the Prophet intercedes for him.' In *Al-Nisa'* 4:69 obedience to God and Muhammad are equated, to gain his follower a place among the prophets, the faithful, the martyrs and the righteous.

A leader in the mosque programme wrote on my notes from a lecture about the need to love Muhammad: 'The Messenger won't enter Paradise without his followers. He will stand at the door saying, "My people, my people," asking God to forgive all his followers and let them enter Paradise.' In this way Muhammad is the 'key to paradise'; entry is contingent and consequent on being his follower.

This conviction finds practical expression in prayers for Muhammad, which are believed to be reciprocated by his intercession for the petitioner. A leader explained to me a cited speech of Muhammad as meaning, 'I am alive in my tomb, the one who sends me a mercy, Allah will send him ten.' Thus I would often see women pause wherever they were with upraised forefinger when they heard the call to prayer, murmuring the (Arabic) invocation, 'Oh God, Lord of this complete petition and of this prayer, give our Messenger Muhammad (the right of) intercession and favour and the highest position you promised him; you are the one who does not change a promise.' A *hadith* has Muhammad saying, 'Who recites this (preceding invocation) when they hear the *adhan*, this one has my intercession on the day of judgement.'[571] This dependence on Muhammad's intercession was evident in the following *du'a*, which were commonly heard in the mosque programme:

> 'Prayers and peace on you, greatest advocate before God.'
> 'Oh Muhammad, we implore you, intercede for us before your Lord.'
> 'Make us from the people of your Beloved, Muhammad, God's prayers and peace be on him.'

Thus in Padwick's extensive survey of Muslim prayer manuals, she describes at least a third of them as variations on the prayer, 'May God call down blessing on our Lord Muhammad and on the family of our Lord Muhammad and greet them with peace.' Prayers for Muhammad bring the petitioner forgiveness of sins, relief from the terrors of the tomb and of judgement and a reward of glory.[572]

Popular vows at tombs seeking the intercession of saints are generally made with regard to the affairs and needs of this world: however for some it includes a belief in the influence of the saints for the next world also.[573]

Women martyrs

Martyrdom offers instant access to Paradise; this is also viewed as a path for women. The *Sheikhah,* teaching her expatriate visitors about Islam and terrorism, specified that those who bombed innocent civilians in the west were not martyrs. However, 'Of course if someone is a martyr, they would go straight to heaven, without having to face an accounting first. Even if they hadn't prayed or carried out the (religious) requirements, if they were a martyr they would not be held to account for it.' And 'women could also be martyrs.'

Another *hadith* returns women's witness to the domestic sphere, describing the woman who dies in pregnancy as a martyr.[574] Hence Schleifer writes:

> Although in Islam, there are many ways to open the doors of Paradise, the vehicle especially chosen for the woman is that of pregnancy, childbirth, nursing and conscientious rearing of her children. ... for every ounce of effort, be it physical, emotional or mental, exerted in this direction, the mother is elevated to a higher position of esteem in the eyes of her family and society, and has thereby gained a place for herself among the successful in the Hereafter.[575]

What Awaits Women?

Good deeds, God's mercy, the intercession of the Prophet of Islam, and martyrdom offer women hope of heaven rather than hell. The latter three offer women more equitable access to heaven than on the basis of merits alone. But when they reach the afterlife, what can they look forward to?

Paradise

A sensuous eternity

The gardens of delight in Paradise are described in luscious detail in the Qur'an. As well as brotherhood instead of bitterness, and no fatigue in Paradise (*Al-Hijr* 15:47-8), *Al-Waaqi'ah* 56:15-24, 35-8 describes the prospect of thrones, bountiful fruit trees and water, non-intoxicating wine served by eternal youths, and the wide-eyed *Hur*, virgin maidens (also *Al-Dukhaan* 44:54, *Al-Rahmaan* 55:56). There are rivers of water, milk, wine and honey (*Muhammad* 47:15, *Al-Baqarah* 2:25). *Al-Insaan* 76 reiterates the raised thrones and hanging fruit, silken garments and silver bracelets, silver and crystal drinking vessels for wine, and the boys of eternal youth. The purified spouses promised to believers (this is interpreted as meaning that they will not menstruate, defecate or urinate)[576] (*Al-Baqarah* 2:25, *Al-'Imran* 3:15, *Al-Nisa'* 4:57) are traditionally associated with the *Hur* (*Al-Saffat* 37:48).

The qur'anic account of the *hur* has evoked much discussion: hence the comment that 'Sexuality, therefore, is like eating and drinking an essential and integral part of the anthropocentric imagery of paradise. Sexuality is always consummated, never postponed.' Speculative exegesis about the *hur* has reemerged in recent years in relation to suicide attacks, and the anticipated rewards of martyrdom.[577]

In response, some have explained to me that women will have male *hur* as companions in Paradise (*hur* is plural for both *huriyah* [female] and *ahwar* [male]).[578] However all the descriptions offered of the *hur* are female. Others argue that the idea of multiple spouses is a less motivating factor for women than for men: 'It is known that women are shy by nature, thus Allaah (sic) the Almighty did not motivate them with something that would embarrass them. Women's longing for men is not as strong as men's longing for women.'[579]

Additional discussions prefer to focus on the higher status of the believing women. Gardet comments that commentaries celebrate the sexual joys

> 'a hundred times greater than earthly pleasure', that the elect will derive from their (the *hur*) perpetual virginity. But the female Believers who have been admitted to Paradise through the merit of their good deeds will rank 70,000 times greater than the Houris in the eyes of God.[580]

Al-Musnad cites a fatwa by *Shaikh* ibn Jibreen to agree that a woman's 'acts of worship and obedience' in this life ensure her superiority over the *hur*.[581] 'Paradise is a reward for the righteous women and men: but the houri is one of the rewards in Paradise.' What the rewards in Paradise are for the women however remains unclear: unspecific recourse is taken in Sahih Muslim's *hadith*, 'In paradise there are things that no ear has heard, no eye has seen and no one could contemplate,'[582] and in *Al-Nisa'* 4:32, promising both men and women a share of what they earned.[583]

Family connections apparently continue: the believers are accompanied by their wives (*Yasin* 36:56, *Al-Aukhruf* 43:70), or also by their believing fathers and children (*Al-Ra'd* 13:23, *Ghafir*

24:4). Jibreen takes *Al-Waqi'ah* 56:35-6 to argue that God will recreate elderly women into virgins (and elderly men into youths).[584] There are no unmarried women in heaven, so if a woman enters Paradise without a husband, she will be married to someone in Paradise. However where a woman has had more than one husband (through being widowed or divorced), some insist that she has no choice, but will be married to her last husband: others offer her the choice of 'the one with the best character and behavior.'[585]

How do the promised *hur* fit into spousal relations? Despite the higher status of the wives, a man's *hur* are on guard to stop his wife annoying him, telling her: 'Do not annoy him, may Allah ruin you. He is with you as a passing guest. Very soon, he will part with you and come to us.'[586] Numerous traditions suggest that each man will have two wives from this world in Paradise, in addition to the *hur,* which lead some to conclude that women will be the majority of the dwellers in Paradise as well as in hell (whether because they outnumber men anyway: or they will be the majority when they are added to the *hur*: or when they have received the due punishment for their sins, they will move from being the majority in hell to being the majority in heaven).[587]

In Paradise earthly delights are said to find fuller consummation. 'Since in this world of ailments, eating and marriage lead to many wonderful and various pleasures, for sure, Paradise, the Realm of Happiness and Pleasure, will contain these pleasures in their most elevated form.'[588] When Paradise is viewed in sensuous terms, the reward for believing women is promised, but generally the nature of the reward remains unclear.

Earthly intimations of heavenly worship

On the other hand, there is an established exegetical tradition that views the qur'anic description of Paradise as metaphorical or allegorical, rather than literal realities.[589] Even in physical descriptions of the pleasures of Paradise, the most perfect bliss is attributed to looking on the face of Allah.[590] In the mosque lectures there was occasional mention of physical attributes of heaven ('each room has trees'): however more often Paradise was alluded to in reference to the fellowship of the mosque community, and particularly during Ramadan.

A woman from mainland China who was studying Arabic in the Middle East came to the mosque programme. Explaining that women were forbidden to attend the mosque where she came from, she twice described the opportunity to pray with women in mosques in the Middle East 'as if I was in Paradise.' The *Sheikhah* encouraged the women in the programme to support one another, because 'on the day of resurrection, who will introduce you, testify to you, more than your sisters or spouse or parents? It will be the women who say that you asked after them.' The early community of Muhammad and his companions was a model for the women now: 'The Prophet was living happily with his friends as if he was already in paradise. The believer feels as if he is in Paradise.'

Ramadan was when faith time and faith community intersected for greater similitude and entry to the coming life. The effectiveness of pious practice in Ramadan towards the afterlife is evident in the saying cited by Mahmood, heard from women in mosque circles: 'The first third of Ramadan is kindness of God, the second third is His forgiveness, and the last third is refuge from hell's fire.'[591] Teaching on worship as Ramadan began, the *Sheikhah* told the women, 'If this is Paradise, how glorious it is. The love of God is greater than the concerns of the world.' Ramadan offered the possibility of experiencing that worship: it was 'The good, blessed month, when the doors of heaven are open, the doors of hell shut, and devils are chained.' The Night of Power was particularly the chance to encounter God's mercy: the *dhikr* prayers in the mosque programme during the week before it included the repeated:

> O God, make us among the family of the night of Power [those who are forgiven].
> There is no one more merciful to us than you.

A young woman described her experience of praying in the community during the night of Power to me:

> It's about weeping and submissiveness. God comes down to the first heaven and answers prayers. It's a seclusion, you and God alone. You feel as if you're flying, pray until tears come, it's a strange feeling, tears come suddenly. You pray to God, feel with everyone, love everyone, feel soft, forget worries – what I feel at night I try to follow in the day, as I am able.

In this exegetical stream, the reward awaiting women in Paradise is not depicted in physical imagery, but rather likened to community worship and God's mercy accessed particularly during Ramadan.

Hell

Paradise is a hoped-for, if vaguely-defined, destination for women: hell is also a reality to be reckoned with. Each *dhikr* session or lecture or recitation of the Qur'an in the mosque programme was preceded by 'I take refuge from the accursed devil.' Thus Glassé comments that 'When traditional Muslims mention hell in conversation, they set off the idea with invocations of God's protection, for themselves and for the listener, for the magic of words is such that even the thought is frightening, and its appearance in speech may be taken as a dreadful omen.'[592] Qur'anic descriptions invoke God's curse, expressed in fire and eternal torment. Conditions are described in grisly detail including skin roasted or faces scalded by boiling water, hooked iron rods of torture and burning fire (*al-Nisa'* 4:56, *al-Kahf* 18:29, *al-Hajj* 22:19-22, *al-Dukhan* 44:44-46, *al-Buruj* 85:10).

In addition to spousal ingratitude, deeds that bring certain damnation include usury (*al-Baqarah* 2:275), murder (*al-Nisa'* 4:93), cowardice in battle (*al-'Anfaal* 8:15-16) and slander (*al-Humazah* 104), as well as unbelief, polytheism and hypocrisy (*al-'Imran* 3:10). Three women and two men are mentioned specifically in the Qur'an as destined for hell: Cain (*al-Ma'ida* 5:29), the wives of Noah and Lot (*al-Tahrim* 66:10) and Abu Lahab and his wife (*al-Masad* 111). (Women are denoted usually by their husband's name: women are nameless in the Qur'an, except for Mariam, mother of 'Isa, who had no husband.) In lectures the *Sheikhah* warned her audience that the arrogant would not enter heaven: and if a child was not taught the difference between right and wrong (by being punished for wrong-doing), both mother and child would face the fire.

Gardet comments: 'Most theologians believe that if the person who entered hell was not an idolater, a *mushrik*, one who associated another reality with God, but a believer, than God could forgive his sins or non-conformities. This could take place immediately, aided perhaps by the intercession of the Divine Messengers whom the believer followed, despite his sins. Or the forgiveness could take place after a sojourn in hell in which the non-conformities had been "burned away."'[593] However other sins, perilously part of everyday life, also culminate in the fire. The *Sheikhah's* instruction to the women to, 'Greet all, even Christians – you don't know who'll go to heaven or hell,' reflects not only a wider understanding of the possibilities of salvation for People of the Book, but also the entrenched uncertainty of one's ultimate destination.

Motivation in this Life for the Next

What future prospects impact daily life?

Not because of heaven or hell

Rabi'a, one of the early mystics of Islam, is described as carrying a flaming torch in one hand and a bucket of water in the other. When asked what they were for, she explained, 'I want to put out the fires of Hell, and burn down the rewards of Paradise. I do not want to worship from fear of punishment or for the promise of reward, but simply for the love of God.'

The *Sheikhah* exhorted her women in similar fashion during Ramadan lectures: 'We offer worship in love, not in fear.' 'We worship God, not to be saved from the fire, but because this is our happiness.' 'It's better for people to be drawn to God through his characteristics in nature than through the fear of hell.' 'Do we worship because of heaven and fire? We seek heaven because God's voice is in heaven.'

Benefits of Fear

However at times the language of reward and punishment was evoked. A leader in the mosque programme noted: 'Worship is God's right ... Because of his mercy, he creates the heaven and fire as a kind of justice to treat the good people differently from the bad ones.' The *Sheikhah* taught, 'There are verses which warn and limit, and others which promise and encourage. There is fear and hope, and a person needs to give thought to the two: to feel happy sometimes, hopeful of paradise -not to be always in fear of punishment. So we need the two,' suggesting the potency of fear among her hearers. On *al-Zumar* 39:20, she commented on the disobedience among those who didn't believe in God, or think of the afterworld and judgement. This is the 'fear that compels one to act virtuously.'[594]

Mahmood vividly describes the evocation of hellfire in a working class mosque in Cairo:

> The rhetorical style employed by the three *daa'iaat* relies heavily on the technique of invoking fear, an emotion invoked through colourful

and graphic depictions of God's wrath, the contortions of death, and the tortures of hell. Women often react with loud exclamations, followed by loud incantations of the gory details of the torture and religious chants to ward off the anticipated pain and evil. In asense, the lessons are a joint production in which both the *daa'iyya* and the listeners play a performative role.

However it is also effective in more upper-middle-income mosques (as was the mosque programme described in this paper).

> Hajja Samira did not simply prescribe fear as a necessary condition for piety, but deployed a discourse and rhetorical style that elicited it as well. In doing so, she punctuated her lessons with evocations of the fires of hell, the trials faced in death, and the final encounter with God after death, all of which served as evocative techniques for the creation of virtuous emotions. [595]

Like the *Sheikhah*, most *da'iyya*s suggest a balance between preaching that evokes love for God and that which creates fear in the hearers. However the emotion of fear is often perceived as more effective in eliciting a response and action. This reflects Wild's description of the 'rhetoric of terror' in the Qur'an, where descriptions of the punishment of hell are designed to evoke fear and turn the listeners to the message of Muhammad.[596]

Conclusion

The uncertainty of what lies beyond the curtain of death is compounded for Muslim women. On the one hand the Qur'an promises equal rewards and penalties for men and women: on the other hand they are the majority inhabitants of hell, and traditional descriptions of the delights of Paradise awaiting the believer are generally cast in male terms. If merits are the basis of entry to heaven, women stand little chance compared to men. The possibility of God's mercy allied with the intercession of Muhammad offers more hope. And promises of heaven are tied to certain family relationships, to memorizing the Qur'an, and to martyrdom, whether in *jihad* or childbirth.

As Muslim women are engaging more with the texts and teachings of their faith, they are finding ways to challenge and reinterpret some of the more troubling gendered passages. However Muhammad himself was unsure of what lay beyond death for him. The same doubt is reproduced in all his followers, with particular precariousness for Muslim women as they approach death and the uncertainty of judgement day.

Finding an End in the Beginning: Eschatological Trends among ex-Muslim Christians

Duane Alexander Miller Botero[i]

Introduction

Ex-Muslim studies are a new and emerging field of studies, calling on a number of different disciplines, ranging from sociology and anthropology to political science, psychology, and Islamic jurisprudence. When individuals or communities leave Islam they generally head towards either some form of atheistic or agnostic secularism, or towards Christianity. This article primarily focuses on the latter groups.

In this article I will seek to describe some general theological trends that I have identified among ex-Muslim Christians. The word 'trends' is chosen carefully, as ex-Muslim Christians are a diverse and heterogeneous group. It is therefore not possible to speak of core eschatological doctrines which are common to all (or most) ex-Muslim Christians. The word eschatological is used in its most inclusive form, encompassing the signs of the end times that are understood as preceding the Messiah's *parousia*, as well as the question of eternal beatitude with God v. eternal separation from God or damnation.

The term 'ex-Muslim Christian', or its equivalent, Christian from a Muslim background (CMB), is also used quite specifically. People familiar with the recent debates within the world of evangelical missiology will be familiar with a host of contested and debated terms like C5 and Messianic Muslim and Insider Movement. These terms usually refer to one of two things: 1) a specific strategy regarding how to missionize Muslims,[597] or 2) an allegation[598] that such a movement among specific people in a specific place, existing apart from Western missions, is being objectively and dispassionately described.[599] Can a family of Muslims continue to

[i] Dr Duane Alexander Miller is professor of Church History and Theology at Nazareth Evangelical Theological Seminary (NETS). He is also adjunct professor in theology at St. Mary's University (San Antonio, TX, USA). His main areas of interest are religious conversion from Islam to Christianity and the history of Protestant mission in the Middle East. A native of Montana, the author is married to Sharon and they have three children. He can be contacted via his blog duanemiller.wordpress.com.

believe in Jesus and the Cross and the Bible while also continuing to (in some manner) honor the Qur'an while their community becomes a church, though they do not call it a church, and while they call themselves Muslims and eschew the label Christian? And can this all be salvific?

I am very glad to ignore the above question in this article. Instead, this article is about people who identify themselves clearly as having been Muslims, and then having undergone a process of religious conversion or 'transfer of tradition'[600]—whether sudden or, as is more often the case, over many years—converted *from* Islam *to* Christianity *qua religio*, which includes not only the attractive person and message of the Messiah but also his troublesome yet somehow indispensable bride—the Church.

Historical background

The field of ex-Muslim studies, of which this theological inquiry is part, is emerging and of recent vintage. Religious conversion between Islam and Christianity has been occurring since the days of the Prophet Muhammad, as when Ubaidah bin Jash left Islam for Christianity while in Ethiopia.[601] There are Christian Saints, like Abo of Tiflis (Tbilisi) who was martyred on January 6th of 786, or St Ahmed the Calligrapher who was martyred on May 3rd of 1682, who were converts from Islam. We have, recently translated into English, an autobiography of John Avetaranian,[602] a Turkish convert, from as early as the 19th Century. But these conversions were sporadic and individual. It is not until the latter half of the 20th Century that we can speak not only of individual converts here and there, but entire families, communities, or towns converting from Islam to Christianity. The first large movement was in Indonesia in the 1960's and the 1970's among the Javanese.[603] After the Iranian Revolution in 1979 tens or, more likely, hundreds of thousands of Iranians, both in the country and in the Diaspora, have converted. There are today Iranian Christian congregations worshipping in Farsi throughout Iran and in major cities throughout the West. Other movements have taken place in Bangladesh, Algeria, Turkey, Kazakhstan, and significant conversions have been seen in countries as traditionally resistant to Christian conversion as Pakistan and Egypt.

Research has already been published on the reasons given by these converts as to *why they convert*.[604] Some of the main reasons given are the attractiveness of Jesus, Christian community, a supernatural experience (like a healing or dream), and just being disappointed in some way with Islam, the Qur'an, or the prophet. These conversion motives often build on each other and work synergistically. Underlying almost all conversion narratives is the conviction that the Christian deity loves unconditionally and reveals this love in Jesus, while the deity of Islam loves conditionally and cannot be relied upon.

Why now? That is another question that surfaces regarding this rather sudden increase in conversions in relation to the very small numbers of known converts in the past. It appears that several characteristics set the latter half of the 20th Century apart from other ages, and in that context multiple factors coalesced which made such movements a possibility.[605] These factors include developments in media from radio to satellite to the internet; an increase in the number of dreams and visions reported by Muslims; greater creativity and innovation in relation to missionary and ministry strategies; advances in translation made possible by the PC and the internet; and increased migration whereby many Muslims have migrated to lands with a Christian heritage, where they are more likely to meet Christians, read a Bible, attend a church, or, broadly speaking, in some way encounter and understand the Christian message.[606]

In sum, the field of ex-Muslim studies is unexplored because the communities being studied did not exist in numbers that would permit systematic and structured scholarship until recently.

Sources of Theological Knowledge and ex-Muslim Christians

Studying the theology of ex-Muslim Christians is not like much other theological research. If one wanted to study eschatological trends among African Anglicans or German Lutherans one could presumably find a number of books or journal articles to be a guide. With ex-Muslim Christians though, there is very little in the way of published, explicitly theological books or articles.[607] There are published materials, but they strongly tend towards apologetics or conversion narratives (or a combination of those two genres in one book). This manner of research entails the sometimes-difficult project of extracting from a personal narrative the traces of a theology. If this seems overly ambitious, it is worth remembering that we do this often with the Scripture, and thus one can extract from 1 and 2 Samuel a theology of kingship, or from Luke-Acts a theology of baptism. I do not mean to imply that all conversion narratives have the same intentionality and complexity as one finds in Luke-Acts or Samuel, but the point of contact holds—that theological truths can be communicated through narratives.

Such texts are one source of theological reflection for ex-Muslim Christians, but I have also done numerous interviews and attended worship events and meetings that included ex-Muslim Christians among a few groups. This includes a number of Arabic-speaking people in/from the Middle East, as well as groups of Iranian Christians in the UK and the USA.[608] Beyond believers from Arab and Iranian backgrounds, I have also interviewed some converts from Azerbaijan, Turkey and South Africa.

Conversion narratives, interviews, participation in their liturgies (loosely defined)—these have been the main sources I have accessed to try to discern some eschatological trends among the ex-Muslim Christians I have studied. Due to the scarcity of the material and the newness of the field, though, I cannot claim to make quantifiable evaluations, e.g. percentages of converts who believe in this or that specific teaching.

Eschatological Trends

Ushering in the Kingdom: Praxis and Justice

The West has a strong tradition of systematization in theology, and of understanding theology as 'certain knowledge,' which has the appearance of, in some way, being supra-cultural and universal. When Calvin wrote his *Institutes* or Aquinas wrote his *Summas* there was the appearance, if not the intention, of laying down the true essence of theological reality—certain knowledge about God in the light of Christian revelation that applied to all people at all times. In other words, it had the appearance of making universal and non-contextual truth claims and '...often attempts have been made to impose the methods and results of theology as sure knowledge in cultural contexts where they do not fit...'[609]

But there are other ways of envisioning what theological knowledge is (and is not). Robert Schreiter outlines some of these in his dense 1985 book *Constructing Local Theologies.* He argues that in some cultures theological knowledge is more properly understood as wisdom. Wisdom is understood as 'the ability to discern the divinely ordained pattern within nature and experience, and then to follow the prescribed way of living well so as to be in right relationship with God'.[610] A wisdom theology is concerned with finding the underlying order in the universe—in the midst of persecution, alienation, solitude, prison, how can one locate the presence and activity of a loving God? While this sort of God-knowledge is not the supra-cultural metaphysical claim one might be familiar with in the field of systematic theology, we do have it in the West in the writings of St John of the Cross[611] and St Teresa of Avila[612] and, more recently, in the Anglo-Catholic tradition, TS Eliot's *'Four Quartets'*.[613] Wisdom theology is also taught in our colleges and seminaries, but normally under labels like pastoral theology or applied theology.

The conversion narratives of these believers contain a great deal of God-knowledge in relation to such pragmatic but important questions: How should one break the news to his family that he has become a Christian? How should one relate to the Islamic government after conversion? How can one form a relationship with a local church? To what extent should the CMB engage in Islamic activities and feasts? And so on. The theology may not be systematic, but rather applied, pastoral and pragmatic.[i] It is still Christian theology though, in that it claims to communicate something about God in the light of his self-revelation in his Messiah. In relation to eschatology, we do not find a great deal of insight in these texts when interpreted as wisdom theology. But when viewed from the angle of liberation theology we do.

Another form of theological knowledge identified by Schreiter[614] is praxis. Praxis is the logical and necessary outcome of theological reflection. Praxis leads to liberation.   It is not the economic liberation sought by the Latin American Catholics of yesteryear, but a liberation whose telos is a reality wherein ex-Muslim Christians will be tolerated within their own Islamic countries, rather than forced into exile, quietism, or prison, or, at worse, executed.[615] The call for human rights and acceptance is present in a number of the texts composed by ex-Muslim Christians. Because of this, I believe (and have argued at length elsewhere)[616] that some of these believers are engaged in a certain type of liberation theology. The

---

[i] Ed: Terms that might also be applied to the theology of Paul in his epistles, for example. The point is not that Paul's writings are in any way haphazard or lacking in depth and structure, but they are almost entirely 'occasional' in nature.

Christian message confronts the realities of Islamic *shari'a* (and especially the law of apostasy, but also the treatment of women and non-Muslims) and finds the latter to be unacceptable given the proclamation of God's just reign entering into human history. The opening up of the Kingdom, the present partial coming of the Kingdom *on earth as it is in heaven*, is in itself an eschatological sign; it is also a reminder that the *fullness* of the Kingdom (and thus of the eschaton) is not yet here. This Kingdom is understood to be centred around the concept of sacrificial power, and ties together eschatology and ethics in that it requires action. The praxis itself is the theological artifact.

The actual praxis takes place in at least two different manners. One is through social activism. An example of this is Hannah Shah's campaign to protect British ladies from an Asian background from being forced into marriages and from the unjust habits that emerge from the honor-shame culture she experienced growing up as a Pakistani girl in the UK.[617] Fatima Al-Matayri was a convert in Saudi Arabia, martyred by her own family for her faith in 2008. We have some of her writings from an online forum which she used to communicate with others, both Christians and Muslims. These writings include a poem (originally in Arabic) that defends the *mutanaasiriin* or converts from Islam to Christianity. Multiple arguments are being made by the author of the poem. These include the insistence that by leaving Islam the converts have not betrayed their country of Saudi Arabia, and an appeal for tolerance and freedom:

> You see Jesus is my Lord and he the best protector
> I advise you to pity yourself and clap hands [in resignation]
>
> And see your look of ugly hatred
> Man is brother of man, oh learned ones!!!!!
> Where is the humanity, and love, and where are you
> And my last words I pray to the Lord of the worlds
> Jesus the Messiah, the light of the clear guidance,
> That he changes your notions and set right the scales of justice
>
> And spreads love among you oh Muslims.[618]

On the one hand in this poem we have an appeal for tolerance and understanding and the hope that Jesus will someday 'set right the scales of justice'. But we also see a second strategy unfolding that will achieve the goal of transforming an Islamic society into a just one in accordance with God's loving will—evangelism.[619]

Evangelizing Muslims is seen by many Muslims as being a deeply subversive act, and in some places it is against the law. So when Al Matayri prays that Jesus himself would change their notions, and spread love among them, this can easily be seen as a prayer for *their* conversion as well. Many of the conversion narratives by ex-Muslim Christians include explicit invitations to Muslim readers to convert, like those of Christopher Alam[620] and Saiid Rabiipour,[621] converts from Pakistan and Iran, respectively. Other writers, like Daniel Ali,[622] a Kurdish convert to Catholic Christianity, emphasizes that folks in the West need to start to actively evangelize Muslims around them. All in all, evangelism is a way of ushering in the eschatological just rule of God. In these cases, political change is sought, but by means of deploying spiritual resources and rhetoric, never by using coercion or violence against the political structures. Such a manner of achieving political change would be too close to what they had seen in the prophet's life and in Islam in general, a way of interpreting and applying power which they intentionally have left behind as they turned from the old and incorrect of Islam to the new and correct of Christianity. This new conceptualization of power which she has learned from Jesus empowers Al Matayri to make the paradoxical claim in that same poem, 'Your swords do not concern me at all.'

The eschatological significance of this liberating praxis as preparation for the parousia should not be pushed to the extreme though. There is no statement here that once religious freedom has been achieved among Muslims that Jesus will return, like some evangelicals envision, say, the reconstruction of the Temple on Mount Zion. But there is a pronounced trend in relation to eschatology which we can identify: the *eschaton*, the righting of the wrong in the world, is something which must be actively worked for *here* and *now*. A complete justice will not be achievable by our own efforts, but substantial justice is possible, as is improving the lot of converts from Islam, even if only incrementally and with great difficulty. Even if the earthly city can never become the City of God, the students of Messiah are the salt of the earth, and thus enrich that earthly city, though it is not their home. Moreover, the reality that the reign of God is at hand compels such a praxis. In other words, though they may not have an over-realized eschatology, they do insist on *some* realization. They express the *already* of the 'already and not yet' in social activism and kerygmatic effort.

Within the evangelical tradition

Inculturation is a useful framework for describing and analyzing the emergence and maturation of these Christ-ward movements from Islam.[i] The definition of inculturation given by Aylward Shorter is '...the creative and dynamic relationship between the Christian message and a culture or cultures'. He clarifies later '...we really are speaking of a dialogue between a [...] Christianized culture of the missionary and the hitherto un-Christianized culture to which he comes'.[623] What is sometimes overlooked is that every instance of the Gospel embodied in a community is already embodied in a specific cultural setting. In the words of Bp Lesslie Newbigin,[624]

> There is no such thing as the gospel pure and simple. Every statement of the Gospel, and every exercise in the living out of the gospel, is culturally conditioned. And yet the gospel exercises and will always exercise a critical function within any culture in which it plays a part.

This is true for the Christianity we encounter in the Bible itself— Jerusalemite Christianity and Antiochian Christianity and Corinthian Christianity each appear to have shared a core *kerygma* and *leitourgia*, but each community in each city was developing and living out their faith in a specific, contextual manner.

This is significant here because the Christian message as it has been encountered by most ex-Muslim Christians in the world today is itself already embodied (I hesitate to use the word 'incarnated'— I feel it has been overused so much as to have become almost meaningless, unfortunately) within a (broad) cultural setting. That cultural setting is global evangelicalism, itself larger than, but disproportionately influenced by, American evangelicalism. There are groups of ex-Muslims who have encountered the Christian message as already clothed in a distinctive manner, like some of the converts to Orthodoxy in Albania or Indonesia, or families who have converted to Roman Catholicism in Kosovo.[ii]

---

[i] In previous articles I have used the tentative term *Islamic Christianity* to refer to movements towards Christ originating in Islam. This term would include also individuals who continue to identify themselves as Muslims who follow Jesus. This article is dealing only with ex-Muslim Christians.

[ii] Liberal Protestantism seems to be the exception—perhaps because the dangerous step of converting from Islam to Christianity is seen as unnecessary or illogical by pastors and leaders in those churches who tend towards universalism. This would make conversion superfluous.

All of this is to say that the default positions of ex-Muslim Christians tend to fall somewhere within the range of evangelicalism, and specifically dispensational, American eschatology. I asked one convert from the Arab world about his beliefs regarding the return of Jesus and heaven and hell— someone whom I met right after his conversion while he was in a safe house and not yet baptized. Eventually he fled to the West where he is today. I asked him about his position on heaven (the Christian term) and paradise (the Islamic term) and his answer is a good indicator of how strong an influence American dispensationalism has made on some ex-Muslim Christians:

> I believe according to the biblical teachings:
>
> I believe in heaven's existence; it's a physical-spiritual place where God rules, where evil can't be [present]. (Rev 14, 20, 21 & 22)
>
> I believe in paradise's existence; it's the place where God had created and put Adam to rule the earth from. And according to its description in Gen 1 & 2 we figure it was somewhere between Iraq and Turkey. (Gen 1, 2 & 3)
>
> I believe we (the Church) will be taken up, or raptured: 'Then we who are alive and remain will be caught up together with them in the clouds to meet the Lord in the air...' (1 Thessalonians 4:17 NASB).
>
> I believe also in the 1000 years of ruling on earth with Christ after that, and I believe that heavenly Jerusalem literally will come down from heaven, as it's stated in Revelation.
>
> I believe also as it's stated in Revelation that after the 1000 years [...] we'll move to heaven also literally in our spirits and with our new bodies as is written in 1 Corinthians 15:40-end and Thessalonians as well.
>
> I believe the moon will turn to a bloody color before the great day of Yahweh as it's written in Joel.
>
> I also believe the earth will melt down as Peter said in his book.[625]

The rapture, a 1000-year reign of Christ from the city of Jerusalem, a reading of Joel's prophecy as applying literally to the moon circling our earth right now—these are mainstays of the American, evangelical, dispensational eschatology formed and popularized by figures like Darby and Scofield.

Another theme from the evangelical tradition which has been adopted by some ex-Muslim Christians is the connection of the practice of evangelism to the nearness of the parousia. Thus

Christopher Alam near the end of his book, states that 'Time is short, and Jesus is coming back to the earth soon. The harvest is plenteous, but the laborers are few. We have preached the gospel to millions, yet millions are still unreached'.[626] Evangelism as an action fulfills two roles simultaneously: it transforms society into one that more resembles the contours of the reign of God (as mentioned above), but evangelism also prepares the world for Messiah's return and the final judgment.

As inculturation has taken place, ex-Muslim Christians have at different times moved away from evangelical orthodoxies (as with the soteriology of penal substitution).[627] In spite of this, on the whole the default position for eschatology will tend to be one of the positions within global evangelicalism, with a strong tendency towards some form of dispensationalism popularized by Americans.

Signs of the Parousia

Trying to predict when Jesus is going to come back is not a key concern for the ex-Muslim Christians I studied. They all believe that he will return, it will be visible, and he will return in bodily form. Nonetheless there is a minor trend that sees the ingathering of Muslims into the Christian faith as a sign of the end times and the immanent return of Messiah.

Once I attended a daylong conference in Scotland that was sponsored by and mostly attended by local Iranian Christians. While most of the teaching was done in Farsi I was able to read the PowerPoint presentation and had partial translation. One of the issues that can cause divisions among Iranian Christians (and ex-Muslim Christians in general) is the topic of the gifts of the Spirit. Are they all still active today, or have some of them (like tongues and prophecy) disappeared for some reason?

The speaker that day was an Iranian priest from the Church of England who ministers to Iranian Christians in the U.K. During a Q&A period one of the young men, a relatively new convert, asked if the age of miracles had passed, that is, had certain gifts (like working miracles) gone away? Taking a strong position either way on this topic may well have occasioned an extended argument as each side on the issue referenced the biblical verses which they felt bolstered their position. The teacher answered that in fact the greatest miracle of the Holy Spirit and sign of his presence was that

Muslims in large numbers were coming to faith in Christ. In other words, the ingathering of Muslims into the Church is an indication that the Spirit is present and active in a unique and special way not yet encountered in human history. As these evangelicals are aware, the pouring out of the Holy Spirit is a sign of the immanent return of Christ (according to Peter's interpretation of Joel in Ac. 2:17-21).

The most extended and clear example of connecting the conversion of Muslims to an eschatological sign of the immanent parousia is found in the book *Here Comes Ishmael*[628] by Pentecostal Pakistani ex-Muslim Faisal Malick. While the book is not very long (124 pages), it is the only book by an ex-Muslim Christian, that I am aware of, which is entirely concerned with eschatology. Therefore a summary of the content of the book is appropriate.

The purpose of the book is to 'define and clarify the season we are in, and to bring understanding and create awareness of the significance of Ishmael and his role in provoking Israel to salvation'. The second section of the book title, written on its cover, is *the kairos moment for the Muslim people*. Kairos, he writes, is a Greek word that points to '...a moment when a portal is opened between time and eternity so that an event can take place in its fullness, as appointed by God, to forever change the destiny of man'.[629] He sets the stage by explaining how Ishmael is a representative of Islam today, and how God knew Ishmael before he was born and named him, and had a special plan for him which is only today being unfolded in this kairos moment.

What is this special role for Ishmael in the end-times? One role is that many of the sons and daughters of Ishmael will convert from Islam to Christianity. Jesus will not return until people from every nation come into the Church, and since the world is 42% Muslim (most population statistics suggest the proportion of Muslims around the world is half this figure), this obviously includes a large number of Muslims. One consequence of this is that nominal and lazy Christians throughout the world will become stirred up as they see the zeal of these new ex-Muslim Christians. But the conversion of many Muslims is going to provoke something else—the conversion of the Jews: 'The glory of God revealed to the Muslim people will anger Israel to seek the face of God. When Israel sees the Shekinah glory they rejected on the mount [sic] manifested among the Muslim people, they will be angered and seek the face of God'.[630] This, he says, will fulfill the Pauline prophecy in Romans that in the end, all Israel will be saved. And the salvation of the Jews is the *sine qua non* of signs of an imminent *parousia*: 'When Israel says, "Blessed is He that cometh in the name of the Lord" (Matthew 23:39), the Lord Jesus shall return'.

This eschatological role for Ishmael does not mean every Muslim will be saved though. Nor does it mean that one should deny the reality and scope of a violent, terroristic community within Ishmael. Where does this come from? Continuing with his allegorical reading of Genesis, Malick points out that Esau married his cousin Mahalath, the daughter of Ishmael (Genesis 28:9). Since then, '...Esau and Ishmael have been mingled together in covenant'. This inclusion of a spirit of Esau explains the contemporary reality of terrorism among some of the children of Ishmael. Esau struggled against Jacob in the womb, he was a man of the sword, and at one point proposed to kill Jacob. The increase in Islamic terrorism represents a waxing of this spirit of Esau among the children of Ishmael, even though the spirit of Ishmael is itself one that is blessed by God. In other words, the two tendencies or spirits are fighting against each other for predominance among Muslims today. As to conversion, it is the *true* children of Ishmael[i] (to whom 'God listens') that will in turn listen to God and turn to Christ. The spirit of Ishmael cries out as the child did in the Genesis narrative, even today:

> We, the Church of God, must intercede for Ishmael like a mother would for a dying child. [...] Today, when God hears the cry of Ishmael, He will use another lady, the Church, to give him water from the well of everlasting life.

Malick then goes on to give some details of how it is that Ishmael will hear and enter the Kingdom. For instance dreams and visions, television and media, the Glory of God expressed in the righteousness of believers and the Church, miracles, signs, and wonders, raising the dead, and Christians' power over witchcraft. Moreover, God himself will 'give creative ideas to the Body of Christ that will position believers in places of financial dominion in times of famine in the world'. And as the sons and daughters of Ishmael turn to Jesus in large numbers, and gain a vision for the end-times harvest of evangelism, they will contribute their own substantial wealth to that evangelistic effort: 'God blessed Ishmael unconditionally [with petroleum] with the intention to fund the

---

[i] Ed: Akin to the Pauline concept (Romans 2) of the 'true Jew'.

end-time harvest in part'. And so the Church will be blessed with 'Wealth and substance coming into the Kingdom...'. In this he sees a fulfillment of Is. 60:1-3 wherein 'Gentiles shall come to thy [ie, the Church's] light, and kings to the brightness of thy rising.' And Is. 60:5-7 wherein gifts and wealth are brought to Israel (presumably replaced by the Church?), including the camels of Midian and Ephah, gold and frankincense of Sheba, the flocks of Kedar, and the rams of Nabaioth. In the end, 'When Ishmael is revived in the presence of God, he will lay his treasures at the feet of Jesus and embrace his destiny'.[631]

This is, one might say, evangelical eschatology at its best and its worst. Its best, because it offers hidden insights into otherwise inscrutable or complex issues. This is what makes so much of evangelical eschatology attractive to the masses and quite marketable in a way that, say, Joseph Ratzinger's fine book *Eschatology: Death and Eternal Life,*[632] will never be. Thus, Muslim terrorism is born from the spirit of Esau within the community of Ishmael, which also explains handily the protracted Arab-Israeli conflict. How to make sense of the vast oil wealth of the fundamentalist and intolerant House of Saud? God has foreseen and planned that in this *kairos* it will be used for the mission of his Church. And so on. The best of evangelical eschatology is very marketable and explains in a very simple way complex and difficult issues (though of course, it may not invariably be correct), and that the apocalyptic interpretation (even if incorrect) is related to a call for greater activity in relation to mission and evangelism.

Nevertheless, we also see the worst of evangelical eschatology because there is no unity to his method for engaging the biblical text within its context, and so the author can jump from a typological exegesis of Genesis, to an eschatological reading of Isaiah wherein the promises of Israel become the promises of the Church, to wherein 'all Israel' (Romans) is once again the Jewish people and related to the secular State of Israel born in 1948! Any one of these hermeneutical methods *may* be correct and fitting and fruitful for understanding Scripture, but to jump between very different passages and interpret them each according to a different standard without explaining why—this is not a very good example of biblical scholarship and reminds us why evangelical eschatology is so often held in disdain (unfairly, at times, to be sure) by other Christians.

Regardless of what one might make of Malick's eschatology or the Iranian priest's opinion that the Spirit was doing its greatest work in drawing Muslims to Christ, we do see a trend among some ex-Muslim Christians linking the recent and historically unprecedented influx of Muslims into the Church to an eschatological-pneumatological sign indicating the proximity of the parousia. Not only is this eschatological writing (i.e. about the End or Destiny of mankind), but it is also more Apocalyptic than anything else in this paper, because it deals with unveiling what was otherwise inscrutable, and frankly involves a pretty fantastic sequence of latter-days signs.

Discontinuous with Islamic eschatology

According to the model of inculturation outlined above, it is also possible for a community to bring forward cultural elements from their original context. In other words, there are treasures old and new. New symbols, concepts, words, rites and doctrines from the (global evangelical) Christian faith meet people within a certain cultural matrix, which already has its (old) symbols, meanings and rites. In the case of Muslims, it is worth noting that often-times culture and religion are construed as being inextricably intertwined. That is, to be a Turk is to be a Muslim, or, to be Malay is to be a Muslim. When a person leaves the 'religious' identity of Islam, their former co-religionists understand them to also be leaving their ethnic identity as a Turk or Malay or Gulf Arab, etc.

One way for converts to disarm critics who charge them of being traitors to their people would be to emphasize the continuity with the beliefs, practices, symbols, and norms of their previous community. Sometimes ex-Muslim Christians do exactly this. Thus, Iranian Christians continue to celebrate the Persian new-year (Nowruz), employ Farsi in their liturgy (songs, preaching, poetry), and often prefer to give their children Persian names rather than Arabic names, which are understood to be superior by many Muslims. Similarly, among Arab converts I have known, some have recommended keeping the Ramadan fast. The fast is kept *not* in relation to soteriological merit, but in reference to intercession for the conversion of other Muslims, especially family. Theology aside, fasting when your Muslim family fasts is, regardless of motive, a way of respecting their customs and community by maintaining some sort of continuity. Trying to find forms of continuity between

Islam and Christianity is not something foreign to the ex-Muslim Christian community.

In the area of eschatology, though, I have found no effort at all to draw on the previous, Islamic concepts in order to emphasize continuity. For instance, it seems possible to find some sort of parallel between the image of the qur'anic paradise or *al janna*,[i] with the image of the garden-city of God which descends from heaven in Revelation 21. One might elaborate on this and note that both the Qur'an and the Bible place humans in fellowship with the Creator in a garden both at the beginning of the metanarrative, and at the end as well, forming a meta-historical chiasm. Also, both faiths teach a bodily resurrection, which, for someone seeking common ground or continuity between Islam and Christianity, is an obvious starting point.

But rather than seeking or emphasizing continuity or commonality, among ex-Muslim Christians eschatology appears to be a locus of *discontinuity*—an arena wherein the community can emphasize the newness of what they have encountered in the Christian message as superior to the old and 'incorrect' doctrine they had learned in Islam. An example of this was seen above in the answer from 'John', who saw in the word *paradise* not eschatological felicity, but only a reference to Eden.

Christian ex-Muslims tend to find the eschatological promises of Islam to be carnal, dangerous, and chauvinistic. The Qur'an makes numerous claims about the abode of the elect:

> Paradise has an eternally moderate climate (76.13), shade is everlasting, grapes and pomegranates abound, rivers of wine, milk, honey and fresh water flow through it (47.15), recalling the four rivers of paradise in Genesis 2.10–14. The believers can call for every kind of fruit (44.55), they receive 'what their souls desire' (43.71), they are clad in silk and brocade, they wear golden bracelets and recline upon 'close-wrought couches' (56.15). Immortal youths offer flesh and fowl, they serve wine out of 'goblets, ewers and a cup from the spring (56.18). [633]

Heaven also promises for the elect (males) *huris*, who according to traditional Islamic exegesis are beautiful, perfectly formed, spotless virgins (Q 44:54, 56:35-38, 55:56).

---

[i] Literally, 'the garden'.

One of the main accusations formed against this image of the eschatological garden is that it has no place for women, or that women are merely sex objects there.[i] Abu Atallah,[634] an Egyptian convert, educator and missionary, answers a question about heaven from a Muslim by making three points. First, he says, in heaven we will see God and live with him, we will relate to him there, and so, he tells his Muslim enquirer, 'This is why we [Christians] say that if you do not have a relationship with God you are dead spiritually'. The second point is that heaven is a state of being wherein there is no suffering or sorrow (citing Rev 21:4), and that there the believer will 'enjoy [God] to the fullest.' The implication is that it is *not* wine or *huris* that are enjoyed in the afterlife. His final point is based in Isaiah 11:2-9, wherein nature itself is transformed. This is why the lion can rest with the lamb in the afterlife, and similarly sexuality also is transformed: 'Another important point to emphasize here is that in heaven there will be no marriage', which is based on Mt 22:30. The author does not need to mention that this is in opposition to the unlimited sex available to the man living in *al-janna*. Each point contradicts in some way the popular image that many Muslims have of the afterlife. No attempt has been made at finding continuity with Islam, but rather in emphasizing how different the Christian teaching is.

Another reason for discarding the Islamic tradition of the afterlife is that it is seen as being intertwined with violence. Nonie Darwish recalls her Islamic education as a child:

> Moslem children at a very early age undergo horrific indoctrination to hate Jews and Christians. We all had to go through Islamic education breeding fear, anger, Jihad and extreme criticism and rivalry of other religions. We were told stories beyond belief about Jews. We were told Jews were hated by God and should be exterminated. They killed Arab children and pregnant Arab women, break treaties with Arabs! Hearing this about other human beings made me extremely scared. I listened day in and day out to religion teachers who only spoke of an angry God, Hell and Heaven, the battles that Mohammed won and the booty his soldiers got. Jihad and martyrdom was the center piece of Moslem education and the certain road to heaven. [635]

---

i Ed: See Moyra Dale's chapter on women and Islamic eschatology.

In this passage, Darwish is implying that the terroristic violence of jihad is directly connected to the eternal felicity of *al-janna*. That martyrdom in Islam is seen as being related to military jihad, which itself is said to be a guarantee of entry into *al-janna*, is an insurmountable pollution for many ex-Muslim Christians. This repudiation of relating violence to entry into the eschatological garden is related to the conviction that the power of God, the Father of Jesus Christ, is intimately bound up with *agape* and self-sacrifice. This is set in contrast to a 'love' demanding obedience and which will resort to coercion or violence in order to obtain it, which is how ex-Muslim Christians tend to understand the deity of Islam. This theory of power is what enables someone like Fatima al Matayri to tell her Muslim compatriots in Saudi Arabia that, 'Your swords do not concern me at all'.[636]

The concept of the afterlife, though it remains rather nebulous in the writings of ex-Muslim Christians, is not like the Islamic concept of *al-janna*. Whatever the details surrounding eternal felicity may be, Bilquis Sheikh summarizes the *relational* core of what eternal beatitude is: 'To know You is joy, to worship You is happiness, to be near You is peace. This is heaven!'[637] In sum, whatever the afterlife is like, it is *not* like *al-janna* of Islam, which is seen as being male-centered, carnal, and even as a motive for terrorism.

Conclusion: 'In my beginning is my end'

T S Eliot wrote, 'In my beginning is my end,' and this verse (taken totally out of context from Eliot's complex philosophy of time and redemption in *The Four Quartets*)[638] comes to mind as we examine some eschatological trends among ex-Muslim Christians. I say this because many of these trends have some parallel in various facets of the contexts wherein these people left Islam and—whether suddenly or gradually—became Christians. That is, the beginning of their faith (conversion) has helped to form their vision of the end or goal of their faith.

One trend was related to working for justice and liberation. Khalil and Bilici, in studying conversion narratives of ex-Muslims, identified two categories of motivations given for why people left Islam:

Intellectual/Ideological Motivations

1. The status of women in Islam.

2. The contradiction between *Shari'a* and human rights.

3. The problematic nature of the Qur'an.

4. The character of the Prophet and other Muslim leaders.

5. Islam as illogical and unscientific (e.g. *vis-à-vis* the theory of evolution).

6. The eternal damnation of good non-Muslims.

7. The unnecessary, strict rules and expectations of Islam.

8. Islam as not universal, but rather Arab-centric.

9. The dubious historicity of the Qur'an and Hadith.

Social/Experiential Motivations

1. Encounters with bad, cruel Muslims.

2. Muslims as oppressive.

3. Muslims as backward.

4. Muslim ill-treatment of women.

5. Muslim ill-treatment of non-Muslims.

6. Muslims in a state of illusion regarding their own religion.[639]

The desire to work for justice and liberation as a trend is in part related to the fact that some had left Islam due to their experiences of Muslims being bad, cruel, oppressive, chauvinistic, and intolerant. Because this is what they had experienced in the past (their beginning), it has influenced what they want to change about the future (their end).

That the eschatologies are largely evangelical by default is likewise not surprising. Historically, it was for the most part evangelicals, both local and foreign, who took the initiative to reach out to Muslims in the first place. This is another way of speaking of the beginning: aside from the abortive effort of Bl. Ramon Lull (c. 1232- c. 1315), which was centuries ahead of its time, it was evangelicals from different countries and traditions who first formed a vision for coordinated, organized, long-term missions that had the goal of converting Muslims and even forming churches made up of such

Christians. This beginning of mission helps to form the vision of these believers in relation to the things of the end.

The discontinuity with Islamic eschatology is also explainable because many of the reasons why these Christians left Islam, such as the perceived poor treatment of women and non-Muslims, and the incompatibility of *shari'a* and Human Rights, are seen as revealing not only the inferiority of Islam to Christianity here and now, but also in the future. For many ex-Muslim Christians these questions related to justice influenced them in their decision to leave Islam, and so they also inform their critique of the Islamic vision of eternal felicity.

For these believers, Islam and Christianity offer two differing perspectives that cannot be reconciled. These perspectives differ regarding how to work for a just society even though it will never be completely achieved, they differ regarding the signs of the return of the Son of Mary, and they differ regarding the joys and pleasures of the afterlife.

Glossary

Term	Description
Abbasids	The dynasty that succeeded the Umayyads, 750-1258.
Adhan	Call to prayer
Ahadith	Plural form of *Hadith*
al-akhira	The afterlife
Alids	Followers of Ali
Amir	Commander
Asbab al-nuzul	Occasions/circumstances of revelation; the historical context in which qur'anic verses were revealed.
Barzakh	Time in the grave between death and resurrection.
Caliph	The successor to Muhammad as political and military ruler of the Sunni Islamic community.
Da'i/ da'iyya	Islamic missionary (male/female)
Da'wa	Islamic 'call', mission
Dajjal	The Antichrist who will appear on earth before the Last Day.
Dar al-Harb	The House of War; the rest of the world not under Islam
Dar al-Islam	The House of Islam; areas where Islam has political dominance.
Dhikr	Form of Islamic devotion involving reciting the names of God, or supplications taken from hadith collections.
Dhimmi	'Protected' non-Muslim communities living under Islamic rule (especially Jews and Christians)

Term	Description
Du'a	Calling upon God; supplication; prayer
Fasiq	Sinner; (Islamic) law-breaker
Fatwa	Legal opinion/advice
Fiqh	Islamic Jurisprudence
Hadith	Authorative traditions recording Muhammad's statements and deeds.
Hajj	Pilgrimage (to Mecca)
Hanafi(te)	One of four Sunni schools of Islamic law founded by Abu Hanifa (d. 767)
Hanbali(te)	One of four Sunni schools of Islamic law
Hijra	Migration of Muhammad and his followers from Mecca to Medina in 622.
Huda	Guidance
Hur	Maidens in the Islamic conception of Paradise.
Ijtihad	Process of legal deduction by which a scholar produces a legal opinion/fatwa.
Imam	(Sunni meaning) leader of congregational prayer in a mosque. (Shia meaning) a recognized authority on Islamic theology and law and a spiritual guide.
Isnad	A chain of transmission identifying scholars who have reported individual hadith accounts down the generations.
Isra'iliyat	a body of narratives found within Islamic literature originating from the Jewish and Christian traditions.
Jahannam-i Kubra	Greatest Hell
Jahiliyya	Paganism/ Ignorance
Jannat-i Uzma	Most Glorious Paradise

Term	Description
Jawi	Malay language written with the Arabic alphabet
Jihad Jehad	Holy war; 'a continuous and never-ending struggle waged on all fronts including political, economic, social, psychological, domestic, moral and spiritual.'[640]
Jinn	Spiritual beings, good or evil; demons
Jizya	Poll tax to be paid by dhimmi communities to Islamic authorities.
Kafir	Unbeliever/ disbeliever/ infidel
Kalam	Islamic theology
Karbala	The site of the martyrdom of Hussein, grandson of Muhammad, in 681.
Khilafa	The Caliphate; the seat of authority of Sunni Islamic from 632-1924.
Kufr	Disbelief
Maliki(te)	One of four Sunni schools of Islamic law founded by Malik ibn Anas (c 715-795)
Maslaha	Public good
Mu'minun	Believers
Mu'tazila	Islamic school of theology based on reason and rational thought that flourished in Iraq in the third/ninth century.
Mujaddid	Renewer of Islam
Mujahiddin	Holy warriors
Munkar and Nakir	Angels who interrogate the dead to test their faith; Munkar (the Denied) and Nakir (the Denier)
Mushrik	Idolater; polytheist
Nur	Light
PBUH	Peace Be Upon Him (stated after each mention of the name of Muhammad)

Term	Description
Qadr/Qadar	That which has been destined; predestination
Qisas	Popular story-based genre of Islamic literature
Salafi	Historically refers to early generations of Muslims close to Muhammad's period; today used to refer to literalist, fundamentalist Muslims who seek to creat strict, Shari'a based societies
Saracens	Name used by Christians for Muslims in the Midle Ages
Seerah	Biography of Muhammad (see Sira)
Shahada	The Muslim Creed: 'There is no God but God and Muhammad is his messenger'
Shahid	Martyrs
Shari'a	Islamic Law
Sheikhah	Islamic teacher/authority (female)
Shifa'ah	Intercession
Shirk	The sin of idolatry or polytheism
Siddiq	Righteous
Sira	Biography of Muhammad
Sufi	Mystical stream of Islam
Sunna	Way or example of Muhammad
Sura	Chapter of the Qur'an
Tafsirs	Qur'anic commentaries
Tahrif	Corruption, distortion (of text)
Taqlid	Uncritical imitation of judgements made by earlier scholars.
Tawbah	Repentance
Tawhid	Oneness of Allah (Sufi meaning) Oneness with Allah

Term	Description
Ulema	Muslim scholars trained in Islam and Islamic law
Umayyads	The Arab dynasty of great imperial expansion, 661-750.
Umma	The worldwide Muslim community.
Ummiyyin	People without a revealed scripture.
Zakat	Almsgiving (Sufi meaning) totally giving oneself to Allah and to a Sufi brotherhood

Endnotes

[1] Hussam S. Timani, "Death and Dying in Islam," in *Ultimate Journey,* ed. Steven J. Rosen Westport, CT: Praeger, 2008, p.68.

[2] Surah 23:100, M.A.S. Abdel Haleem

[3] Mokrane Guezzou, trans., *Tanwir al-Miqbas min Tafsir Ibn 'Abbas,* Amman, Jordan: Royal Aal al-Bayt Institute for Islamic Thought, 2007, p.383.

[4] William C. Chittick, "Your Sight Today is Piercing: The Muslim Understanding of Death and Afterlife," in *Death and Afterlife,* ed. Hiroshi Obayashi, New York: Praeger, 1992, p.137.

[5] Muhammad M. Khan, *The Translation of the Meanings of Sahih Al-Bukhari,* 9 vols. Medina: Islamic University, 1981, Bukhari 1.4.215.

[6] Jane I. Smith, "Reflections on Aspects of Immortality in Islam," *Harvard Theological Review* 70:1-2 (Jan-Apr 1977), pp.85-98, http://ezproxy.ciu.edu:2055/eds/pdfviewer/pdfviewer?sid=f92385a0-8907-40a2-a1be-231a3d841589%40sessionmgr112&vid=10&hid=116 (accessed May 14, 2013), p.85.

[7] Timani, p.69

[8] Einar Thomassen, "Islamic Hell," *International Review for the History of Religions* 56:2-3 (Apr 2009, 401-416, http://ezproxy.ciu.edu:2055/eds/pdfviewer/pdfviewer?sid=a82452a3-8338-471f-b817-142af08f5ef1%40sessionmgr10&vid=7&hid=7 (accessed May 28, 2013), p.413.

[9] Ibid., p.413

[10] *Tanwir al-Miqbas min Tafsir Ibn 'Abbas*, p.26

[11] Ibid., p.348

[12] *Tanwir al-Miqbas min Tafsir Ibn 'Abbas*, p.385

[13] Feras Hamza, trans., *Tafsir al-Jalalayn*, Amman, Jordan: Royal Aal al-Bayt Institute for Islamic Thought, 2007, p.352.

[14] Surah 4:56

[15] Bukhari 2.23.455

[16] Muhammad M. Khan, trans, *The Translation of the Meanings of Summarized Sahih Al-Bukhari,* Riyadh: Maktaba Dar-us-Salam, 1994, p.342.

[17] *Tanwir al-Miqbas min Tafsir Ibn 'Abbas*, p.329

[18] Al-Ghazali, *The Remembrance of Death and the Afterlife*, trans. T.J. Winter, Cambridge: The Islamic Texts Society, 1995, pp.137-138.

[19] Ibid., p.138

[20] *Tanwir al-Miqbas min Tafsir Ibn 'Abbas*, p.647

[21] Surah 101:6-10

[22] Smith, "Reflections on Aspects of Immortality in Islam", p.93

[23] Ibid.

[24] Bukhari 8.75.376

[25] Bukhari 2.18.159

[26] Jane I. Smith, "Islam," in *How Different Religions View Death and Afterlife*, ed. Christopher J. Johnson and Marsha G. McGee, Philadelphia: The Charles Press Publishers, 1991, p.194.

[27] Surah 6:111

[28] *Tanwir al-Miqbas min Tafsir Ibn 'Abbas*, p.147

[29] Smith, "Islam", p.194

[30] *Tanwir al-Miqbas min Tafsir Ibn 'Abbas*, p.541

[31] Annabel Keeler and Ali Keeler, trans., *Tafsir al-Tustari*, Amman, Jordan: Royal Aal al-Bayt Institute for Islamic Thought, 2007, p.193.

[32] Bukhari 2.23.422

[33] Leor Halevi, "The Torture of the Grave: Islam and the Afterlife", *New York Times*, http://www.nytimes.com/2007/05/04/opinion/04iht-edhalevi.1.5565834.html (accessed February 23, 2013).

[34] 2 Corinthians 5:7-8

[35] Robert H. Smith, "Paradise Today: Luke's Passion Narrative", *Currents in Theology and Mission* 3:6 (Dec 1976), pp.323-336, http://ezproxy.ciu.edu:2055/eds/pdfviewer/pdfviewer?sid=d6765326-f296-410e-973b-eda1fdf4b7d1%40sessionmgr111&vid=2&hid=110 (accessed May 28, 2013), p.330.

[36] Wayne Grudem, *Systematic Theology*, Grand Rapids, MI: Zondervan, 1994, p.816.

[37] One of the 99 books in Al-Bukhari's collection focuses on "Afflictions and the End of the World" 9: 172-250.

[38] Muslim 1

[39] Muslim 1352

[40] Al-Bukhari 9:237

[41] Al-Bukhari 1:30; 9:204, 205

[42] Al-Bukhari 4:176, 177, 791. Where a variety of references is given, the account in the text will be a composite of all the references, since one reference may include details that the others lack.

[43] Muslim 1350

[44] Al-Bukhari 4:178, 787, 788, 789, 790

[45] Q.18:91-99. 'Q' stands for the Qur'an, with the appropriate chapter and verse/s listed.

[46] Q.21:96

[47] Al-Bukhari 4.565,566, 797; 7:215

[48] Abu Dawud 1051

[49] Abu Dawud 1054

[50] Al-Bukhari 1:85; 2:146; 9:237

[51] Al-Bukhari 1:56; 8:503

[52] Al-Bukhari 8:504

[53] Al-Bukhari 7:158

[54] Al-Bukhari 7:158

[55] Al-Bukhari 2:146

[56] Al-Bukhari 9:237

[57] Tirmidhi 1459

[58] Al-Bukhari 2:146

[59] Al-Bukhari 9:237

[60] Muslim 1352

[61] Al-Bukhari 6:159, 160; 8:513; 9:237

[62] Tirmidhi 1450

[63] Al-Bukhari 1:85; 2:146; 7:158; 9:237

[64] Al-Bukhari 4:808; 6:577; 9.64,65,66; Tirmidhi 1008

[65] Al-Bukhari 9:237

[66] Al-Bukhari 9:232

[67] Muslim 1371

[68] Al-Bukhari 2.663

[69] Al-Bukhari 1:85; 2:146; 9:237. He may be referred to in Q. 27:82

[70] Al-Bukhari 4:799

[71] Al-Bukhari 4:798; 9:210

[72] Al-Bukhari 9:237, 231

[73] Al-Bukhari 4:834

[74] Al-Bukhari 4:835

[75] Al-Bukhari 9:237

[76] Abu Dawud 2004, 2005

[77] Abu Dawud 2006

[78] Abu Dawud 2007, 2009
[79] Tirmidhi 1449
[80] Abu Dawud 2008
[81] Abu Dawud 2007, 2008
[82] Abu Dawud 2008
[83] Muslim 1371
[84] Muslim 1370
[85] Muslim 67, 1352, 1377
[86] Al-Bukhari 3:425, 656; 4:567
[87] Muslim 1371
[88] Abu Dawud 2025
[89] Muslim 1370, 1371
[90] Muslim 1370, 1371
[91] Muslim 1370, 1371
[92] Al-Bukhari 9:237; 8:513
[93] Al-Tirmidhi 1446
[94] Al-Bukhari 2:146; 9:237
[95] Al-Tirmidhi 410
[96] Abu Dawud 401
[97] Abu Dawud 400
[98] Al-Bukhari 9:181
[99] Al-Bukhari 4:565, 797; 9:249
[100] Tirmidhi 1455
[101] Al-Bukhari 1:795; 2:459; 6:230; 8:378, 386, 387, 388
[102] Al-Bukhari 8:188
[103] Tirmidhi 1454
[104] Tirmidhi 1451
[105] Al-Bukhari 2:468
[106] Muslim 490
[107] Al-Bukhari 2:539; 9:171
[108] Abu Dawud 1030
[109] Al-Bukhari 1:184
[110] Al-Bukhari 1:795; 2:459; 4:76, 77; 6:230; 8:375, 376, 377, 378, 381, 385, 386, 387, 388
[111] Al-Bukhari 2:454
[112] Muslim 1371
[113] Al-Bukhari 4:581, 556
[114] Al-Bukhari 6:236
[115] Tirmidhi 1458
[116] Tirmidhi 1460
[117] A-Bukhari 4:568; 6:149
[118] Al-Bukhari 6:265; 8:537
[119] Tirmidhi 1462
[120] Tirmidhi 1464
[121] Muslim 49, 50, 1387; Abu Dawood 330, 403, 498
[122] Tirmidhi 215, 1464
[123] Tirmidhi 1463
[124] Al-Bukhari 1:770; 8:577; 9:532A
[125] Al-Bukhari 9:532B
[126] Al-Bukhari 1:770; 8:577; 9.532A
[127] Al-Bukhari 1:529; 9:529
[128] Al-Bukhari 9:530
[129] Al-Bukhari 9:531
[130] Al-Bukhari 1:770; 8:577; 9.532A (cf. Q.75:22-23)
[131] Al-Bukhari 9:532A

132 Al-Bukhari 9:532.2 c.f. Q.68:42 "the day when the *sāq* (shin) will be laid bare".
133 Muslim 1371
134 Muslim 417
135 Al-Bukhari 1:239; 2:1,21; 4:693; 8:621; 9:26, 160, 587
136 Al-Bukhari 1:770; 8:577; 9.532A
137 Al-Bukhari 1:770; 8:577; 9.532A
138 Muslim 83
139 Tirmidhi 1461
140 Tirmidhi 1472
141 Tirmidhi 56
142 Al-Bukhari 6:265; 8:537; Muslim 1371
143 Al-Bukhari 2:422; 6:371, 372, 373; 8:654; 9:481, 541
144 Tirmidhi 1518
145 Al-Bukhari 6:265; 8:537; Muslim 1371
146 Al-Bukhari 1:770; 8:577; 9.532A
147 Tirmidhi 1475
148 Al-Bukhari 4:556; 6:236
149 Al-Bukhari 4:556; 6:236
150 Al-Bukhari 4:556; 6:236
151 Al-Bukhari 4:556; 6:236; 4:581
152 Al-Bukhari 4:556; 6:236
153 Al-Bukhari 4:556; 6:236
154 Al-Bukhari 5:374
155 Tirmidhi 1467. However Tirmidhi reports that this is a *gharib* tradition (related by a single line of transmission, or carrying additional material).
156 Al-Bukhari 4:556; 6:236
157 Tirmidhi 1469
158 Al-Bukhari 9:532B
159 Tirmidhi 1470
160 Tirmidhi 1471
161 Tirmidhi 1473
162 Abu Dawud 1042; Tirmidhi 1067
163 Al-Bukhari 9:532B
164 Tirmidhi 1472
165 Tirmidhi 1474
166 Muslim no.82
167 Al-Bukhari 1:770; 8:577; 9:532A
168 Al-Bukhari 3:620; 8:542
169 On which see David Cook, *Contemporary Muslim Apocalyptic Literature*. Syracuse, NY: Syracuse University Press, 2005, and Jean-Pierre Filiu, *Apocalypse in Islam* (M.B. DeBevoise, trans), Berkeley: University of California Press, 2011.
170 Again, see Cook, *Contemporary Muslim* and Filiu, *Apocalypse*.
171 Filiu, *Apocalypse*, p.xii.
172 David Cook, *Studies in Muslim Apocalyptic*, Princeton: Darwin Press, 2002, pp.301-302.
173 d. 855.
174 There are other key signs, such as the death of Muhammad, the conquest of Jerusalem, the assassination of caliph(s), the disappearance of the Qur'an from human hearts, etc. Some signs, like the burning of the Ka'ba, have at times been classified as 'greater,' at times as 'lesser'. Compare D. Cook 'Messianism in the Mid-11th/17th Century as Exemplified by al-Barzanji (1040-1103/1630-1691),' *Jerusalem studies in Arabic and Islam* 33, 2007, pp.264-265.
175 Volume.Book.Number (available online at: http://www.sahih-bukhari.com/, accessed June 24, 2013).
176 Cf. Q 27.82.

[177] See Cook, *Studies*, pp.23-27. A popular, non-canonical, early collection is that of Nu'aym b. Hammad, (*Kitab*) *al-Fitan* (A.M.M. 'Arafa ed), Cairo: al-Maktaba al-tawfiqiya, n.d. (Nu'aym died ca. 843.)

[178] *asbab al-nuzul.*

[179] Cf. Cook, *Studies*, pp.277f.

[180] Cf. J.J. Collins, 'Apocalypses and Apocalypticism, Early Jewish Apocalypticism,' in *The Anchor Bible Dictionary*, v. 1, New York: Doubleday, 1992-1996, p.283.

[181] David Olster, 'Byzantine Apocalypses', in *The Encyclopedia of Apocalypticism*, v. 2, New York: Continuum, 2000, pp.60-64. D. Cook suggests that the Christian apocalypses of the early Islamic period may be considered the earliest Christian polemic against Islam (*The Beginnings of Islam in Syria during the Umayyad Period*, vols. 1-2. PhD diss. University of Chicago, 2002, pp.230-231). Cf. Kevin Van Bladel, 'The Alexander Legend in the Qur'an 18:83–102,' in *The Qur'an in Its Historical Context*, London: Routledge, 2008, p.188.

[182] In the bitter invective the 'degenerate' Shi'i followers of Dajjal may be connected to the Jews because their Mahdi will rule according to the rule of the house of David. See http://www.sunniforum.com/forum/showthread.php?p=377969 (accessed September 10, 2009).

[183] Examples throughout John C. Reeves, *Trajectories in Near Eastern Apocalyptic, A Postrabbinic Jewish Apocalypse Reader*, Atlanta: SBL, 2005. See further, Olster, *Byzantine Apocalypses*, pp.52-53.

[184] Muhammad b. Jarir al-Tabari, *The History of al-Tabari*, v.12 (Y. Friedmann trans), Albany: SUNY Press, 1992, p.190; Olster, *Byzantine Apocalypses*, 64, pp.66-67; Saïd Amir Arjomand, 'Islamic Apocalypticism in the Classical Period,' in *The Encyclopedia of Apocalypticism*, v. 2, New York: Continuum, 2000, p.247; Pseudo-Methodius (in Francisco Martinez, ed. and trans, *Eastern Christian Apocalyptic in the Early Muslim Period: Pseudo-Methodius and Pseudo-Athanasius*, vols. 1-2, PhD diss., Catholic University of America, 1985, pp.152-153.

[185] Cook, 'Messianism', p.277.

[186] E.g., Bukhari 4.55.657 (cf. 3.43.656); Muslim 1.71.242-243; 52.20.110; Ibn Majah v.5, 36.33.4078, p. 386; Abu Da'ud v.3, p. 1203, no. 4310.
Muslim b. al-Hajjaj, *Sahih Muslim, The Authentic Hadiths of Muslim with Full Arabic Text*, vols. 1-4 (M.M. al-Sharif trans), Beirut: Dar al-Kotob al-Ilmiyah, 1426/2005 [Volume.Chapter.Number]/Ibn Majah al-Qazwini, *Sunan Ibn-e-Majah, With Arabic Text*, vols. 1-5, revised edn, (M.T. Ansari trans), New Delhi: Kitab Bhavan, 2004 [Book.Chapter.Number]/ Abu Da'ud, *Sunan Abu Dawud, English Translation with Explanatory Notes*, vols. 1-3 (A. Hasan trans), New Delhi: Kitab Bhavan, 1990.

[187] Indeed, in most Muslim apocalyptic, the explicit historical and social concerns of the writer are thoroughly submerged under the spare presentation of the ancient hadiths. Cf. Cook, 'Messianism', pp.261-262

[188] Filiu, *Apocalypse*, pp.30f.

[189] For biographical information see, *inter alia*, Muhammad Husayn al-Dhahabi, *Al-Tafsir wa al-Mufassirun*, v. 1, Cairo: Dar al-Hadith, 1426/2005, pp.210-214; H. Laoust, 'Ibn Kathir' in *EI²*, v. 3, Leiden: Brill, 1971, pp.817-818 and *idem*, 'Ibn Kathir Historien,' *Arabica* 2, 1955, pp.42-88; J.D. McAuliffe, *Qur'anic Christians, An Analysis of Classical and Modern Exegesis*, Cambridge: CUP, 1991, pp.71-76.

[190] Hereafter, '*Tafsir*'. *Tafsir al-Qur'an al-'Azim*, vols. 1-4 ('Abd al-Qadir al-Arna'ut, ed), Riyad and Dimashq: Dar al-Salam and Dar al-Fayha, 1418/1998. [English abridgement: *Tafsir Ibn Kathir, Abridged*, vols. 1-10, (S-R Al-Mubarakpuri, ed), Riyadh: Darussalam, 2000.]

[191] Hereafter, '*Nihaya*'. *Al-Nihaya fi-al-Fitan wa al-Malahim* (A. 'Abd al-Shafi, ed), Bayrut: Dar al-Kutub al-'Ilmiya, 1408/1988. This work is paramount in the current essay. It is a large tome relatively evenly divided between a more-or-less chronologized emphasis on the last-days events prior to the End and then on traditions about resurrection/judgment and reward/punishment. [English translation with occasional gaps or alterations: *The Book of the End: Great Trials and Tribulations* (A. Ahad ed/F. Shafiq trans), Riyadh: Darussalam, 2006.]

171

[192] Multiple examples in M.R.K. al-Nadawi, *Al-Imam Ibn Kathir—Siratuhu wa-Mu'alafatuhu wa Minhajuhu fi Kitabat al-Ta'rikh*, Dimashq wa Bayrut: Dar Ibn Kathir, 1420/1999, pp.96-99; al-Dhahabi, *Al-Tafsir*, v.1, 210-211, p.214.

[193] This is true of many of his works. Online abridgements of his *tafsir* may be found at [http://www.qtafsir.com/index.php?option=com_content&task=view&id=3000&Itemid=731] and [http://www.quran4u.com/Tafsir%20Ibn%20Kathir/Index.htm], both accessed December 1, 2012.

[194] J.D. McAuliffe, 'The Tasks and Traditions of Interpretation,' in *The Cambridge Companion to the Qur'an*, Cambridge: CUP, 2006, p.196.

[195] Walid A. Saleh, 'Preliminary Remarks on the Historiography of *tafsir* in Arabic: A History of the Book Approach', *JQS* 12, 2010, 15, pp.33-34. Cf. Neal Robinson, *Christ in Islam and Christianity*, Albany, NY: SUNY Press, 1991, 1, pp.73-75, 191; R. Williams, 'Ibn Kathir,' Oxford Encyclopedia of the Islamic World, New York: OUP, 2009 (online entry at Oxford Islamic Studies Online, accessed March 30, 2011; A-M. Mujahid in *Tafsir Ibn Kathir, Abridged*, v. 1, p.5.

[196] R. Tottoli, *Biblical Prophets in the Qur'an and Muslim Literature* (M. Robertson trans), London: Routledge, 2002, p.187. See also Al-Arna'ut, the editor, in Ibn Kathir, *Tafsir*, v. 1, p.7.

[197] Cook, *Studies*, p.292.

[198] W. Saleh, 'Ibn Taymiyya and the Rise of Radical Hermeneutics: An Analysis of *An Introduction to the Foundations of Qur'anic Exegesis*', in *Ibn Taymiyya and His Times*, Oxford: OUP, 2010, pp.123-124, 148, 153.

[199] That is, the idealized, 'faithful' generation who had been with the prophet and those immediately following them. Cf. Robinson, *Christ in Islam*, pp.73-75.

[200] Saleh, 'Ibn Taymiyya', pp.123.

[201] Saleh, 'Ibn Taymiyya', pp.125, 154.

[202] Saleh, 'Ibn Taymiyya', p.148.

[203] See Mohammad Ahmad Masad, *The Medieval Islamic Apocalyptic Tradition: Divination, Prophecy, and the End of Time in the 13th Century Mediterranean*, PhD diss., Washington University in St. Louis, 2008, pp.142-155, 159-163, esp. 154; Tariq al-Jamil, 'Ibn Taymiyya and Ibn al-Mutahhar al-Hilli: Shi'i Polemics and the Struggle for Religious Authority in Medieval Islam,' in *Ibn Taymiyya and His Times*, Oxford: OUP, 2010, pp.229-246.

[204] Saleh, 'Ibn Taymiyya', pp.150-153, provides the basic argument of this paragraph.

[205] See, for example, A-M. Mujahid in the 'Publisher's Note' in *Tafsir Ibn Kathir, Abridged*, v. 1, p.5.

[206] See glossary and Robinson, *Christ in Islam*, pp.73-74.

[207] See in the introduction to the *Tafsir* in v. 1, p. 7. Similar praise and mild censure in Al-Nadawi, *Al-Imam Ibn Kathir*, p.96.

[208] Cf. Ibn Kathir, *Nihaya*, pp.10, 29; Bukhari 5.57.2-3; 9.88.188; Muslim 44.52.210-216; Tirmidhi→ رسول الله عن الفتن → منه → no. 2206 (http://hadith.al-islam.com/Page.aspx?pageid=192&BookID=26&TOCID=1504 [accessed December 17, 2012]); Nu'aym, *Fitan*, 1.1.46, p. 39. Parallel traditions noted in note to no. 46 on page 39 of Nu'aym's *Fitan*.

[209] There is no space here for a detailed analysis, but for some sense of the sectarian environment and theological concerns of Ibn Taymiyya and his school one might start with the following sources: Y. Rapport and S. Ahmed, eds, *Ibn Taymiyya and His Times*, Oxford: OUP, 2010; Jon Hoover, 'The Apologetic and Pastoral Intentions of Ibn Qayyim al-Jawziyya's Polemic against Jews and Christians,' *MW* 100.4, 2010, pp.476-489; Yahya Michot, 'Between Entertainment and Religion: Ibn Taymiyya's Views on Superstition,' *Muslim World* 99, 2009, pp.1-20. Primary texts: Rifaat Ebied and David Thomas, eds and trans, *Muslim-Christian Polemic During the Crusades, The Letter from the People of Cyprus and Ibn Abi Talib al-Dimashqi's Response*, Leiden: Brill, 2005; Ibn Taymiyya, *Muslims Under Non-Muslim Rule* (Yahya Michot ed and trans), Oxford and London: Interface Publications, 2006; M.U. Memon, *Ibn Taimiya's Struggle against Popular Religion, with an Annotated Translation of his Kitab*

iqtida' as-sirat al-mustaqim mukhalafat ashab al-jahim, The Hague: Mouton, 1976; T.F. Michel, ed and trans, (abridged) *A Muslim Theologian's Response to Christianity; Ibn Taymiyya's Al-Jawab Al-Sahih*, Delmar, NY: Caravan Books, 1984.

210 E.g. Memon, *Kitab iqtida'*, pp.90-96; Ibn Taymiyya, *Muslims*, p.100.

211 Memon, *Kitab iqtida'*, pp.97, 108-111.

212 Memon, *Kitab iqtida'*, pp.121-131, 167f.

213 Ibn Kathir, *Nihaya*, pp.9, 23-27. Cf. Ibn Kathir, *Tafsir*, v. 3, p.402.

214 Cf. Ibn Kathir, *Tafsir*, v.1, pp.768-777; Ibn Kathir, *Qisas al-Anbiya'*, 2nd edn, Beirut: Dar Al-Kotob Al-Ilmiyah, 1422/2001, p.432.

215 But, see Gabriel Said Reynolds, 'The Muslim Jesus, Dead or Alive?' *BSOAS* 72.2, 2009, pp.237-258.

216 *Nihaya*, p.10.

217 *Nihaya*, pp.10, 12-14.

218 Ibn Kathir, *Nihaya*, p.11; Masad, *Medieval Islamic Apocalyptic*, p.4.

219 E.g., Ibn Kathir, *Nihaya*, pp.50-51.

220 Interestingly, on occasion Ibn Taymiyya attacked 'Sufi excess' by forwarding the Dajjal and his wonders as the paradigmatic model for the Sufi mystics and their alleged miracles. Memon, *Kitab iqtida'*, p.64.

221 On the Dajjal, see A. Abel, 'al-Dadjdjal,' *EI²* v. 2, Leiden: Brill, 1965, pp.76-77.

222 Ibn Kathir, *Tafsir* v.1, pp.768-777.

223 Cf. Bukhari 3.43.656; 4.55.657-658; Muslim 1.71.242-244; 15.34.216; Abu Dawud v. 3, p. 1203, no. 4310; Ibn Majah, *Sunan*, v. 5, 36.33.4078, p. 386; *Musnad Ahmad Ibn Hanbal* → باقي مسند المكثرين → مسند أبي هريرة رضي الله عنه → no. 8226 (accessed online at http://al-islam.com/Page.aspx?pageid=695&BookID=30&PID=8077&SubjectID=30284, September 2, 2010). Also, Ibn Kathir, *Qisas al-Anbiya'*, p.432.

224 Cf. 1 Thess. 5.3.

225 Ibn Kathir, *Tafsir* v.1, pp.773-774.

226 Ibn Kathir, *Nihaya*, p.98, is parallel.

227 The Messiah with heavenly warriors is a ubiquitous notion.

228 See too Ibn Kathir on Q 4.157-158 (*Tafsir* v. 1, 764). Here the pre-ascension Jesus appears with his head *dripping water*. As Jesus, '*the anointed*,' departs, so he returns (cf. Ac. 1.11). This may suggest a sort of timeless occultation in heaven until his return.

229 Cf. 2 Thess. 2.8. On the 'breath' *topos*, see also Isa. 11.4, 15; 30.27-33; 33.11; Rev. 1.16; 2.16; 11.5; 19.15, 21; 1Q28b (=1QSb) 5.24-25; *Sefer Zerubbabel* in Reeves, *Trajectories*, pp.62, 66.

230 Ibn Kathir also carries reports from Ibn Hanbal and Tirmidhi paralleling this demise of the Dajjal in Palestine/Israel. E.g., Tirmidhi, → رسول الله عن الفتن← مريم ابن عيسى قتل في جاء ما الدجال← no. 2244 (http://hadith.al-islam.com/Page.aspx?pageid=192&BookID=26&TOCID=1528), accessed December 22, 2012. [الدجال باب لد بباب الدجال مريم ابن يقتل]

231 Ibn Kathir, *Tafsir* v.1, pp.774-775; Muslim, 52.23.116; also in Ibn Kathir's *Nihaya*, p.94.

232 Cited here with respect to the Judgment are Q 37.24; Q 73.17; Q 68.42.

233 Ibn Kathir, *Tafsir* v.1, p.775.

234 *Tafsir* v.1, 775-776; *Nihaya*, p.98; cf. *Qisas al-Anbiya'*, pp.432-433.

235 *Tafsir* v.1, p.772. In *Nihaya*, pp. 61 and 98, he notes other reported locations as well, including Jerusalem, 'the Jordan,' a mountain in Syria, and 'the midst of the Muslim camp.' Jerusalem seems to be the site in the early *Tafsir Muqatil b. Sulayman* v. 3 (A. Farid, ed.), Beirut: Dar Al-Kotob Al-Ilmiyah, 2003, pp.194-195.

236 Ibn Kathir, *Tafsir* v.1, pp.771-773 [see also *Nihaya*, 66]; Ibn Majah, *Sunan*, v.5, 36.33.4077, pp. 378-386. While from an authoritative book, this *hadith*'s *isnad* is open to objection. The tradition is remarkably lengthy, incorporating many stock elements of the apocalyptic storyline and some unusual elements.

237 Cf. *Nihaya*, p.70.

238 There are differing interpretations of '*bab ludd*.' Cf. Ibn Kathir, *Nihaya*, pp.92-93; also, Ibn Majah v. 5, 36.33.4075, on p.376; v. 5, 36.33.4077 (Arabic ref. to Lod Gate on p.380). Musnad Ahmad Ibn Hanbal no. 18984 (accessed online at http://al-islam.com/Page.aspx?pageid=695&BookID=30&PID=18661&SubjectID=30284, September 2, 2010) and no. 23946 (accessed online at http://al-islam.com/Page.aspx?pageid=695&BookID=30&PID=23329&SubjectID=30284, September 2, 2010).

239 On this prevalent motif see *Nihaya,* 75, and throughout.

240 For example, *Nihaya*, pp.92-93.

241 *Tafsir* v.1, 770-771; *Nihaya*, pp.78-79.

242 *Musnad Ahmad Ibn Hanbal* → مسند الشاميين →
حديث عثمان بن أبي العاص عن النبي صلى الله عليه وسلم → no. 17443 (accessed online at http://al-islam.com/Page.aspx?pageid=695&BookID=30&PID=17228&SubjectID=30284, September 2,2010).

243 For more on the pattern of 'thirds' and the Dajjal, see also *Nihaya*, 79, pp.92-93.

244 Cf. Q 4.171.

245 Compare Abel, 'al-Dadjdjal', p.76.

246 Compare Muslim 1.75.274; Bukhari 4.55.608, 648-650. It is best to consult the Arabic texts in these instances because the translations of the terms for the skin colour can vary.

247 The Dajjal is compared to Ibn Qatan, supposedly a Khuza'a tribesman who died in the *jahiliyya*. Cf. *Nihaya*, pp.97-98.

248 Cook, *Studies*, pp.99-100.

249 *Tafsir* v.1, pp.770-771; *Nihaya*, pp.78-79; *Musnad Ahmad Ibn Hanbal* → مسند الشاميين →
حديث عثمان بن أبي العاص عن النبي صلى الله عليه وسلم → no. 17443 (accessed online at http://al-islam.com/Page.aspx?pageid=695&BookID=30&PID=17228&SubjectID=30284, September 2, 2010).

250 Apparel associated with foreigners. See E.W. Lane, *An Arabic-English Lexicon* (vols. 1-4), London: Williams and Norgate, 1885, *s.v.* ج سوج → ساج and also طلس → طيلسان.

251 See too W. Saleh's chapter, 'The Woman as a Locus of Apocalyptic Anxiety in Medieval Sunni Islam,' in *Myths, Historical Archetypes, and Symbolic Figures in Arabic Literature*, A. Neuwirth *et al*, eds., Beirut: Franz Steiner Verlag Stuttgart, 1999, pp.123-145.

252 Compare Muslim 52.18.6266; Abu Dawud v.3, p. 1198, no. 4292.

253 See below.

254 Ibn Kathir, *Nihaya*, pp.102-103.

255 It must be remembered, of course, that both these books are dependent on traditions stemming from the prior collections on which Ibn Kathir relied and which we often reference here alongside the primary citations of Ibn Kathir's work.

256 See the familiar Ibn Kathir, *Tafsir* v.1, pp.771-773 [see also *Nihaya*, 66]; Ibn Majah, *Sunan*, v.5, 36.33.4077, pp.378-386.

257 See Abel, 'al-Dadjdjal,' pp.76-77 (comparing St. Ephraem and Pseudo-Methodius). Also, N. Robinson, 'Antichrist,' *Encyclopaedia of the Qur'an* v. 1 (J. D. McAuliffe, ed.), Leiden: Brill, 2001, p.110. Cf. Bukhari 2.17.147 and 9.88.214 (troubles from the *Najd* in the Arabian Peninsula). See also the Tamim al-Dari tale below.

258 See especially *Nihaya*, p.84, following sentences as well.

259 It is interesting to note the later mahdist claim of the Iranian Imami Shaykh Fazlallah al-Astarbadi, Ibn Kathir's younger contemporary, who dreamt that his 'right eye had absorbed the supernatural brilliance of an eastern star' (Filiu, *Apocalypse*, p.56).

260 *Nihaya*, pp.89-93.

261 *Nihaya*, p.92.

262 *Nihaya*, pp.89-90.

263 *Nihaya*, p.92.

264 *Ibid*.

265 Again, Ibn Kathir, *Tafsir* v.1, pp.771-773.

[266] Cf. Q 75.23 (i.e., if you are still in this earthly existence and can see the Dajjal, then he is not God). Cf. Muslim 52.19.95c, pp.730-732; *Nihaya*, p.53.
[267] See, e.g., see the examples contained in *Nihaya*, pp.68-71, 73.
[268] Cf. previous note and also *Nihaya*, p.82.
[269] Compare Mt. 13.47-50; 25.31-46. Also Isa. 49.16; Ezek 9.4-6; Rev. 3.12; 7.3; 9.4; 13.1, 16-18; 14.1, 9; 17.3; 19.12-16; 20.4; 22.4.
[270] On the *topos*, but not the Dajjal, see Bernard McGinn, *Antichrist, Two Thousand Years of the Human Fascination with Evil*, New York: Columbia University Press, 2000, p.93.
[271] Sometimes, Ibn Sa'id. Bukhari 2.23.437; 3.48.806; 4.52.290d; 8.73.193; 8.73.194; 8.77.615; Muslim 52.19 (باب ذكر ابن صياد), p. 724f. and 52.20 (باب في ذكر الدجال وصفته وما معه), p. 734f.; *Abu Dawud* v.3, pp.1205-1206.
[272] *Nihaya*, pp.52-53.
[273] Cf. Bukhari 4.52.290; Muslim 52.19.95 (p. 728-731); 52.19.86.
[274] *Nihaya*, pp.59-60. Cf. Muslim 50a.16.67, v. 4, p. 634-635 (كتاب صفة القيامة والجنة والنار); 52.19.87.
[275] *Nihaya*, pp.52-53. Bukhari 4.52.290, pp.184-186; Muslim 52.19.95a-95b, pp.728-731.
[276] Ibn Sayyad or b. Sayyad mean 'son of Sayyad.'
[277] See *Nihaya*, 52 n3, for the editor's attempts to defend or ameliorate the scene.
[278] *Nihaya*, pp.59-60.
[279] *Nihaya*, p.61.
[280] *Nihaya*, p.54; Muslim 52.19.98.
[281] Compare Hebrew, גרה.
[282] The climactic trauma of the destruction of the Jewish temple (70 AD) was attributed by some to gratuitous hatred (תאנש מניח). See, e.g., Talmud tractate Yomah in chapter one (http://www.sacred-texts.com/jud/t03/yom06.htm#fr_6, accessed online December 24, 2012).
[283] For example, see *Abu Dawud* v.3, p. 1206, no. 4316. Also, *Nihaya*, pp.54, 59; Bukhari 9.92.453; Muslim 52.19.94; Abu Dawud v.3, p. 1205, no. 4314; v. 3, p. 1206, no. 4317.
[284] *Nihaya*, p.88; Tirmidhi→ الفتن عن رسول الله → ما جاء في ذكر ابن صائد → no. 2248 (http://www.al-islam.com/Page.aspx?pageid=695&BookID=26&PID=2174&SubjectID=30272), accessed December 25, 2012. See also D. Halperin, 'The Ibn Sayyad Traditions and the Legend of al-Dajjal,' *JAOS* 96, 1976, pp.223-224. He mentions the lone tradition that Ibn Sayyad is born one-eyed and circumcised (224 n100)!
[285] *Nihaya*, p.54. Literally, 'a small man' (perhaps in view of the outsize nature of the coming Enemy).
[286] E.g., Muslim 52.19.89-91; Tirmidhi→ الفتن عن رسول الله → ما جاء في ذكر ابن صائد → No. 2246 (http://hadith.al-islam.com/Page.aspx?pageid=192&BookID=26&TOCID=1529), accessed December 24, 2012.
[287] *Nihaya*, p.54.
[288] Cf. *Nihaya*, p.60.
[289] *Nihaya*, pp.48-51; cf. Bukhari 9.88.237; Muslim 52.18.83; 15.18.84; Abu Dawud v.3, p. 1206, no. 4319-4320.
[290] E.g., *Nihaya*, pp.50-51, 71-72. Cf. Muslim 42.4.21(b).
[291] Variations on this *hadith* may be seen, for example, at Muslim, 52 (Chapter entitled باب قصة الجساسة) pp.750-758; Abu Dawud v.3, p. 1203-1205, no. 4311-4314; Ibn Majah v.5, 36.33.4074, pp.370-373.
[292] *Nihaya*, pp.55-59.
[293] Cf. B. Carra de Vaux, 'Al-Dadjdjal,' *EI*[1] v. 2, Leiden: Brill, 1987, pp.886-887.
[294] *Nihaya*, pp.56, 58.
[295] *Ibn Kathir*, *Nihaya*, p.56. In the Muslim apocalypse, Gog and Magog are thought to drink the lake dry.
[296] Medina (*Nihaya*, p.56). The inviolability of Mecca and Medina before the Dajjal is a recurrent theme. See also the traditions in Bukhari, under the chapter 'باب لا يدخل الدجال المدينة' (9.88.246-248). See also *Nihaya*, pp.87, 105-106. This hardly implies immunity from all

eschatological travail for these cities (cf. *Nihaya*, pp.46f., 103; Filiu, *Apocalypse*, p.9). On various counts Jerusalem presents some competition for the two harams in the hadiths; so on occasion, Jerusalem too is said to be immune to the Imposter (*Nihaya*, p.75).

[297] *Nihaya*, p.55.

[298] E.g., Bukhari 9.88.242.

[299] *Nihaya*, pp.60-61f.

[300] *Nihaya*, p.88.

[301] *Nihaya*, p.88, remainder of this paragraph, paraphrased.

[302] Or, 'divinity.' (Compare English translations such as *Book of the End*.)

[303] E.g., see McAuliffe, *Qur'anic Christians*, pp.119-120, on Ibn Kathir's 'hardline' interpretation of Q 2.62.

[304] See further examples in *Nihaya*, p.74.

[305] Compare Al-Nadawi, *Al-Imam Ibn Kathir*, p.168, on Ibn Kathir on the transmutation to 'apes and pigs' of Q 2.65; 7.166.

[306] *Nihaya*, p.46.

[307] *Nihaya*, p.81; Muslim, 52.18.82. Cf. *Nihaya*, p.75; Bukhari 4.52.177; 4.56.791; Muslim 52.18.79-82; Tirmidhi, → الفتن عن رسول الله ← ما جاء في علامة الدجال → no. 2236 (http://hadith.al-islam.com/Page.aspx?pageid=192&TOCID=1522&BookID=26&PID=2162), accessed January 3, 2013.

[308] Muslim 52.18.65.

[309] Contrast, Tirmidhi, →
ما جاء من أين يخرج الدجال ← الفتن عن رسول الله → no. 2237 (http://hadith.al-islam.com/Page.aspx?pageid=192&BookID=26&TOCID=1523), accessed January 3, 2013.

[310] *Nihaya*, p.81.

[311] *Ibid*.

[312] Again, Ibn Kathir, *Tafsir* v.1, pp.771-773 [see also *Nihaya*, 66]; Ibn Majah, *Sunan*, v.5, 36.33.4077, pp.378-386.

[313] See also Bukhari 92.5.7061; *92.24.7121. Similar, not identical, is* Muslim 52.23.116.

[314] Cf. *Nihaya*, 62; Abu Dawud v.3, p.1202, no. 4307.

[315] *Nihaya*, p.88.

[316] *Nihaya*, pp.88-89.

[317] Cf. Bukhari 9.88.246; Muslim 52.21.113.

[318] As in the familiar Ibn Kathir, *Tafsir* v.1, pp.771—773.

[319] Cf. *Nihaya*, p.86; *Qisas al-Anbiya'*, p.318. On al-Khidr in the *Qisas* see pp.274-279, 309-321. Also, Muslim 52.21.112.

[320] Again, *Tafsir* v.1, pp.771-773 [see also *Nihaya*, p.66].

[321] Cf. Rev. 11.13.

[322] Cf. *Musnad Ahmad Ibn Hanbal* → باقي مسند الأنصار →
حديث السيدة عائشة رضي الله عنها → no. 23946 (accessed online at http://al-islam.com/Page.aspx?pageid=695&BookID=30&PID=23329&SubjectID=30284, September 2, 2010).

[323] Ibn Kathir, *Tafsir* v.1, pp.771-773. Cf. Rev. 13.3; 17.8.

[324] *Nihaya*, pp.90-92. Cf. Nu'aym, *Fitan*, 7.61.1520, pp.404-405

[325] The parallel for this part of the tale: Nu'aym, *Fitan*, 8.65.1594, p. 423.

[326] The Arabic in my edition of the *Nihaya* (p.91) appears confused here. The text is difficult in any case.

[327] The sharpness of this polemic became clearer to me in a conversation with Lisa Neely.

[328] *Nihaya*, p.90.

[329] External disfiguring signaling ritual, spiritual, or moral impurity. Cf. Lev. 21.16-23.

[330] *Nihaya*, p.74.

[331] Recall biblical motifs of two latter-day witnesses or of angels attesting to the Messiah's resurrection or accompanying his return.

[332] *Nihaya*, p.71.

333 Ibn Kathir notes that though this unique tradition was carried by the great Ibn Hanbal and that though its 'isnad is not objectionable… [Nonetheless,] in the matn are strange and improbable elements.'

334 Ibn Kathir brings further narratives from the Musnad which emphasize the Dajjal's acting like Jesus in healing those born blind (الأكمه) and lepers; it is also underlined that the returned Jesus confirms Muhammad's revelation and kills the Enemy (Nihaya, p.72).

335 Compare the Antichrist of Pseudo-Methodius (Martinez, Eastern Christian, pp.153-154).

336 Nihaya, pp.92-93.

337 Nihaya, p.83.

338 He brings a mysterious cache of gold with him as well (Nihaya, p.84).

339 Cf. Rev. 11 and traditions on Elias and Enoch at the End [Abel, 'al-Dadjdjal,' p.76]. Interestingly, in terms of Shi'i 'passion' theology, there are tendencies to identify the suffering young man who is killed and raised by the Dajjal as the Mahdi himself. See, for example, http://www.endoftimes.net/08mahdiandtheendtimes.html (accessed September 11, 2009).

340 Cf. Jesus' reign in Nihaya, 64-66 (and parallel in the Tafsir); Ibn Majah, 36.33.4077, pp.378-386.

341 Nihaya, pp.83-84.

342 Ibid.

343 Compare Ibn Taymiyya on the reality and spiritual invalidity of the Dajjal's miracles (Michel, Muslim Theologian, p.298).

344 Cf. Michot, Between Entertainment.

345 Nihaya, p.84. Following sentences as well.

346 Nihaya, p.84.

347 Cf. Nihaya, p.83.

348 Nihaya, p.90.

349 Ibn Kathir, Tafsir v.1, pp.771-773.

350 A common locution. Cf. Nihaya, pp.68-71, 73.

351 Cf. Q 21.69.

352 On these themes, including Sura 18, cf. Tafsir, v.1, pp.773-774; Muslim 52.20.110.

353 Nihaya, pp.72-73.

354 Nihaya, p.73. Cf. Muslim 52.25.126. (See Nihaya, p.74, subsection: ليس في الدنيا فتنة اعظم من فتنة الدجال) Cf. Didachē, Chapter 16 (http://www.earlychristianwritings.com/text/didache-roberts.html--accessed July 13, 2013).

355 Nihaya, pp.61-63; Muslim 52.20.110; Ibn Majah, Sunan v.5, 36.33.4075, pp.373-377; Tirmidhi→ الفتن عن رسول الله → ما جاء في فتنة الدجال → no. 2240 (http://hadith.al-islam.com/Page.aspx?pageid=192&BookID=26&TOCID=1525) accessed January 1, 2013. Cf. Abu Dawud v.3, p.1202, no. 4307 and Musnad Ahmad Ibn Hanbal → حديث → مسند الشاميين → النواس بن سمعان الكلابي الأنصاري رضي الله تعالى عنه → no. 17177 (accessed online at http://al-islam.com/Page.aspx?pageid=695&BookID=30&PID=16973&SubjectID=30284, September 2, 2010).

356 Cf. Nihaya, pp.49, 64 (par. Ibn Majah, Sunan v. 5, 36.33.4077, pp.378-386), p.74.

357 Nihaya, p.62.

358 Nihaya, p.88.

359 Nihaya, p.83; Muslim v. 4, Chapter 22 (p. 746-747); 38.6.32.

360 Again, for example, Ibn Kathir, Tafsir v.1, pp.771-773 [cf. Nihaya, p.66].

361 In other cases Ibn Kathir deftly excises or reinterprets hadith which point to early and specific dates for the end (e.g., Nihaya, pp.9-14).

362 Once again, implicit commentary on the contemporary scene is in fact a pattern and partial purpose of malahim and fitan collections. See D. Cook, 'Hadith, Authority and the End of the World: Traditions in Modern Muslim Apocalyptic Literature,' Oriente Moderno 21, 2002, p.35.

363 This topic is dealt with in Nihaya, pp.84-86.

364 Nihaya, pp.84-85.

365 Tirmidhi← الله رسول عن القرآن تفسير ← الأنعام سورة من و← no. 3072 (http://hadith.al-islam.com/Page.aspx?pageid=192&TOCID=1839&BookID=26&PID=2998), accessed January 10, 2013.

366 *Nihaya*, p.85.

367 *Nihaya*, p.86.

368 *Nihaya*, p.86. Cf. also p.4. See also Bukhari 7.70.569.

369 *Nihaya*, p.86.

370 Ibid.

371 Ibid. Compare the converted sorcerers' challenge to Pharaoh in Q 7.120-126.

372 Cf. Cook, 'Hadith, Authority, and the End of the World,' p.43; R. Tottoli, '*Hadiths* and Traditions in Some Recent Books Upon the Dajjal (Antichrist),' *Oriente Moderno* 21, 2002, pp.63-65.

373 Tottoli, '*Hadiths* and Traditions', p.61. See Filiu, *Apocalypse*, pp.187-189, for a modern writer who acknowledges Ibn Kathir but relies *in practice* even more on Nu'aym's unauthorized collection.

374 Tottoli, '*Hadiths* and Traditions', pp.58-59; Filiu, *Apocalypse*, p.85; cf. pp.91, 166.

375 Cook 2005, pp.15-49 and Cook, 'Hadith, Authority, and the End of the World', pp.31-53 (e.g. the Dead Sea Scrolls as a source—p.44).

376 Cook, 'Hadith, Authority, and the End of the World', p.40.

377 See Cook, 'Hadith, Authority, and the End of the World', p.35.

378 Cook, 'Hadith, Authority, and the End of the World', p.33.

379 See Tottoli, '*Hadiths* and Traditions', pp.55-75.

380 Cf. Cook, 'Hadith, Authority, and the End of the World,' 45, and Tottoli, '*Hadiths* and Traditions', p.66.

381 Cook, 'Hadith, Authority, and the End of the World', p.36. Cf. Cook, *Contemporary Muslim*, 164 n10, p.207.

382 Tottoli, '*Hadiths* and Traditions', p.71 n93.

383 Cf. Laoust, 'Ibn Kathir Historien', *Arabica* 2, 1955, pp.86-87. Remember, the *Nihaya* was also presented as the conclusion to Ibn Kathir's book of universal history.

384 A pattern (outside the Islamic context) articulated very ably in the work of Bernard McGinn.

385 Compare McGinn, *Antichrist.*

386 E.g., Abu Dawud v.3, p.1183, no. 4246; v.3, p.1185, no. 4249; Nu'aym, *Fitan*, 1.1.12-1.1.14, pp.29-30.

387 Yahya Birt, 'Lies! Damn Lies! Statistics and Conversions', *Q-News*, October 2003, p.20.

388 H. A. Mustofa, 'Keadaan dalam Kubur dan Keberatannya', in *Kumpulan Khutbah Jum'at Pilihan*, Surabaya: Penerbit Al Ikhlas, 1986, p.212.

389 Hamka, *Pelajaran Agama Islam*, Jakarta: Bulan Bintang, 1956, p.279.

390 M. S. Seale, *Qur'an and Bible: Studies in Interpretation and Dialogue*, London: Croom Helm, 1978, p.93.

391 Al-Samarqandi, 'Tanbih al-ghafilin' (The Arousement of the Heedless), cited in A. Jeffery (ed.), *A Reader on Islam: Passages from standard Arabic writings illustrative of the beliefs and practices of Muslims*, The Hague: Mouton & Co., 1962, p.202.

392 Al-Samarqandi, 'Tanbih al-ghafilin', pp.208-209.

393 P. Voorhoeve, "Bajan Tadjalli", *Tijdschrift voor Indische Taal-, Land- en Volkenkunde*, 23/1, 1952, pp.91-93.

394 R. Arnaldez, 'Al-Kurtubi', *Encyclopaedia of Islam, New Edition*, vol. V, Leiden: Brill, 1986, p.512.

395 Shlomo Dov Goitein, 'The Jews Under Islam 6th – 16th centuries', in Kedouri, Elie (ed.) *The Jewish World: Revelation, Prophecy and History*, London, Thames & Hudson, 1979, p.184.

396 Hamka, *Pelajaran Agama Islam*, Jakarta: Bulan Bintang, 1956, p.300.

397 Abu Hanifa, 'Testament', cited in Peters, F. E., *A Reader on Classical Islam*, Princeton: Princeton University Press, 1994, p.402.

398 Al-Nasafi, 'Bahr al-Kalam fi 'Ilm al-Tawhid' (Sea of Discussion on the Science of Theology), cited in Jeffery, *A Reader*, p.436-437.

399 Ibn Qudama, 'Creed', cited in A. Rippin, & J. Knappert (eds.), *Textual Sources for the Study of Islam*, Chicago: University of Chicago, 1986, p.123.

400 Seale, *Qur'an and Bible*, p.93.

401 Taken from al-Ghazali's *Dhikr al-Mawt wa-ma ba' duh Kitab al-Aghani*, cited in Seale, *Qur'an and Bible*, pp.93-94.

402 H. A. Mustofa, 'Keadaan dalam Kubur dan Keberatannya', pp.217-18.

403 Hamka, *Pelajaran Agama Islam*, Jakarta: Bulan Bintang, 1956, p.281.

404 C. Brakel-Papenhuyzen, 'The tale of the skull; An Islamic description of hell in Javanese', *Bijdragen tot de Taal-, Land- en Volkenkunde* 158/1 (2002), Leiden, p.6.

405 H. A. Mustofa, 'Keadaan dalam Kubur dan Keberatannya', p.218.

406 Cf. Bukhari 8.76.534, and Muslim 40. 6844.

407 Al-Samarqandi, 'Tanbih al-ghafilin', p.230.

408 Al-Samarqandi, 'Tanbih al-ghafilin', p.207.

409 Hamka, *Pelajaran Agama Islam*, Jakarta: Bulan Bintang, 1956, pp.270ff.

410 Attributed to Abu Dharr. Muslim 1.192.

411 Attributed to Abu Hurayrah. Muslim 1.195.

412 H. Gatje, *The Qur'an and its Exegesis: Selected Texts with Classical and Modern Muslim Interpretations*, Oxford: Oneworld Publications, 1996 [1976], p.178. Cf. Abi Sa'id al-Baydawi, *Tafsir al-Baydawi al-musamma Anwar al-Tanzil wa Asrar al- Ta'wil*, Beirut: Dar al-Fikr 1996, vol. 5, p.519.

413 Gatje, *The Qur'an and its Exegesis*, p.182. Cf. A. a. al-Zamakhshari, *al- Kashshaf 'an haqa'iq al-tanzil wa 'uyun al-aqawil*, Beirut: Dar al-Fikr, n.d., vol. 2, p.293.

414 Nurcholish Madjid, 'Konsep-Konsep Kebahagiaan Dan Kesengsaraan', in Budhy Munawar-Rachman, *Kontekstualisasi Doktrin Islam Dalam Sejarah*, Jakarta: Penerbit Yayasan Paramadina, http://unix.lib.itb.ac.id/~hutri/private/islam/bahagia.htm, accessed April 30, 2003. Madjid cites Q11:105-108 in support of this statement.

415 Hatem Bazian, 'Translation of the hijacker letter', http://www.mindfully.org/Reform/Photos-Hijackers-DOJ27sep01.htm, accessed February 21, 2014.

416 Ayatollah Khomeini, *Islamic Government*, Tehran: The Institute for Compilation and Publication of Imam Khomeini's Works [International Affairs Division], trans. Hamid Algar, p.23.

417 Ibrahim Ayati, *A Probe Into the History of Ashura*, Karachi: Islamic Seminary Publications, 1985, http://al-islam.org/ashura/

418 Ibid.

419 Sayyid Muhammad Taqi Musawi al-Isfahani, *Mikyal al-Makarim fi Fawa'idi Du'a lil Qa'im*, vol. 2, p.75. http://www.rizvia.com/ziarat/nahiya/1.htm

420 *Uyun Akhbar al-Ridha*, vol. 1, p. 299, Hadith 58; *Bihar al-Anwar*, vol. 44, p.285, Hadith 23. http://www.rizvia.com/ziarat/nahiya/1.htm

421 Mohammad A.Shomali, *Shi'i Islam: Origins, Faith & Practices*, London: ICAS, 2003, p. 93.

422 Ibid., p.16.

423 Ibid., p.109.

424 Michael Axworthy, *Revolutionary Iran: A History of the Islamic Republic*, London: Allen Lane, 2013, pp.76-77.

425 Khomeini, *Islamic Government*, pp.29, 86.

426 Shomali, *Shi'i Islam: Origins, Faith & Practices*, p.93.

427 Imam Jafar Sadiq (AS) said: He whose eyes shed tears for our blood which has been shed, or for our rights which have been usurped, or for the humiliation meted out to us or to one of our Shi'ites, Allah shall accommodate him in paradise for a long time. *Amali Al-Shaikh Al-Mufid*, p.175.

[428] Khomeini, *The Ashura Uprising*, p. 59f. The hadith to which he refers is *Bihar al-anwar*, v. 44, p.288.

[429] Hezbollah, *Hezbollah: Identity and goals*, http://www.hizbollah.org/english/info.htm#1 2001.

[430] Naim Qassem, *Hezbollah: The Story from Within*, London: Saqi, 2005, p.45.

[431] Ibid, pp.169f.

[432] Ibid., p.270.

[433] Patrick Cockburn, *Muqtada al-Sadr and the Fall of Iraq*, London: Faber & Faber, 2008, p. 167.

[434] Ibid., p.7.

[435] Cockburn, *Muqtada al-Sadr and the Fall of Iraq*, p.66.

[436] Oliver Roy, 'Has Islamism a future in Afghanistan?' in Maley, William (ed.), *Fundamentalism Reborn?: Afghanistan and the Taliban*, London: Hurst & Co., 2001, p.202; Rashid, Ahmed, *Taliban: The Story of the Afghan Warlords*, London: Pan, 2001, p.204.

[437] Muhammad ibn al-Hassan and Ali ibn Muhammad has narrated from Sahl ibn Ziyad and Muhammad ibn Yahya from Ahmad ibn Muhammad, all from Ja'far ibn Muhammad al-Ash'ari from 'Abd Allah ibn Maymun al-Qaddah and Ali ibn Ibrahim from his father from Hammad ibn 'Isa from al-Qaddah from abu 'Abd Allah who has said the following. 'The Holy Prophet has said, "If one sets out on a journey to seek knowledge Allah will lead him to the way that would take him to paradise. The angels will stretch their wings for the pleasure of the seeker of knowledge"...' (*Usul al-Kafi*, H 57, Ch. 4, h1)

[438] Ahmad has narrated through his chain of narrators from the Imam (a.s.) the following. 'Allah disdains to make the people's time set for it (reappearance of the one who will rise with Divine Authority) to come true.' (*Usul al-Kafi*, H 941, Ch. 82, h 4) Al-Husayn ibn Muhammad has narrated from Mu'alla ibn Muhammad from al-Hassan ibn Ali al-Khazzaz from 'Abd al-Karim ibn 'Umar al-Khath'ami from al-Fadl ibn Yasar who has said the following. 'I asked abu Ja'far, "Is there a definite time for this matter (the rise of al-Mahdi with Divine Authority and power)?" He said, "Those who set a definite time have lied, those who set a definite time have lied, those who set a definite time have lied..."' (*Usul al-Kafi*, H 920, Ch. 82, h 5)

[439] Allamah Muhammad Baqir al-Majlisi, *The Promised Mahdi: English Translation of Biharul Anwar, Volumes 51-52-53*, Part II, Mumbai: Ja'fari Propagation Centre, Undated, 30.41, p.104.

[440] Ibid., p.112.

[441] Khomeini, *Islamic Government*, p.92.

[442] Ibid., p.93.

[443] Ibid., p.82.

[444] Ayatollah Ibrahim Amini, *Al-Imam al-Mahdi, The Just Leader of Humanity*, London: Translated by Dr. Abdulaziz Sachedina, 1996, http://al-islam.org/mahdi/nontl/Chap-12.htm

[445] Muhammad ibn Yahya has narrated from Ahmad ibn Muhammad from Ali ibn al-Hakam from Dawud al-'Ijli from Zurara from Humran from abu Ja'far, Who has said the following. 'As Allah, the Most Holy the Most High, created the creation... He then made the 'Ulu al-'Azm messengers to testify and covenant to this fact: "I am your Lord, Muhammad is, Ali is the commander of the believers and his successor, after him are people who possess My authority and are the reservoir of my knowledge. That al-Mahdi, is one whom I make to lend support to my religion. Through him I will establish my kingdom on earth make my enemies to pay for their crimes. Through him I will them to worship me willingly or otherwise".' (*Usul al-Kafi*, H 1434, Ch. 1c, h 1)

Muhammad ibn Yahya has narrated from Ahmad ibn Muhammad from Ali ibn al-Hakam from 'Abd Allah ibn Bukayr from a man who has said the following:
...Abu Ja'far, said, '...Whoever will find himself with our al-Qa'im (al-Mahdi) and will come out with him to do away with our enemies he will have a reward equal to that for twenty martyrs and whoever will be killed supporting our al-Qa'im his reward will be equal to that for fifteen martyrs.'(*Usul al-Kafi*, H 2237, Ch. 94, h 4)
Narrated by Imam Baqir
The Mahdi resembles his grandfather Muhammad (peace be upon him and his progeny) in the way in which the latter began his struggle with the sword. He will kill the enemies of God, His Prophet, and those who have oppressed the people and have led them astray. He will gain victory through sword and creating fear [in the enemy]. None of his army will face defeat. (*Bihar al-anwar*, Vol 51, p.218)
[446] It is reported that the Prophet ('s) said, 'Among my progeny is the Mahdi. When he emerges, Jesus the son of Mary will descend to help him, then Jesus will send him ahead and pray behind him.'
(*Bihar al-anwar*, 14, 349)
Khaythama reported that Abu Ja'far said, '..... Dajjàl appears and Jesus ...descends from the sky, and Allah will kill Dajjàl by his hands...' (*Bihar al-anwar*, 24, 328, 46)
The Apostle of Allah said, 'How can a community perish when I am at the beginning of it, Jesus the son of Mary will be at the end of it and al-Mahdí will be in the middle of it.' (*Dala'il al-Imamah*, 234)
[447] Ayatollah Morteza Motahari, *Jurisprudence and Its Principles*, New York: Tahrike Tarsile Qur'an, 2002, pp.9-40.
[448] Muhammad Ali, *The Split in the Ahmadiyya Movement*, p. 22ff, Lahore: Anjuman Ahmadiyya, n.d.
[449] *Sunan Abu Dawud*, vol. 4, Hadith 4291, Beirut: Dar al-Jil, 1988.
[450] *Sunan Ibn Maja*, vol. 2, Hadith 4039, Beirut: al-Maktaba al-Ilmiyyah, n.d.
[451] Ghulam Ahmad, *Izala Auham*, part II, p. 474, R.K., vol. 3, p.354, London: Additional Nazir Isha'at, 1984. The abbreviation R.K stands for *Ruhani Khazayan*, series 1 in 23 volumes. These volumes hold all the books of Ghulam Ahmad. The English translations of the quotations from Ghulam Ahmad's books are that of the author of this essay.
[452] Ghulam Ahmad, *Taudih Maram*, p. 1, R. K., vol.3. p.51.
[453] Ibid
[454] http://www.ahmadiyya-islam.org/bm/islam/six-main-articles-of-faith-in-islam/the-belief-in-the-day-of-resurrection (accessed December 2, 2013).
[455] Al-Qurtubi, *Al-Jami li-Ahkam al-Qur'an*, Beirut: Dar al-Kutb al-Ilmiyya, n.d, vol. 11, p.44; Al-Zamakhshari, *Al-Kashshaf*, Beirut: Dar al-Kitab al-Arabi, n.d, vol. 2, p.748; Al-Baydawi, *Anwar al-Tanzil*, Beirut: Dar al-Kutub, 1988, vol. 2, pp.23-24; Ibn Kathir, *Tafsir al-Qur'an al-Azim*, Beirut: Dar al-Jil, n.d, vol. 3, p.103; Al-Shawkani, *Fath al-Qadir*, Beirut: Dar al-Kutb al-Ilmiyya, 2000, vol. 3, p.389.
[456] Ghulam Ahmad, *Shahadat al-Qur'an*, p. 15, R. K., vol. 6, p.311.
[457] Ghulam Ahamd, *Shahadat al-Qur'an*, p. 16, R. K., vol. 6, p.312.
[458] Al-Zamakhshari, *Al-Kashshaf*, vol. 2, pp.746-757, footnote 2.
[459] Al-Qurtubi, *Al-Jami' li-Ahkam al-Qur'an*, vol. 11, p.38.
[460] Al-Zamakhshari, *Al-Kashshaf*, vol. 2, p. 746; Al-Baydawi, *Anwar al-Tanzil*, vol. 2, p. 22; Al-Shawkani, *Fath al-Qadir*, vol. 3, p.386.
[461] Ghulam Ahmad, *Izala Auham*, p. 509, R. K., vol. 3, p.373.
[462] Ghulam Ahmad, *Shahadat al-Qur'an*, pp. 14-15, R. K., vol. 6, p.310-311.
[463] Ibid, p. 18, R. K., vol. 6, p. 314. However, the head of the dissident group of the Ahmadiyya, Muhammad Ali (d. 1952), stated that it refers to the transformation brought by Muhammad 'first in Arabia, and later on in the whole world' (Muhammad Ali, *The Holy Qur'an: Arabic Text, English Translation and Commentary*, p.1198, Lahore: Anjuman Ahmadiyya, 1963.

[464] Ghulam Ahmad, *Shahadat al-Qur'an*, p. 19, R. K., vol. 6, p.315.

[465] Ibid; also his: *Chashma Ma'rifat*, pp. 73-74, R. K. vol. 23, pp.81-82.

[466] *Musnad Imam Ahmad*, Beirut: Alam al-Kutb, 1998, vol. 4, pp.283, 306, 456; *Sunan al-Tirmidhi*, Beirut: Dar al-Kutb al-Ilmiyya, 2000, vol. 4, p.273; Al-*Muttaqi al-Hindi, Kanz al-'Ummal*, Beirut: Dar al-Kutub-Ilmiyah, 1998, vol. 14, p.89; Ibn Kathir, *Tafsir al-Qur'an al-'Azim*, vol. 4, p.476; Al-Shawkani, *Fath al-Qadir*, vol. 5, p.482.

[467] Ghulam Ahmad, *Mahmud ki Amin*, p. 46, R. K. vol. 12, p.372.

[468] Ghulam Ahmad, *Tuhfa Golarwiyya*, p. 90, R. K., vol. 17, p.243.

[469] Ghulam Ahmad, *Shahadat al-Qur'an*, p. 19, R. K., vol. 6, p.315; *A'iyna Kamalat Islam*, p. 469, R. K. vol. 5, p.469.

[470] Ghulam Ahmad, *Government Angrizi awr Jihad*, p. 16, R. K., vol. 17, p.16.

[471] Ghulam Ahmad, *Shahadat al-Qur'an*, p. 22, R. K., vol. 6, p.318; *Haqiqat al-Wahy*, p.198, R. K., vol. 22, p.206.

[472] Ibn Kathir, *Tafsir al-Qur'an al-'Azim*, vol. 4, p. 477; Al-Shawkani, *Fath al-Qadir*, vol. 5, p.483.

[473] Ghulam Ahmad, *Shahadat al-Qur'an*, pp.21-22, R. K., vol. 6, pp.317-318. Similar statements are found in his other publications: *Haqiqat al-Wahy*, p. 198, R. K., vol. 22, p.206; *Kashti Nuh*, p. 8, R. K., vol. 19, p.8; and *Chashma Ma'rifat*, pp.306-307, R. K. vol. 23, pp.321-322.

[474] His son and second successor, Bashir al-Din, suggested that it could mean that 'zoos will be made or that barbarous people will become civilized or they would be uprooted from their lands as happened in America and Australia' (Bashir al-Din Mahmud Ahmad, *Tafsir-i Saghir*, Qadian: Muhtamim al-Isha'at, 1972, p.806.

[475] Ghulam Ahmad, *Shahadat al-Qur'an*, p. 22, R. K., vol. 6, p.318.

[476] Ibid, p.22, R. K., vol. 6, p.318.

[477] Ibid, p.22, R. K., vol. 6, p.318; also his, *Haqiqat al-Wahy*, p.198, R. K., vol. 22, p.206.

[478] Ghulam Ahmad, *Shahadat al-Qur'an*, p.22, R. K., vol. 6, p.318; *Haqiqat al-Wahy*, p.198, R. K., vol. 22, p.206.

[479] Tabari, *Tafsir al-Tabari*, Beirut: Dar al-Kutub al-Ilmiyah, 1990, vol. 12, pp.464-465; Al-Qurtubi, *Al-Jami' li-Ahkam al-Qur'an*, vol. 20, p.152; Al-Zamakhshari, *Al-Kashshaf*, vol. 4, p.708; Al-Baydawi, *Anwar al-Tanzil*, vol. 2, p.572; Ibn Kathir, *Tafsir al-Qur'an al-'Azim*, vol. 4, p.479; Al-Shawkani, *Fath al-Qadir*, vol. 5, p.484.

[480] Ghulam Ahmad wrote, 'There is an allusion [in this passage] to the present situation of the country where such wicked deeds are being committed' (*Zia' al-Haq*, p. 9, footnote, R. K. vol. 9, p. 338). Bashir al-Din, however, suggested that a time was to come when 'the burial of a living daughter would become a criminal offence' (Bashir al-Din Mahmud Ahmad, *Tafsir-i-Saghir*, p.806).

[481] Ghulam Ahmad, *Shahadat al-Qur'an*, p. 22, R. K., vol. 6, p.318.

[482] Ghulam Ahmad, *Aiyna Kamalat Islam*, p. 478, R. K. vol. 5, p.478. Bashir al-Din takes the passage to mean that 'the advances in the knowledge of astronomy will increase.'(Bashir al-Din, *Tafsir-i Saghir*, p.806.)

[483] Ghulam Ahmad, *Shahadat al-Qur'an*, p. 22, R. K., vol. 6, p.318.

[484] Ibid, p. 24, R. K., vol. 6, p.320.

[485] Ghulam Ahmad, *Shahadat al-Qur'an*, p. 24, R. K., vol. 6, p.320.

[486] Ghulam Ahmad, *Khutba Ilhamiyya*, pp. 120-123, R. K., vol. 16, pp.120-123.

[487] There are several narratives of Ahadith which state that Gabriel, as a stranger or a companion, asked Muhammad, 'What is belief?' to which Muhammad replied, 'That you should believe in God, in the last day, in His angels, His book, His prophets, in paradise, and fire and that everything good and bad is decided by God (Al-Muttaqi al-Hindi, *Kanz al-Ummal fi Sunan al-Aqwal wa al-Aa'l*, vol. 1, p.146; *Sahih al-Bukhari*, vol. 6, pp.285-286 [tr: Muhammad Muhsin Khan], Ankara: Hilal, 1978; *Musnad Imam Ahmad Hanbal*, vol. 1, p.191).

[488] Ghulam Ahmad, *Surma Chashm Arya*, p.93, R. K., vol. 2, p.141.

[489] Ghulam Ahmad, *Surma Chashm Arya*, p.95, R. K., vol. 2, p.143; *Aiyna Kamalat Islam*, p.145, R. K., vol. 5, p.145.

[490] Ghulam Ahmad, *Malfuzat*, vol. iii, pp.28-29.

491 Ghulam Ahmad, *Islami Usul*, p.70-71, R. K., vol. 10, pp.411-412.

492 Ghulam Ahmad, *Kitab al-Bariyya*, pp.52-53, R. K., vol. 13, pp.70-71.

493 Ghulam Ahmad, *Chashma Ma'rifat*, pp.159-160, R. K., vol. 23, pp.167-168.

494 Ghulam Ahmad, *Izala Auham*, pp.356-357 R. K., vol. 3, p.282.

495 Ghulam Ahmad, *Malfuzat* vol. 1, p.290; *Al-Hakam*, vol. 3, no. 3, pp.2-3, 23rd January, 1899, Qadian: Qadian Press.

496 Ghulam Ahmad, *Al-Haq: Mubahitha Dehli* (held in October 1891), p.85 R. K., vol. 4, p.215.

497 Sirhindi, *Maktubat-I Rabbani*, Lahore: Idara Islamiyat, 1988, Daftar III, vol. 2, pp.428-429.

498 Ghulam Ahmad, *Islami Usul*, pp.88-93 R. K., vol. 10, pp.411-412.

499 Ghulam Ahmad, *Izala Auham*, p.358, R. K., vol. 3, p.283.

500 Ibid, p.359, R. K., vol. 3, p.284.

501 Ibid, pp.360-361, R. K., vol. 3, pp.284-285.

502 Ibid, pp.360-361, R. K., vol. 3, pp.284-285.

503 Ibid, pp.360-361, R. K., vol. 3, pp.284-285.

504 Ibid, p.364, R. K., vol. 3, p.287.

505 Ghulam Ahmad, *Islami Usul ki filosfy*, pp. 88-93, R. K., vol. 10, pp.411-412.

506 He believed that there were *darajat* in hell and paradise. *Izala Auham*, pp.359-360, R. K., vol. 3, p.284.

507 Ghulam Ahmad, *Malfuzat*, vol. 3, pp.61-62; *Izala Auham*, p.356, R. K., vol. 3, p.282.

508 Ghulam Ahmad, *Izala Auham*, p.359, R. K., vol. 3, p.284.

509 *Sahih al-Bukhari*, vol. 1, p.427.

510 Ghulam Ahmad, *Ayna Kamalat Islam*, p.147, R. K., vol. 5, p.147.

511 *Sahih al-Bukhari*, vol. 6, p.288. A similar version is found in the Bible: Isaiah 64:4 and I Corinthians 2:9.

512 Ghulam Ahmad, *Islami Usul ki filosfy*, pp.82-84, R. K., vol. 10, pp.411-412.

513 *Ibid*, pp.98-99, R. K., vol. 10, pp.411-412.

514 Ghulam Ahmad, *Zamima Barahin Ahmadiyya*, v. p.213, footnote, (R. K., vol. 21, p.387).

515 Ghulam Ahmad, *Surma Chashm Arya*, p.109, R. K., vol. 2, p.157.

516 Ghulam Ahmad, *Surma Chashm Arya*, p.109, R. K., vol. 2, p.157.

517 Ghulam Ahmad referred to the Qur'an, Sura 14:24: 'Don't you see how God sets forth a parable? A divine word is like a good tree, whose roots are firmly fixed and its branches [reach] the heaven' (*Surma Chashm Arya*, p.110, R. K., vol. 2, p.158).

518 Sura 52:20. Similar statements appear for example in Sura 37:48-49; 44:54; 56:35-37.

519 *Musnad Imam Ahmad*, vol. 4, p.191; *Sunan Tirmidhi*, Beirut: al-Maktaba al-Ilmiyyah, n.d, vol. 3, p.399. Jabiya is in Syria and San'a is the capital of Yemen.

520 *Sunan Tirmidhi*, vol. 3, p.399.

521 Maulana Muhammad Ali, *The Religion of Islam*, Lahore: Anjuman Ahmadiyya, n.d, p.223.

522 Ibid, p.219, 221.

523 Ghulam Ahmad, *Islami Usul ki Filasafi*, pp.94-99, R. K., vol. 10, pp.411-412.

524 Ibid, pp.71-79, R. K., vol. 10, pp.411-412.

525 Bashir al-Din, *Ahmadiyyat or The True Islam*, Qadian: Talif-o-Isha'at, 1924, p.63.

526 Ghulam Ahmad, *Lecture Lahore: Islam awr is mulk kay dusray madhahib*, [September 1903], p.24, R. K., vol. 20, p.170.

527 Ghulam Ahmad, *Chashma Masihi*, p.47, R. K., vol. 20, p.369.

528 Ibid, pp.47-48, R. K., vol. 20, p.369.

529 *Encyclopaedia of Islam, New Edition*, Leiden: E. J. Brill, 1960- , vol. I, p.69.

530 Fritjof Schuon, *Dimension of Islam*, Lahore: Suhail Academy, 1985, p.137.

531 Ibn Arabi, *Fusus al-Hikam*, p.169, cited by A. E. Affifi, *The Mystical Philosophy of Muhyid Din Ibnul 'Arabi*, Lahore: Muhammad Ashraf Publications, 1964, pp.167-168.

532 Sirhindi, *Maktubat-I Rabbani*, 266, Daftar I, vol. 1, pp.518-519.

533 *Ibid*, p.519

534 *Ibid*, p.524.

535 *Ibid*, p.524.

[536] Ghulam Ahmad, *Chashma Masihi,* p.47, R. K., vol. 20, p.369; *Lecture Lahore: Islam awr is mulk kay dusray madhahib,* [September 1903], p. 24, R. K., vol. 20, p.170); Bashir al-Din, *Tafsir al-Saghir,* p.844; also his *Ahmadiyyat or the True Islam,* p.396 and *Invitation to Ahmadiyyat,* p.182; Muhammad Ali, *The Religion of Islam,* Lahore: Anjuman Ahmadiyya, n.d, p.233.

[537] Eleanor Abdella Doumao, *Getting God's Ear. Women, Islam, and Healing in Saudi Arabia and the Gulf,* New York: Columbia University Press, 2000, p.182. Also Muhammad Ali al-Hashimi, *The Ideal Muslimah,* Trans. Nasiruddin al-Khattab, Riyadh: International Islamic Publishing House, 2005, pp.520-1.

[538] Goolam Vahed, 'Religious Practices: Religious Commemorations' in *Encyclopedia of Women & Islamic Cultures,* Vol.5, ed Suad Joseph; Leiden-Boston: Brill, 2007, p.364.

[539] Oliver Leaman, 'Death' in *The Qur'an: an Encyclopedia,* ed. Oliver Leaman: London & New York: Routledge, 2006, p.176.

[540] Lilia Lakidi, 'Funerary Practices: North Africa' in *Encyclopedia of Women & Islamic Cultures,* Vol.3, (2006), pp.122-124.

[541] Iman Roushdy-Hammady, 'Health Policies: Western Europe' in *Encyclopedia of Women & Islamic Cultures,* Vol.6, (2007), p.124. Also Doumato, *Getting God's Ear,* p.137.

[542] Ingrid Pfluger-Schindlbeck, 'Language: Use by Women: The Caucasus' in *Encyclopedia of Women & Islamic Cultures,* Vol.5, (2007), p.233.

[543] Cyril Glassé, *The Concise Encyclopaedia of Islam* 3rd ed.; London: Stacey, 2008, p.144.

[544] Constance Padwick, *Muslim Devotions. A Study of Prayer-Manuals in Common Use,* Oxford: Oneworld Publications, 1961, p.211.

[545] See also http://www.islamicinsights.com/religion/religion/the-journey-continues-barzakh-and-beyond.html, http://www.turntoislam.com/threads/the-first-night-in-the-grave-barzakh-day-of-judgement-and-life-after-death.24213/, accessed April 24, 2013.

[546] 'Umar S. al-Ashqar, *The Minor Resurrection (What Happens After Death) In the Light of the Qur'an and Sunnah,* 2nd English ed.; Riyadh: International Islamic Publishing House, 2005, pp.96-8, 100-102.

[547] Reuven Firestone, 'Islam: Jewish and Muslim Sources, Discourses, and Interactions' in *Encyclopedia of Women & Islamic Cultures,* Vol.5, pp.218-9. Also al-Ashqar, *The Minor Resurrection,* pp.77, 98; and http://islamqa.info/en/ref/21212/grave, accessed April 4, 2013.

[548] Ed: Compare Walid Saleh, 'The Woman as a Locus of Apocalyptic Anxiety in Medieval Sunni Islam' in *Myths, Historical Archetypes, and Symbolic Figures in Arabic Literature,* A. Neuwirth et al, eds. Beirut: Franz Steiner Verlag, 1999, pp.123-145.

[549] Jane I. Smith, 'Representations: Afterlife Stories' in *Encyclopedia of Women & Islamic Cultures,* Vol.5, p.401.

[550] Muhammad al-'Areefi, The End of the World. Signs of the Hour Major and Minor, Riyadh: Darussalam, 2010. http://www.squidoo.com/End-Times-Islam#module12932773, http://gmiah.hubpages.com/hub/Islam-2012-What-Are-The-Consequences, http://www.islam.tc/prophecies/qiyaam2.html, accessed April 24, 2013.

[551] Book #6, Hadith #301: also in eight other Bukhari hadith - 2:28, 3:101, 18:161, 24:541, 54:464, 62:125, 126, 76:146: and in al-Muslim.

[552] Ahmad Jad, *Fifty of the Counsels of the Prophet to the Women,* Lebanon: Dar Al-Kotob Al-Ilmiyah, 2009, p.27.

[553] http://www.islamweb.net/emainpage/index.php?page=articles&id=151196, accessed October 15, 2012. See further, http://www.ahlesunnat.net/media-library/downloads/regularupdates/wifeduties.htm, accessed October 15, 2012

[554] Barbara Freyer Stowasser, *Women in the Qur'an, Traditions and Interpretation,* New York & Oxford: Oxford University Press, 1994, pp.41, 43.

[555] Also Saba Mahmood, *Politics of Piety. The Islamic Revival and the Feminist Subject,* Princeton & Oxford: Princeton University Press, 2005, p.96.

[556] Bukhari Book #2, Hadith #40, Book #76, Hadith #498, Book #93, Hadith #592: Sahih Muslim Book #001, Hadith #0235.

557 Chawkat Moucarry, *The Search For Forgiveness*, Leicester: IVP, 2004, pp.29, 37.

558 Bukhari Book #8, Hadith #466, Book #11, Hadith #620:. Emerick suggests twenty-seven times more. Yahiya Emerick, *What Islam Is All About*, Kuala Lumpur: A.S.Noordeen, 2002, p.138.

559 Abu Dawud Book#3, Hadith #1062

560 Syed Abdul A'ala Mawdudi, *Purdah and the Status of Woman in Islam*, 2nd ed.; Delhi: Markazi Maktabi Islami, 1981, pp.202-3. Also cited in Jad, *Counsels of the Prophet*, pp.36-37.

561 Julia Meltzer & Laura Nix, *The Light in Her Eyes*, DVD, Clockshop & Felt Films, 2012.

562 Bukhari, Book #24, Hadith #499, Book #73, Hadith #24.

563 http://authentichadīths.blogspot.com.au/2012/03/authenticity-on-hadīth-paradise-is.html, http://islam.about.com/od/elderly/a/mothers.htm, accessed July 17, 2012.

564 For example, *Al-Nisa'* 4:110, *Al-'a'araaf* 7:23, *Al-Naml* 27:44. See also Padwick, *Muslim Devotions*, p.192.

565 Bukhari, Book #2, Hadith #42. Also Book #9, Hadith #532B, in Muhammad Taqi-ud-Din Al-Hilali & Muhammad Muhsin Khan, *Translation of the Meanings of the Noble Qur'an*, Medinah: King Fahd Complex for the Printing of the Holy Qur'an, 1404 A.H., pp.781-3.

566 L.Gardet, 'Djahannam' in *Encylopaedia of Islam, New Edition*, Leiden & London: Brill, Luzac & Co., 1983, vol. II, p.381. See also Abdul-Halim ibn Muhammad Nassar As-Salafi, *Description of Paradise in the Glorious Qur'an*, Riyadh: Darussalam, 2010, p.173.

567 Moucarry, *The Search For Forgiveness*, pp.25-35.

568 L. Gardet, 'Hisaab', in *Encylopaedia of Islam, New Edition*, vol. II, pp.465-466.

569 al-Hilali & Khan, *The Noble Qur'an*, p.38.

570 Glassé, *Concise*, p.366.

571 Bukhari, Book#11, Hadith #588.

572 Padwick, *Muslim Devotions*, pp.152-162.

573 Doumato, *Getting God's Ear*, p.116.

574 Abu Dawud, Book #20, Hadith #3105.

575 Aliah Schleifer, *Motherhood in Islam*, Cambridge: The Islamic Academy, 1986, p.58. Also Wanda Krause, *Women in Civil Society. The State, Islamism, and Networks in the UAE*, New York: Palgrave Macmillan, 2008, p.122.

576 Note in al-Hilali & Khan, *The Noble Qur'an*, p.6.

577 Stefan Wild, 'Paradise' in *The Qur'an: An Encyclopedia*, ed. Oliver Leaman; London & New York: Routledge, 2006, p.487.

578 Hans Wehr, *A Dictionary of Modern Written Arabic*, Beirut & London: Librairie Du Liban, and Macdonald & Evans, 4th edn.1974, p.212. Also Wild, 'Paradise,' p.487; and http://sheikhynotes.blogspot.com.au/2010/01/womens-reward-in-paradise-in-islam.html, accessed February 27, 2013.

579 http://islamreligion1.wordpress.com/2011/07/15/the-hoor-al-ayn-of-jannah-paradise/, accessed May 8, 2013. Also http://www.islamweb.net/emainpage/index.php?page=articles&id=158781 , accessed February 27, 2013.

580 L. Gardet, 'Djanna' in *Encyclopaedia of Islam, New Edition*, Vol II (1983), p.449. Tafsir As-Sharbini Vol 4:181 suggests seventy times. *Sheikynotes.blogspot*, accessed February 27, 2012.

581 Muhammad bin Abdul-Aziz Al-Musnad. *Islamic Fatawa Regarding Women*. Riyadh: Darussalam, 1996, pp.55-6. Also islamreligion1.wordpress, accessed May 8, 2013. http://www.ummah.com/forum/showthread.php?289565-The-hoors-of-jannah-the-paradise accessed May 8, 2013.

582 Sahih Muslim, Book #001, Hadith #0363, Book #040, Hadith #6783

583 Sheikynotes.blogspot, accessed May 8, 2013.

584 Al-Musnad, *Fatawa*, p.55-6.

585 Al-Musnad, *Fatawa*, p.56.

586 As-Salafi, *Paradise*, 213; also Islamreligion1.wordpress, citing Ibn-i-Majah vol3:2014 p.212, accessed May 8, 2013.

[587] http://www.islamweb, http://www.ummah.com, islamreligion1.com, accessed May 8, 2013.

[588] Beiuzzaman Said Nursi, *The Words. The Reconstruction of Islamic Belief and Thought*, New Jersey: Light, 2010, p.145.

[589] Wild, 'Paradise,' p.487.

[590] As-Salafi, *Paradise*, pp.257-283.

[591] Mahmood, *Politics*, p.49.

[592] Glassé, *Islam*, p.198.

[593] Gardet, 'Djahannem', p.381.

[594] Mahmood, *Politics*, p.142.

[595] Mahmood, *Politics*, pp.91, 144.

[596] Stefan Wild, 'Hell,' *The Qur'an: An Encyclopaedia*, p.261.

[597] K Gustafson, *An Insider View*, Minneapolis, Minnesota: Common Ground Consultants, Inc., 2007.

[598] Bill Nikides, 'The Emergence of Insider Movements', *St Francis Magazine* Vol. 7:3 (Aug. 2011), pp.46-57. It is worth noting that the very existence of these movements has been called into question.

[599] Rebecca Lewis, 'Strategizing for Church Planting Movements in the Muslim World', *International Journal of Frontier Missions* Vol. 21:2 (Summer 2004), pp.73-7; 'Promoting Movements to Christ within Natural Communities', *IJFM* Vol. 24:2 (Summer 2007), pp.75-6; 'Insider Movements: Honoring God-given Identity and Community', *IJFM* Vol. 26:1 (Spring 2009), pp.16-19; 'The Integrity of the Gospel and Insider Movements' *IJFM* Vol. 27:1 (Spring 2010), pp.41-48. Lewis alleges the existence of such groups, but offers no evidence.

[600] Lewis Rambo, *Understanding Religious Conversion*, New Haven, London: Yale University Press, 1993, p.14.

[601] Muhammad Ibn Ishaq & Alfred Guillaume *The Life of Muhammad: a transl. of Ibn Ishaq's Sirat Rasul Allah*, Lahore, 1967, p.99.

[602] John Avetaranian, *A Muslim Who Became a Christian*, trans. John Bechard and Richard Schafer, Hereford, UK: Authors OnLine Ltd., n.d.

[603] Avery T Willis, Jr. *Indonesian Revival: Why Two Million Came to Christ*. Pasadena, California: William Carey Library, 1977.

[604] Cf. J. Dudley Woodberry and Russell G. Shubin, 'Muslims tell ... "Why I chose Jesus"', *Mission Frontiers*, March 2001, accessed September 9, 2009.
< www.missionfrontiers.org/pdf/2001/01/muslim.htm>;
Jean-Marie Gaudeul, *Called from Islam to Christ: Why Muslims become Christians*, Oxford: Monarch. 1999.
Abu Daoud, 'Apostates of Islam', *St. Francis Magazine* Vol. 3:4 (March 2008), pp.1-8.

[605] D. A. Miller, *Woven in the Weakness of the Changing Body: The Genesis of World Islamic Christianity:* Presented at *Coming to Faith in Christ 2*, Buckinghamshire, UK, February 2010.< www.nazarethseminary.org/datadir/en-events/ev61/files/Duane%20A%20Miller%20Genesis-of-World-Islamic-Christianity.pdf>

[606] D. A. Miller, 'The Secret World of God: Aesthetics, Relationships, and the Conversion of "Frances" from Shi'a Islam to Christianity', *Global Missiology* Vol. 9:2 (Jan. 2012), <globalmissiology.org>, pp.1-14.

[607] Ziya Meral, *Turk Teolojisine Dogru*, Yeni Yasam Yayinlari, 2007.

[608] D. A. Miller, 'Iranian Diaspora Christian in the American Midwest & Scotland: Historical Background, Present Realities, & Future Challenges', *Global Missiology*, Vol.2:9 (January 2012), pp.1-9, <globalmissiology.org>

[609] Robert Schreiter, *Constructing Local Theologies*, London: SCM Press, 1985, p.91.

[610] Philip Sheldrake ed., *The New SCM Dictionary of Christian Spirituality*, London: SCM Press, 2005, p.643.

[611] St. John of the Cross, *Dark Night of the Soul*.

[612] St. Teresa of Avila, *The Interior Castle*.

[613] T. S. Elliot, *Four quartets*, New York: Brace and Co., Harcourt, 1988.

[614] Schreiter, *Constructing*, p.91.

[615] In accordance with the hadith from *Sahih al Bukhari* 4:52:260 'Whoever changes his religion, slay him.' The oft-quoted 'There is no compulsion in religion' (Q 2:256) is interpreted in traditional Islamic jurisprudence as meaning that one cannot be forced *to become* a Muslim. The verse has no relevance for those who are already Muslims though. The four major schools of Islamic jurisprudence (*madhahhib*) agree that the male apostate must be executed. Regarding female apostates there are some who opine that the woman should be imprisoned indefinitely, while others prescribe execution.
Abdullahi Ahmed An-Na'im, 'Islamic Law of Apostasy and its Modern Applicability: A case from the Sudan', *Religion* Vol. 6 (1986), pp.197-224.
Tarek Fatah, *Chasing a Mirage: The Tragic Illusion of an Islamic State*, Mississauga, Ontario: Wiley, 2008.

[616] D. A. Miller, '"Your swords do not concern me at all": The Liberation Theology of Islamic Christianity', *St. Francis Magazine* Vol. 7:2 (2011), pp.228-260; D. A. Miller, '"It is okay to question Allah": The theology of freedom of Saiid Rabiipour, a Christian ex-Muslim', *Mary's Well Occasional Papers* Vol. 1:4 (September 2012), <nazarethseminary.org/datadir/en-events/ev91/files/MWOP_Miller_Duane_on_Saiid_Rabiipour.pdf>, accessed June 26, 2014.

[617] Hannah Shah, *The Iman's Daughter*, Grand Rapids: Zondervan, 2010.

[618] Fatima Al-Matayri, *The Way of Fatima: A collection of articles, messages and poems related to Fatima Al-Matayri who was martyred in August 2008, in the Kingdom of Saudi Arabia, for her faith in the Lord Jesus Christ.* July 2009. http://www.strateias.org/fatima.pdf, accessed June 20, 2014.

[619] D. A. Miller, 'Iranian Diaspora Christians in the American Midwest & Scotland: Historical Background, Present Realities, & Future Challenges', *Global Missiology* Vol. 9:2 (January 2012), p.5.

[620] Christopher Alam, *Out of Islam*, Lake Mary, Fla.: Charisma House, 2006.

[621] Saiid Rabiliipour, *Farewell to Islam*, Maitland, Fla.: Xulon, 2009.

[622] Daniel Ali, *Out of Islam: 'Free at Last'*, Mustang, Okla.: Tate Publishing & Enterprises, 2007.

[623] Aylward Shorter, *Toward a Theology of Inculturation*, Eugene, Ore.: Wipf & Stock, 1999, pp.11-12.

[624] Lesslie Newbigin, *Signs amid the Rubble: The Purposes of God in Human History*, Grand Rapids, Mich.; Eerdmans, 2003, p.81.

[625] E-mail, 2012. The grammar and punctuation has been corrected.

[626] Alam, *Out*, p.181.

[627] Emir Rishawi, *A Struggle that Led to Conversion: Motives for a Gospel-based Faith*, trans. Unk. Villach, Austria: Light of Life, 1993. See for instance, the final chapter where he explicitly disagrees with penal substitution and, apparently, proclaims his agreement with the Orthodox soteriology of *theosis*.

[628] Faisal Malick, *Here Comes Ishmael*, Belleville, Ontario: Guardian Books, 2005.

[629] Malick, *Here*, pp.16, 121.

[630] Malick, *Here*, pp.39, 50-54, 62-63, 73.

[631] Malick, *Here*, pp.75-78, 80-83,101-107.

[632] Joseph Ratzinger, *Eschatology: Death and Eternal Life*, Washington, DC: CUA Press, 2007.

[633] Oliver Leaman, ed., *The Qur'an: An Encyclopedia*, London & New York: Routledge, 2006, p.487.

[634] Abu Atallah, *Heaven*, www.jashow.org/Articles/_PDFArchives/islam/IS4W0100.pdf, accessed Jan. 2013, pp.1-2.

[635] Nonie Darwish, 'Escaping "Submission', *Front Page Magazine*, February 11, 2003. www.freepublic.com/focus/news/840385/posts, accessed June 9, 2010.

[636] Al-Matayri, *The Way*.

[637] Bilquis Sheikh and R. Schneider, *I Dared to Call Him Father*, Lincoln, Va.: Chosen Books, 1978, p.54.

[638] Elliot, *Four:* 1st verse of 'East Coker'.

[639] Mohammed Hassan Khalil and Mucahit Bilici, 'Conversion out of Islam: A Study of Conversion Narratives of Former Muslims', *Muslim World* Vol. 97 (Jan. 2007), p.118.

[640] S.K. Malik, *The Quranic Concept of War*, Delhi: Adam Publishers, 1992, p.54.

CPSIA information can be obtained at www.ICGtesting.com
Printed in the USA
LVOW01s1116150415

434672LV00002B/4/P